D1623807

A New Innings

Manoj Badale & Simon Hughes

Clink Street

London | New York

Published by Clink Street Publishing 2020

ISBNs:
978-1-913568-50-4 Hardback
978-1-913568-51-1 Paperback
978-1-913568-52-8 Ebook

Contents

Preface

The production of this book has been a multiyear project, starting in 2012. Originally, the book was intended to be a summary of the extraordinary journey of the Rajasthan Royals in the Indian Premier League (IPL) – from winning (against all predictions) in Season 1, having our champions league debut thwarted by the Mumbai terrorist attacks, and then taking over South Africa in Season 2, as the tournament moved with four weeks' notice. That version was called 'You couldn't script it!' The next version was focused on getting the facts written about the complexities of the 'Business of Cricket in India', as we found ourselves at the centre of a series of national controversies – from termination, to player spot fixing and then a two year suspension. That version was called 'Fast, and at times, unplayable!' The next version tried to distil the lessons that the IPL, one of the most successful sporting league launches in history, has for the business of sport. This focused on the importance that all sport must seek constant reinvention to grow and survive – a challenge for a game like cricket which is an iconic symbol of tradition. That version was called 'Infinite Boundaries'.

And then just as we were about to publish in March 2020 (yes, that had to be the year given the sport), the game has been hit by its most existential crisis – the cancellation of all forms of play, for an indefinite period of time, due to the coronavirus. Publishing against the backdrop of such a global catastrophe felt futile, but as we reflect on the 'new normal' every individual, every business, and every government is facing a 'once in a generation' reset. Sport is no exception. So, our hope now is that through the lens of the 'Royals journey', the lessons from the reinvention of one of the world's oldest sports will perhaps inform the requirements for that 'reset' or, as they now say, the 'new normal'.

Our fundamental assertion for cricket is that many of the business lessons from the launch of the IPL define a set of strategic imperatives for the game as a whole, that have simply become more urgent. Coronavirus has changed the world irreversibly in many ways, but the importance of sport remains. However, the competition between sports will now be more intense than ever before, given the pressure on the consumer as we enter a period of economic recession. The need for cricket's next reinvention has simply accelerated. Cricket must now collaborate (like it has not done before). Cricket must make tough choices. Cricket must build from the many lessons (good and bad) of the IPL, if it is to survive and grow. It might seem strange to discuss survival after an extraordinary year for the game – with one of most exciting IPL finals, a dramatic World Cup final, and an incredible Ashes Test match series. However, after perhaps its greatest year, cricket must now face a 'New Innings[1]'.

---

[1] An Innings is the period in a game of cricket in which a team or player bats (=tries to hit the ball and score)

Acknowledgements

The people I must thank are many, so please bear with me. First are my family, who have endured a promise of 'the book' for multiple years. Thanks to 'Team Badale' for riding the Rajasthan Royal rollercoaster for 12 years – Katie Yirrell, my strong and extremely patient wife who has consistently facilitated and supported our family through our thirty two year partnership; Hari, Asha and Ravi; my mother Madhuri and my late father Madan – for all tolerating the highs (of which there were many) and the lows (of which there were as many). The patience you have shown, and the support that you have given is greatly appreciated.

Secondly, I must thank Charles Mindenhall, my business partner of the past 22 years. He has patiently reviewed multiple versions, advised on approach, and as with our 40 business ventures together, he has been eternally optimistic and supportive.

I must also acknowledge the team that have built the Rajasthan Royals, through whose lens the book is written. The playing heroes are well known. The franchise has been led by great players, such as Shane Warne, Rahul Dravid, Shane Watson, Ajinkya Rahane and most recently, Steve Smith. They have each helped to define our culture and our style of play, and to inspire our fans. Zubin Bharucha has been our constant 'cricket brain'. He is slowly, but surely, reinventing the way we play the game. He has been supported by incredible coaches – Darren Berry, Jeremy Snape, Paddy Upton, Amol Mazumdar, Sairaj Bahutule and now Andrew McDonald.

However, less acknowledged are the off-field heroes – led by Ranjit Barthakur, our India based chairman and friend for the last 25 years. He has been there from day one, calmly navigating every crisis, helping seize every opportunity, and providing a strong backbone. As he is now allowed to take up the role he was promised (that of a part-time not full-time chairman!) he can focus on his environmental and social work. We have had many great professional leaders – Raghu Iyer (our CEO for many years), Santanu Chari (our COO for many years), Rohit Katyal, Saurabh Arora and the current team led by, Jake Lush McCrum, the ever present Harvinder Sahni, Girish Manik, Romi Bhinder, Rajeev Khanna, Rohit Sareen, Astha Thapliyal, Amit Gupta, Sangeeta Menezes and Sonali Bhatia – amongst the many devoted and hard-working members of the RR commercial and operations teams. Our legal team has sometimes outnumbered our cricket team, led by Harish Salve and Rohan Shah, with support from the late Mr Ashok Desai, Mr Janal Dwarkadas, Dr. Milind Saathe, Mr Darius Khambatta, Anish Dayal and Deep Roy, have protected the franchise on several occasions.

I must thank our co-investors Suresh and Amisha Chellaram, Lachlan Murdoch (and Paul Wilson) for their trust, support and co-investment. We all learnt a lot together, and also had some fun on the way. We should acknowledge Raj Kundra and Shilpa Shetty who created visibility, and provided some 'Bollywood' to the franchise. Our London RR team of Manoj Bithal, Steve Quinn, Tom Scowsill, Sam Clark and Ann Dearden must also be mentioned. Without these people, there would have been no franchise, no learning, no story and no fun.

A mention to the people who willingly gave up their time to be interviewed for this book, especially Lalit Modi, N Srinivasan, Rahul Dravid, Steve Smith, Paddy Upton, NP Singh, Sanjay Gupta, Raghu Iyer, Catherine Simpson, Rahul Johri, Hemang Amin, Zubin Bharucha, John Gloster, Rajesh Aravamudhan, Cathy Craig, Alex Marshall and Shane Warne. Andrew Wildblood and Peter Griffiths, two of the original architects of the IPL,were helpful on both facts, reviews and insights.

We must thank our outstanding Indian Advisory Board of S. Ramadorai, Vijay Singh, Piyush Pandey, Ravneet Singh Gill, Ravneet Pawha and Rohan Shah. I would also like to think the late Shri Arun Jaitley, who became a great friend and counsellor over many years. He is a huge loss to the government of India.

I have to thank the original co-investors in Investors in Cricket, led by Peter Wheeler, Paris Moayedi, Rick Haythornthwaite and Glenn Earle. And thanks to friends, Jim Murgatroyd, Ed Wray, Mark Davies, David Grant, Mark Onyett and Phil Jansen for starting the trend for the annual May Bank Holiday visit from the UK!

I would also like to acknowledge the time and work put in by the 'book team' – particularly Neville Chesan, Ann Dearden and C.P. Thomas for his review. Thanks to Grant Feller for his consistently honest advice. Thanks also to Lee Fairbrother for his cover design and to Nicola Lush and Gwen McCann for their invaluable editorial advice. Thanks too to Gareth Howard and Peter at Authoright for their enthusiasm and quick response and Maddy Hurley for getting the project 'over the line'. I learnt a lot about the publishing industry, and self-publishing should definitely be the 'new normal'!

Last and certainly not least, I want to thank 'the Analyst' Simon Hughes, my co-author and friend for over 30 years: without whom the book would never have been completed; without whom the book would have been unreadable; and whose own research, insights and debate have greatly enhanced the end product. Simon joined the project two years ago. He is one of the game's great writers, great thinkers and great innovators. The production innovations created by 'the Analyst' during Channel 4's ground-breaking coverage of the game have been borrowed, copied and evolved by all sports broadcasters.

An important personal thank you to Doug Yeabsley, my cricket master at Haberdasher's Aske's school for inspiring my love of cricket, and to all of the teachers and coaches across the world who 'feed' the game with its next generation.

Thanks also to the amazing health workers across the world who have been on the front line of the coronavirus challenge, helping all sports to be able to restart in an environment of safety. All proceeds from the book will go to the emergency coronavirus appeal for South Asia (India, Pakistan, Bangladesh and Sri Lanka), which is being led by the British Asian Trust. While coronavirus has been a challenge for all, for the 500 million South Asians who still live on less than one dollar a day, this virus has been a catastrophe. Hopefully, cricket will soon be back for the region, and for the whole world, as without the passion of the fans, there would be no commercially viable game of cricket – let alone, one that is ready for an even brighter 'New Innings'.

Manoj Badale

The Ultimate Game

World Cup final 14 July 2019 Lord's

7.42pm: Two to win. Thirty thousand spectators are transfixed with excitement as England's new pace sensation Jofra Archer (a Rajasthan Royal) bowls the final ball of the World Cup final super over – cricket's equivalent of the penalty shoot-out – to Martin Guptill, New Zealand's hard-hitting batsman. The delivery homes in at the toes of the batsman. Guptill intends to slog, hack or slice the ball somewhere, anywhere, it doesn't matter how, for the two runs New Zealand need to win. But the delivery is too full and direct for him to get any leverage and he can only shovel it towards the short Grandstand boundary where Jason Roy, one of the sharpest of England's fielders, swoops on it, pauses briefly and fires the return back to wicketkeeper Jos Buttler (another Royal). Buttler gathers the ball and hurls himself sideways, demolishing the stumps as Guptill dives desperately for the line. He is a metre short. After 48 matches over six weeks and a final lasting more than nine hours England have won a first World Cup by, in commentator Ian Smith's words, "the barest of margins!" The super over is tied, but England have clinched the cup by scoring more boundaries during the day. Everyone is in suspended animation until the replay on the big screen confirms the verdict.

The crowd erupts. Lord's, the legendary 'home of cricket', a place where matches were first staged two centuries before and which still has a reputation for tradition and decorum, is a scene of wild emotion. The England players career into each other in uninhibited ecstasy, Archer sinks to his knees in grateful submission to a superior being and is embraced by the team's rejuvenated star Ben Stokes (also a Royal). The England supporters punch the air in triumph, the New Zealand players stumble around the field dazed and confused. One or two are in tears. These images are relayed live around the world by more than 30 high definition cameras to almost one billion people.

1

That decisive super over required less than five minutes to complete. Yet those six balls encapsulated so much of cricket's transformation from an often meandering, baffling, exclusive game to one of speed and bravado and compelling melodrama that now regularly captivates a quarter of the world's population. It is a transformation effected by the advent of the Twenty20 (T20) format in general and, in particular, the Indian Premier League (IPL).

The precision and deception of a high-speed bowler (Archer); the fearless batsmen totally undaunted by trying to score 16 off one over to win (Guptill and Jimmy Neesham); the outrageous strokes enabling a batsman to deposit an almost perfect 90mph toe-crusher far over the midwicket boundary for four or six (Buttler); the cool, calm leadership (Eoin Morgan) and the slick, athletic fielding (Roy, Buttler, Stokes) under the severest pressure; the continuous uncertainty at the eventual outcome keeping the capacity crowd and vast TV audience in constant thrall. All these, and indeed the super over concept itself, are hallmarks of the IPL, a tournament that has completely reconfigured cricket as a dynamic sport for the masses – a real-life soap opera – that conjured unprecedented riches for the organisers, the investors and the participants. Ten of England's World Cup winning team have honed their skills in it, and eight of the gallant losers, New Zealand.

This book, initiated, originally written with the many diagrams, and then co-authored by the lead owner of the Rajasthan Royals, Manoj Badale, delves deeply into the anatomy of the IPL to examine how it has revolutionised the game. Badale, a lifelong cricket fan, was in the World Cup final crowd that day.

Manoj Badale: As I watched the game, I realised that most of the spectators had never seen a super over. The atmosphere was electric. The mayhem at Lord's made me momentarily feel as if I was at an IPL match at an Indian Cricket Ground – everyone standing, jumping and screaming at every ball. Ten years previously, our IPL team, the Rajasthan Royals had played in one of the very first ever super overs in Cape Town. And now, three current Royals – Stokes, Buttler and Archer – had the starring roles in the super over to win the World Cup for England. It felt like cricket's reinvention was finally on show at the historic 'Home' of the game. It was a brilliant advert for modern cricket.

The IPL, launched only in 2008, has reinvented cricket, making it universally watchable, sellable and phenomenally profitable. Using a unique business model, it is now one of the world's biggest sports leagues. Silicon Valley technology funds now explore investment in IPL teams and media behemoths such as Amazon and Facebook seek to leverage the league's invaluable access to the global market. In 2019 it was valued at $6.3bn. Men like Virat Kohli and Ben Stokes can earn $2m in six weeks playing in it. It is the jewel in 21st century India's growing economy, spawning copycat leagues within India and all over the world, in a variety of sports. How has it achieved this in little more than a decade? And what are the lessons learnt? And how can these lessons inform the business of sport as it faces one of its biggest ever financial crises?

We go behind the scenes with one of the founding IPL teams, the Rajasthan Royals – the league's first winners, led by Shane Warne. We learn of their development under Rahul Dravid. And explore how the franchise became home to England's World Cup stars Stokes, Buttler and Archer and Australia's run-machine Steve Smith. We sample the vital ingredients of the IPL and how, through its impact on cricket and its impact on India, it has revolutionised the business of sport.

We learn about league design. We see how to build valuable media rights. We appreciate how the IPL has transformed players' lives. We look at how to build brand value within franchises. We discover digital innovation kickstarting a new era of unprecedented commercial growth for broadcasters, rights holders, sports organisations and players. We also examine the many challenges that the IPL has faced, the growing power of the Indian cricket boards and the lessons for sports governance. We analyse the growing influence and impact of gambling within sport and the temptations for players to engage in illegal acts. And we learn how continuous innovation remains the only protection for sport, as it grows in both economic influence and societal importance.

Exactly a year later, the world is currently gripped by the global pandemic – Covid-19. Sport has been affected across the board, the Olympics cancelled, all major leagues and tournaments suspended indefinitely. Cricket has not been spared. IPL Season 13 was postponed. The English season has been decimated. And the global finances of the game put under huge pressure. In industry and in business, reinvention is often created by either a visionary group of leaders (as in the IPL) or by an existential crisis. The lessons, good and bad, from an analysis of cricket's most recent reinvention – the IPL – have never been more important than in a post-Covid world. Across the world industries, businesses, governments and individuals are being forced to reflect and reset. Cricket is no exception, and the game must make many difficult choices in the coming years. If it rests on the laurels of 2019, it will stagnate and retrench. It is time for a 'New Innings'.

Waking the Giant

Life before the IPL

Cricket is one of the oldest ball sports in the world. There are mentions of a crude version of it played in England in 1300. It was first codified in 1744. The size and shape of its essential raw materials – the bat, the ball and the pitch – are still largely the same today. It is a game that has overcome numerous crises and scandals and constant fears for its survival in a fast-paced world that doesn't have the patience for a match that can take several days to complete.

In England by the turn of the 21st century interest in cricket had really begun to wane. The national side were poor, many domestic teams were close to bankruptcy and participation was on the slide. The introduction in 2003 of a new format – Twenty20, (T20) enabling a game to be done and dusted in under three hours in the evening – threw cricket a potential lifeline. There were many mutterings of 'it's not cricket' from the traditionalists, but the concept quickly caught on. County grounds (the English domestic game is organised across 18 regional county teams) that were usually characterised by swathes of empty seating were suddenly full on a Friday night and pavilion bars ran out of beer. Three years on – helped by England defeating their ancient rival Australia for the first time in 18 years in 2005, in a compelling series of five-day Test matches – numbers and general interest were picking up. Then the English administrators sold all of the exclusive live rights to a subscription channel (Sky) and the game started to lose mainstream visibility again. The modestly supported counties were mostly reliant on central hand-outs of £1.3m from the board to survive. By 2007 cricket, especially in the UK, was once again on the wane.

India, where cricket was initially spread by the Parsees (a religious community of Zoroastrians descended from Persia) in the 1870s, was emerging as cricket's new financial powerhouse. Attendances for Test matches were low but one-day internationals drew huge crowds attracted by big names like Sachin Tendulkar and the Indian Board sold the domestic TV rights for a hefty $150m a year (in 2006 this was three times what any other country had managed). India were starting to call the shots at the international table because they could guarantee significant broadcast income, much to the distaste of the old cricket power base within England. And yet, in spite of being easily the most populous cricketing nation, India's performances were underwhelming. In 2006 they occupied a lowly position in the world rankings, and despite the millions of kids playing cricket on the fields and maidans of the subcontinent of an evening, most dreamt of an appearance on *Deal or No Deal* rather than playing cricket for India. As with much of the cricket world, if you didn't play for your country, you couldn't make much of a living from the game. In 2006, cricket didn't feel much like something to invest in.

Investors in Cricket

Born in India but brought up in England, Manoj Badale had long coveted the idea of a serious involvement in cricket. He was a cricket obsessive, playing at school and university, and we first met when I was breaking into the Middlesex county team of the 1980s, and then later in West London reconnecting through our kids. He was given a close insight into professional cricket through our conversations, and friendships with Nasser Hussain and Mike Atherton. But it was the opportunity to apply business learnings – from his 20-year business-building partnership with Charles Mindenhall (through their company Blenheim Chalcot) – to invest in the game (and ultimately the IPL) that forms the backbone for the content in this book. Working together, with me as narrator (and researcher), Manoj's views are captured through quotes (in italics), and drive our overall conclusions.

> *Manoj Badale: Back in 2006, it felt like the game needed new ideas, and new sources of investments. The key to improving the financial fortunes within English cricket was to harness the Indian (and South Asian) eyeball. If a business could have some sort of platform in the game – perhaps an English county – there were a multitude of opportunities. Along with my business partner Charles Mindenhall, we set about a business plan, which had three main*

strands, all of which were about updating a traditional niche sport (cricket) ready for the opportunity presented by hundreds of millions of new Indian consumers with increasing wealth and increasing leisure time.

At that time, for every conversation that took place about reaching new cricket fans, there were a hundred about protecting the traditional formats of the game. Changing lifestyles, new technology, and broader competition for people's leisure time required a change in those formats. Cricket, like every sport, needed to embrace this change rather than resist it. It was becoming imprisoned by its own history.

Badale and Mindenhall diverted investment from their usual focus on digital technology, to build a new company – Investors in Cricket – which began by acquiring the commercial rights to run an English county – Leicestershire. The investment thesis was to point the club squarely at the Indian opportunity. In much the same way that English Premier League clubs were battling it out for the fan bases of China, India and the US, Badale and Mindenhall saw the possibility to create 'India's most popular' team in the UK. Leicestershire – with its large Asian contingent in the city – seemed the perfect fit. It had had limited financial success for many years but had acquired a strong position in T20. Great history, strong position in the growth part of the game, and an untapped local Asian opportunity. However, the venture failed.

Transforming existing mindsets and traditions was always going to take time. While T20 evenings were income generating, the vast majority of the fixture schedule was not.

Manoj: We underestimated the time-consuming decision processes within county cricket clubs. Our biggest mistake was to think that you could build a market, when you fundamentally don't have control of the 'product', which was controlled by the ECB (English Cricket Board). Sport is a product that is consumed by fans, which justify the investment of sponsors, who pay for the media coverage, which in turn grows the fans – all of which directly, or indirectly, funds the clubs. Cricket is no different, but how do you build a business if you have no control of the product? We also learnt the commercial reality of 'club ownership economics'. That is, without a share of valuable media rights, owning clubs is a pretty unattractive investment proposition – other than to create community and social benefit or to massage the ego!

At that time (2008) the people who did control the 'product', the England and Wales Cricket Board (ECB) were making the wrong strategic and commercial choices. Under Giles Clarke they refused to see that there were too many counties. They resisted outside investment into their one growth shoot – T20. They took cricket away from terrestrial television and put it behind a paywall. They expanded the number of international (Test Match Status) grounds, creating unnecessary competition, expense and confusion. They did negotiate ever larger TV contracts with Sky, allowing them to hand out a £1.3m subsidy to each county once a year (and secure important votes in a governance structure that voted by majority). But poorly run businesses that survive due to a central hand-out rarely build a thriving industry. The English game remained governed by a forum of those counties presiding over a game that continued to decline in terms of participation. It was a flawed governance process, which to this day constrains the game's potential.

Seeking inspiration from football, Investors in Cricket tried something different. In September 2006 they staged a 'Champions League' of cricket featuring the top T20 teams from England, Pakistan, South Africa and Sri Lanka. To get meaningful TV coverage required Indian players participating. They were not forthcoming, so they created an international XI with some Indian players. The tournament was a muted success but the organisers had made a fatal error. They had not got the governing bodies (the ICC and the ECB) onside and had no prospects of doing so anytime soon. The venture failed.

So, Investors in Cricket immediately turned their attention to investing in, rather than simply benefitting from, the economic growth of the game in the subcontinent. In such a large country, there was always enormous debate about whether the best 11 players always made up the national team. One reason was the regional nature of selections, and another the regularity of changes in selection panel. It was logical in a country of that size and population that there would be plenty of undiscovered talent. Latching onto the boom in reality TV, Badale and his team, of which I was a part, created *Cricket Star* – a cricketing version of *Pop Idol*. The show was fully endorsed by the BCCI and in 2006 it ran for 12 weeks on Zee TV.

It did not turn anyone into the sporting versions of One Direction or Simon Cowell, although Zee Television were enthusiastic partners. The content just wasn't engaging enough to sustain regular viewers in prime-time slots over 12 weeks. Also, Zee were turning their attention to the creation of their own cricket property, the Indian Cricket League (ICL), a domestic tournament based on the short T20 form of the game. Though disappointed with the failure of *Cricket Star*, Badale and team were unaware that this was excellent preparation for a much bigger investment opportunity.

Manoj: With our technology businesses at Blenheim Chalcot, all of which we build from scratch, we always emphasise the importance of 'getting on the pitch' with a new business, to really learn where the greatest potential for disruption or value creation exist. You build knowledge and relationships. Most of our businesses 'pivot' or change plans multiple times. Cricket was proving to be no exception!

The Catalyst

If you've ever been to India to play or watch cricket, you'll know two things. One, their obvious, unbridled passion for the sport and the abundance of fantastic talent everywhere you look. Two, the terrible state of most of their cricket grounds – before 2006 anyway. I remember peering out through cracked windows from the concrete carbuncle that was the Nagpur media centre at the 2006 India v England Test, reporters overpowered by the stench of raw sewage emanating from nearby drains. The stadium was dilapidated and the outfield rutted and ropey.

Indian cricket was stuck in a rut. Their star players had huge power and determined the approach. If changes to the game, or to training, were not popular – fitness training, practice matches, the Decision Review System – they didn't happen. They were over-reliant on brilliant batsmen – Sachin Tendulkar, Rahul Dravid, Virender Sehwag, VVS Laxman and Sourav Ganguly – and their fielding was dire. Their performances at international level were wildly inconsistent. Scheduling lacked appropriate rigour. Home internationals were divvied out to different states according to which local administrators wielded the most influence – political or otherwise.

Cricket's T20 format had not yet caught on in India, or anywhere else except the UK for that matter. (It was perhaps not that surprising that the version was popular in England since 20-over cricket had actually been played at clubs and schools there since the Second World War. But it had taken a clairvoyant ECB marketing executive, Stuart Robertson, to persuade the professional counties to adopt the idea – they voted 11–7 in favour.) And despite 27,000 fans turning up to Lord's for the Middlesex v Surrey encounter – the largest crowd at a domestic match (other than a cup final) for 50 years – this short-form style did not gain universal approval.

Manoj: Many cricket fans, and even players, regarded T20 as a gimmick. The former England captain Nasser Hussain, now a seasoned commentator, used to refer to it as 'club cricket'! Many of the older fans were appalled by the coloured clothing, the loud music, and the aggressive style of play.

The Test playing countries staged the odd T20 international, but there was no sign that this three-hour version of cricket would be its salvation. There was a jovial feel to the inaugural T20 match between New Zealand and Australia in 2006; both teams were kitted out in retro-coloured strips as a tribute to the first days of 'pyjama' cricket in the 1980s (remember that New Zealand beige?) and some players sported moustaches and hairstyles of the time. Glenn McGrath even mimicked Trevor Chappell's notorious 1981 underarm delivery. The top professionals did not see it as serious cricket – not like 'Test Match Cricket' played over five days.

India were actually the last Test nation to play a T20 international (on 1 December 2006). The BCCI, wedded to the lucrative broadcast and advertising income of longer formats, had paid scant attention to T20. Yet less than a year later, and despite their total lack of experience, India won the inaugural ICC World T20, staged in South Africa. The final – between India and Pakistan – was the media's dream with an estimated TV audience of 400m. The last over finish, exhilarating competition, six hitting, all captured the Indian public's imagination. This triumph instantly quelled the vast discontent surrounding India's abject failure at the 2007 (50 over) World Cup six months earlier. It was not just their first global success for a quarter of a century. It was the catalyst for the explosion of T20. It was like an open sesame to the gold rush of the 1880s.

T20 World Cup Final Scorecard
Johannesburg

	INDIA			PAKISTAN	
	157-5			**152 all out**	
G Gambhir		75 (54)	Imran Nazir		33 (14)
RG Sharma		30 (16)	Misbah-ul-Haq		43 (38)
	Over 20			**Over 19.3**	
Mohammad Asif		1/25 (3)	IK Pathan		3/16 (4)
Umar Gul		3/28 (4)	RP Singh		3/26 (4)
	India won by 5 runs				

Fig. 1

A brand-new competition – the ICL conceived before the T20 World Cup triumph, was launched straight afterwards. It was the brainchild of Subhash Chandra, an Indian media magnate, owner of Zee TV that had broadcast Investors in Cricket's television show *Cricket Star* the year before. The ICL had been developed under the radar through 2007, targeting peripheral players from the domestic Indian circuit, intertwined with the odd former star player. Tony Greig, heavily involved recruiting players for Kerry Packer's original World Series Cricket in the late 1970s, was a central figure again. The great Indian allrounder Kapil Dev was the ICL's figurehead. With the official governing body of cricket – the ICC – not at all focused on T20 cricket, the ICL looked a daring but inspired idea, despite the less-than-celebrated status of many of the signed players. However, with the ICL there were limited city connections and competition, as all of the teams were owned by one entity. Fans didn't care who won or lost. And Zee made another crucial mistake. They did not seek the backing of cricket's real powerhouse, the BCCI.

A man with a vision

Enter Lalit Modi, who was quickly becoming a driving force within the BCCI. Throughout history, whenever a sport has been at the crossroads there has been one visionary, one risk-taker, one impresario who has led the way into the future. Formula One was transformed by Bernie Ecclestone, baseball had Bud Selig, David Stern drove basketball's expansion, the establishment of the English Premier League was driven by Rick Parry, chief executive of the EFL. In 1977 Kerry Packer was cricket's original game-changer, introducing coloured shirts, floodlights and reinventing the one-day game. In 2007 Lalit Modi stepped into world cricket's power vacuum.

The son of the now late, famous Indian industrialist, KK Modi, whose business empire included tobacco, chemicals and entertainment, Modi was himself driven towards sports and entertainment. He was heavily influenced in his ideas by his time working with Disney in the US. His professional interest in cricket dated from the mid-1990s. He was convinced the game offered a massive opportunity. He managed to win election to the cricket association of the small Himalayan state of Himachal Pradesh, then wrested control of the Rajasthan Cricket Association. Within months he was part of the BCCI and promptly recognised within the board as the new commercial leader. He proceeded to raise $150m for the BCCI from a pair of sponsorship deals – with Nike and Sahara – and then an unprecedented $620m from selling the four-year broadcast rights for Indian cricket to Nimbus, a domestic broadcaster.

Having an intimate knowledge of American sports from his student days helped him recognise the potential in India for a professional cricket league. "I'd be sitting all alone in an American college on Sunday and Monday nights while everyone else was watching NFL," Modi says. "Fat guys running around a field chasing a ball. Everybody was glued to it. Or basketball which was also alien to me. Or ice hockey or baseball. They were so passionate about it. All the ESPN executives who I worked with later would talk about was sport. I knew that sport in India was untapped, and that cricket had enormous potential. But I recognised I must know the market, know what I'm doing and execute it with perfection. I'd only have one chance."

He had been doing the groundwork throughout 2007, with many meetings with businessmen and entrepreneurs. The framework for a brand-new competition was well established. But someone else (Zee TV and Subhash Chandra) had got there first. If anything, that encouraged Modi more.

Manoj: Lalit had the strengths of all entrepreneurs. He had a big vision. He had a good commercial instinct. He had resilience and self-confidence. He had courage, and an attention to detail. His global education meant he had international standards, which he wanted to achieve with the IPL. His appetite for celebrity and parties, meant that these ingredients would be important to the design of the format off-the-field. He loved the media, and his usage of it to build awareness was extraordinary.

He also, like all of us, had weaknesses. He could be autocratic and short-tempered. He controlled too much and didn't always build his organisations – too much would go through him. And he was too focused on the media. He even had his own camera crew that followed him around during matches.

He saw the opportunity for the short format early, and originally planned to launch a league in 2009. However, with the arrival of the ICL, he needed to advance his plans. One of the first things that he had to do was stop the ICL. With the full backing of the BCCI he slowly dismantled Zee's plan to create a domestic T20 league.

Showing extreme agility, the BCCI had already acted. In June 2007 they refused to endorse the ICL and threatened all players who signed up to the league with life bans from domestic and international cricket and forbade the major cricket stadiums from staging the matches. Playing fees for accredited domestic competitions were doubled. The ICC fell in line with the BCCI and would not officially recognise the ICL. That ensured that it quickly became a semi-rebel league for the 'has-beens' and 'not-quite-made-its'.

In September 2007 the BCCI also announced the launch of their own domestic, franchise-based T20 league and a supplementary international T20 competition (the Champions League) in harness with the Australian, English and South African cricket boards. Sachin Tendulkar, Rahul Dravid, Sourav Ganguly and Glenn McGrath were among the star players who attended the launch event.

Modi had initially planned to launch in 2008, with season one in 2009, but India's unexpected World T20 victory created new urgency. The board would own the league but private investors could own the teams and receive a large proportion of central revenue. It would be called the Indian Premier League.

Initial Tournament Format (2008-2010)

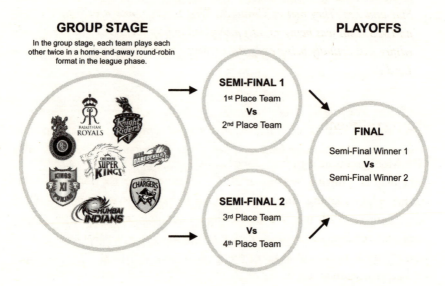

Fig. 2

India at the time had an annual growth rate in the economy of 8.8%, a massive reduction of people on the breadline (from 93% of the population in 1987 to 54% in 2007) and a huge growth in the middle class. In 2007, there were 50m Indians regarded as middle class by their earnings (between $25,000 and $118,000). That figure was expected to jump to 590m by the year 2025. That's a lot of disposable income. Lalit Modi was the right man in the right place at the right time.

He worked with several from the BCCI and partnered with sports consultancy IMG, led in that area by Andrew Wildblood, a cricket loving executive, to formalise the IPL format. They were hugely influenced by the obvious lack of public interest in India's regional cricket, principally the Ranji Trophy played between state sides since the 1930s at deserted grounds. "In the big metros," Wildblood explained, "where the money is in India, people identify much more with their city than with their state."

Manoj: Lalit Modi first mentioned the idea of a city-based league in early 2007. He was totally focused on a mega TV deal. I suggested a conversation with Kunal Dasgupta, who was running Sony, and who was investing heavily in cricket (through his SET Max channel) – which had been dominated by Star and Zee. They met in Chiswick, West London, and a mile up the road an IMG team was being rapidly assembled to help the BCCI. The whole IPL edifice was actually being designed in West London just a stone's throw from Lord's!

Star recruitment

Lalit Modi recounts how he assembled the vital ingredients of his enterprise – the players – during September 2007. "I went all over the place talking to the best players saying 'don't sign with the ICL, their strategy is not good – sign a contract with me. We are having an auction, come for a low reserve price and you'll make a lot of money in the auction – if you're good.' Or I gave them the option of a fixed price and they could still go in the auction. I'll keep the money, up or down. A lot of them opted for the fixed price. I won them over by working out the highest salary that international players were being paid at the time – about $200,000 – and doubling it. I offered [the great West Indian batsman] Brian Lara half a million dollars – as a minimum. He didn't sign. He said 'I want a million.' I said 'I ain't guaranteeing you a million dollars, but you'll make far more than that if you go with my system.' He missed the boat."

Modi headed to South Africa for the 2007 World T20 to sign up the Indian team for the IPL. He had a plan. "The tournament hadn't really caught alight. I went into the Indian dressing room in Durban. I said 'anybody who hits six sixes in an over, or takes six wickets in an over, will get a Porsche!' I'm standing in Kingsmead on the sidelines and Yuvraj Singh hits his first six – off Stuart Broad. Then a second six. Then a third. I woke up. I said to myself 'Shit this could be it!' Yuvraj is looking at me. He hits his fourth six. Fifth six. He hit the sixth six. And he came running towards me and he said 'My Porsche! My Porsche!!' I said 'It's done.' And he went running back and I said, 'Wait! Give me your bat!' And he came back and he gave me his bat and changed it for another. And I said 'That's mine now.' Everybody was so excited.

"That was the start of the IPL! I thought I don't need to market this anymore. It is going to market itself. Now we have to win this T20 World Cup thing. And we did. We created history. And I said to Mr Sharad Pawar [BCCI president] 'India have won the World T20 and they are returning to India tonight. We should felicitate them on behalf of the Board and the IPL when they land. Open top buses, a reception. Like the Italians did with their soccer team.' We got three buses to the airport. I told the media to cover it live. I gave them a bus. I said – anybody who covers it live will get an interview with the team. Then 144 channels went live! LIVE!! I estimated it would take two to three hours to get to the Wankhede Stadium for the reception. The team arrived at the airport at 6am. It took us 11 hours to get to the stadium. *Eleven* hours!! Five million people were on the streets. It was a wall of human beings!"

The Indian players were overnight heroes. The public were dying to see more of them. And within a few months they could. Every night for six weeks in the IPL. Modi could see it all unfolding in front of his eyes. The IPL exploded onto the scene in April 2008 in a cacophony of fireworks and a blaze of sixes from the bat of New Zealand's Brendon McCullum. The genius of the IPL is the way those explosions have not only continued but grown louder and resonated far and wide as the years have passed.

This story examines how a league dreamt up by an Indian entrepreneur and backed by an assortment of investors has transformed sport the world over. We also examine the lessons for sport, as it responds to an existential crisis created by coronavirus, the pandemic from China. In much the same way that Indian cricket responded to the sudden change in public opinion induced by their 2007 T20 World Cup win, cricket must now embrace the need for even more fundamental change and will have to get ready for a 'New Innings'.

Chapter 1

Designing the Optimal Sports League

Create a level playing field and ensure unpredictable outcomes

Attracting investment

What draws people into watching sport? Fundamentally it is two main aspects. First, the exhibition of brilliant skill on an individual or team basis. Spectators love to marvel at the exploits and precious gifts of exceptional sportsmen or women. They give sport its 'wow' factor. A poor standard of play is a turn off. Second, an uncertainty about the outcome. Predictable or one-sided matches are boring. Spectators want a contest. Top class sport is part entertainment, part escapism. If you know the result long before the end (or even at the start) it doesn't really serve its purpose.

Lalit Modi's intimate acquaintance with American sport had taught him these two essentials. The founder of the IPL understood to make a new cricket league successful he had to hire the top talent. He knew that the only way to guarantee attracting the best players in the world was to pay them more than anyone else. To have enough capital to do that he had to sell the team franchises to wealthy private investors. He describes this: 'Wooing them required three guarantees: the promise of a decent return; No risk of relegation from the league ; and a level playing field, with transparent access to players.'

The super-talent had to be spread evenly amongst the eight teams so everyone had a chance of winning. It would get the best out of the players too if the teams were relatively equal. The brilliance of Modi's construction was how he reconciled both those principle aims – ensuring enough money to attract the star players and then making sure that players could be purchased through a transparent auction – so ensuring balanced teams and unpredictable outcomes for the games. He started by tapping up his circle of friends for some prospective team owners.

Manoj: He first explained the concept of a franchise auction in October 2007. When he first said that his target was to raise $100m for the new franchises, I laughed. I decided to discuss the opportunity with Lachlan Murdoch, son of Rupert, with whom I had been loosely exploring media investments in India. There was nothing better to give a sports league some credibility than an association with a Murdoch. This was perhaps going to be important.

It was clear, early on, that Lalit Modi was driving the conception, design and running of the league. We needed to put together a consortium as, even with Lachlan, we had only raised a proportion of the investment. I approached his brother-in-law, Suresh Chellaram, a successful businessman based in Nigeria, whom I had met socially, and who was rumoured to be looking for a passive investment, like Lachlan, which was perfect for me.

The design of the league had many enticing aspects. There was no framework to assess a sport's league's attractiveness, so we applied many of the principles I had learnt working at Monitor Company, a management consulting firm founded by Michael Porter. We applied Porter's framework for assessing the attractiveness of an industry to evaluating the viability of a sports league.

Porter essentially looks for five characteristics – low competition (the more competitors, the lower the profit margin e.g. grocery retail), high barriers to entry (to prevent new competitors e.g. government awarded licences), low supplier power (so costs can be controlled – e.g. airline manufacturing), low power of customers (so they are less price sensitive – e.g. luxury handbags) and no substitute products (so consumers have limited choice e.g. Facebook or Google).

From an investment opportunity the IPL seemed to have it all. A small fixed number of teams with no promotion or relegation, therefore limited competition with no risk of costly relegation or threat of new teams (high barriers to entry). An effective salary cap limiting cost structures by managing player costs (managed supplier power), and a massive market with engaged fans creating an attractive customer base (managed customer power) while a powerful board can ensure calendar exclusivity (no substitute products).

Application of Porter's 5 Forces on Sports League Attractiveness

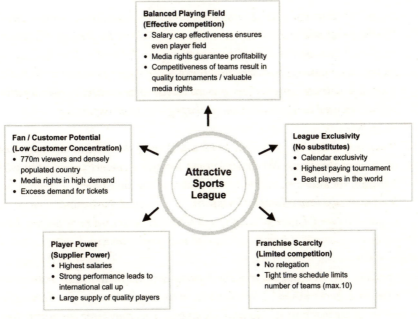

**Balanced Playing Field
(Effective competition)**
- Salary cap effectiveness ensures
  even player field
- Media rights guarantee profitability
- Competitiveness of teams result in
  quality tournaments / valuable
  media rights

**Fan / Customer Potential
(Low Customer Concentration)**
- 770m viewers and densely
  populated country
- Media rights in high demand
- Excess demand for tickets

Attractive Sports League

**League Exclusivity
(No substitutes)**
- Calendar exclusivity
- Highest paying tournament
- Best players in the world

**Player Power
(Supplier Power)**
- Highest salaries
- Strong performance leads to
  international call up
- Large supply of quality players

**Franchise Scarcity
(Limited competition)**
- No relegation
- Tight time schedule limits
  number of teams (max.10)

Fig 3.

The economics of the business plan forecast also looked attractive. Many people overlooked the fact that the payment terms for the franchise fee were likely to be over ten years. Our financial projections showed an assumed three years of losses, suggesting that our peak funding requirement to acquire the franchise was $20–25m, and that was assuming a 'headline' purchase price of $60–70m.

As an investment, the economics seemed highly attractive as a fair proportion of the central revenue was being shared with the franchises (see below) and we already knew that Sony were contemplating spending a considerable sum on it for exclusive TV rights. Our chief concern, at that time, was the potential challenge of doing business in India. But effectively we were co-investing with India 'Inc'. Our interests would be aligned with some of the subcontinent's most powerful business people. If we failed, they failed, and they were unlikely to let that happen.

The IPL financial share out:

The organisers (the BCCI) would receive revenue from:
- media (broadcast rights)
- event and on-ground sponsorship
- official suppliers

The franchises would receive revenue from:
- an equal share of broadcast and sponsorship income from the Board
- gate income at own matches
- franchise title and shirt sponsorship
- local sponsorship
- licensing and merchandising programmes
- hospitality
- franchise own media platforms

The would-be investors were encouraged by two particular guarantees: a share of the media rights (on a sliding scale per year, with 80% of the broadcast revenue divvied out among the franchises in the first year) and a cap on player costs, combined, theoretically, with a transparent purchase process. The major American leagues have figured this out, after years of experimentation with different models, from salary caps (NFL) to luxury taxes on teams that spend excessively on players (MLB and NBA).

On January 10, 2008, Emerging Media (an offshoot of Investors in Cricket) transferred to the BCCI the $5m deposit that was a condition of entering the franchise bidding process. Other individuals or parties rumoured to be interested in running a team included the Oscar-winning actor Russell Crowe (a cousin of New Zealand Test players Martin and Jeff Crowe), various Bollywood personalities, giants of Indian industry like the Ambani family and Vijay Mallya, owner of the Kingfisher group of companies. They were all stepping into the unknown. Little did they realise the tectonic waves the concept would make on the cricket world.

Sale of the century

The first step was the broadcast deal. In late January 2008 Lalit Modi announced that he had secured the IPL broadcast rights to Sony and the World Sports Group for $1bn. A billion dollars for a cricket competition that didn't yet have any team names or players. It was an extraordinary coup prompting the inevitable Billion Dollar Baby headlines. "I knew that once we had the TV deal, the rest would follow," Modi says. "Although the deal was for $1bn, I told the broadcasters I only needed $60m in year one. Let's get the first year done. We will worry about the rest later. I promise if we don't achieve what we set out to achieve I won't carry the IPL on after year one."

The next step was the franchise auction. Modi had spent six weeks frantically marketing the teams – at a time when the world's economies were reeling from the crises in the financial system. The plan now was to allocate the eight franchises to eight bidders. No one would be allowed to own more than one team. The bids were all to be presented in sealed envelopes. It was clear that the major cities like Mumbai and Delhi would attract the largest sums, so Emerging Media opted to pitch instead for either Jaipur (Rajasthan) or Mohali (Punjab.) On January 24 the prospective owners arrived in a selection of limousines (Mallya's was a red Bentley) then battled through a sea of photographers and journalists at Mumbai's Wankhede Stadium to make their bids.

Manoj: We arrived in a Honda, and everyone assumed that we were from the press! We entered the main boardroom, submitted our sealed bids at 2.45pm and then took seats at the table, watching much frenzied activity. I was sitting next to Fraser Castellino (who was to be our Season 1 CEO) and an empty chair, which was subsequently filled by a young woman in big sunglasses who seemed to be attracting most of the attention from the male-dominated room. "Hello, what do you do?" I asked her, at which point I received a firm jab into my ribs from Fraser. "She is one of India's leading Bollywood actresses, Preity Zinta!" he whispered, at which point I tried to clumsily adjust my question. "I mean, which team are you bidding for?" "We have bid for a few," she responded, "but we think that we will only get a chance for Hyderabad, Jaipur or Mohali." Clearly, we had competition for one of the smaller cities – not good news.

The allocation of franchises began in mid-afternoon. The names of the nine hopeful bidders were called out one by one, starting with the highest offer. This was from Mukesh Ambani's Reliance Group with an eye-popping $112m to buy a team in a competition that so far didn't exist. It gave them first choice. They selected Mumbai. They also won the rights to host the final. Next the flamboyant Vijay Mallya, who had offered $110m, chose Bangalore which would also stage the opening ceremony. An unexpected third bidder – the *Deccan Chronicle* – won control of their chosen Hyderabad with their $107m pitch. Chennai ($91m) and Delhi ($84m) went next. The sixth winning bid was Shah Rukh Khan, the Bollywood star, who plumped for Kolkata.

Manoj: Six down, two to go. A handful of bidders remained. When the seventh winning bidder was announced as Preity Zinta, with a bid of $75m, I was sure that it was game over for us. There were only two franchises left for them to choose from, Punjab and Rajasthan. Eventually, after extensive deliberations, they announced their choice – Punjab. We were still in, but only just. It was now 7pm. 'Emerging Media, which includes Lachlan Murdoch, win the eighth franchise' declared the BCCI. None of the press recognized us, so we were able to slip away while the media frenzy focused on everyone else.

There was an owners' celebration party on the rooftop of the Dome, in the Intercontinental Hotel. It carried on into the early hours and was like nothing that I had ever seen in Mumbai before. Everyone seemed to be the son or daughter of a mega-Indian businessman, with the major business houses of the Wadia's, Burman's all represented. Money was clearly not an issue, and everyone seemed to know everyone else – apart from me of course.

In the space of a month, the BCCI had raised $1.8bn for a tournament that still actually had no players, no teams and no schedule. This was for a sport that, a little more than 20 years before, the board had to *pay* the national broadcaster, Doordarshan, to show. There was inevitable delight and fascination in India, not least that the concept had lured industrial bigwigs and, even more significantly, Bollywood icons, to invest substantial sums. "Bollywood takes to the field," declared *The Economic Times*. It was the first time that India's two big passions – cricket and movies – had been harnessed together.

"People in India watched two things: Bollywood and cricket," Modi says. "If you fixed the two together it would be so powerful and dynamic. If we had no interference inside the rope and an explosion outside the rope – complete controversy – we had a fantastic product. It would be a reality show beyond comprehension because you can't predict what's going to happen next."

Elsewhere there was a fair amount of cynicism. The ECB, in particular, were privately outraged that some Indian executive was capitalising on a format they had invented – a sort of 'reverse colonialism'. They immediately declared that English players wouldn't be available (on the basis that the IPL clashed with the start of the domestic programme, a problem which was of course quite soluble). Guided by the board, the 18 English first class counties – existing mostly hand to mouth – closed ranks. They were ruled by myopia. They were like hens clucking about in the yard over scraps while this big unruly Indian beast rampaged untethered about the place. They were privately convinced it would soon come to grief.

The player auction: fantasy cricket for real

A phone conversation in February 2008 between old school cricketing pals Andrew Wildblood, the seasoned sports media consultant, and Richard Madley, the TV auctioneer, set the wheels in motion for one of the most revolutionary events in the history of sport.

"Madders? It's Wildblood. Ever been to India before?"

"Not yet Wildy"

"Well we'd like you in Mumbai next week to conduct an auction of cricket players"

There have been many alternative ways to select sports teams from the traditional two captains taking-it-in-turns method of the school playground to the draft system in American sports where the lowest-finishing team gets the first pick of the new college intake. In the NFL draft, each of the 32 teams receives one pick per round in reverse order to their most recent finishing position (so last place gets first pick and so on). It's a method for keeping a league that doesn't have promotion and relegation competitive. But never before had professional sportsmen been literally auctioned off to team owners.

The idea was conceived by Modi and Wildblood to circumvent the multiple challenges with salary caps. They had to find a way round the prospect of a wealthy team owner buying a player publicly for say $100,000 – keeping well within salary-cap limits – while securing him with a large private sponsorship offer. "Traditional salary caps are always broken," Modi says. "I knew if you tried to impose a salary cap on a variety of rich businessmen there was a strong chance they'd find a way round it. Because there was going to be no promotion and relegation, it was critical that we had a way of ensuring a level playing field across the teams, and a well-executed salary cap is the key to achieving this.

"I got the idea of the auction because we had a partnership with Sotheby's auction house in India. Where you offer the item to the highest bidder. What's wrong with that? Great transparency. I also knew it would be the talk of the town – extremely controversial. This was the central part of my strategy.

"With the IPL consisting of only eight teams, if two of the eight – owned by the richest men – always win, it would soon become boring. You have to keep it interesting. The auction was a way of controlling how players were allocated to the teams. There's an auction 'purse' for each team and if you can't spend more than the purse then it's no advantage being the richest – it's like a transparent salary cap – it completely shines a light on how players are allocated. We also wanted to reassure owners that their asset wouldn't fall off a cliff if they got relegated, which is why we guaranteed the number of teams, and no relegation."

So, for the first time in history, top sportsmen were going to go under the hammer like works of art or rare antiques. It was an intriguing idea that immediately created a buzz among the players speculating on who would be regarded as the most valuable, and who would be sold for a pittance. Five 'icon' players – Sachin Tendulkar, Sourav Ganguly, Rahul Dravid, Virender Sehwag and Yuvraj Singh – were removed from the auction. "We wanted Sachin to play for the Maharastra (Mumbai) team because that's where he's from," Wildblood remembers. "Like a sort of Gerrard of Liverpool idea – we didn't want him playing for a city he had no connection with, similarly Sourav is from Kolkata so we wanted him playing for them. We knew it would get the fans excited.

But we also wanted to do that so that these players were certain to get paid the most, as their participation was critical to the success of the league."

Each franchise could have as many as eight non-Indian players in their initial 16-man (minimum) squad (though only a maximum of four overseas players were allowed in the playing XI) and they had $5m available to assemble their team. This meant an average player's salary of around $350,000 for about six weeks' work.

A group of us sat in Badale's front room in Chiswick, with the glossy IPL brochure, selecting cricketers as if we were choosing holidays. We were playing fantasy cricket for real. We discussed whether (the recently retired) Glenn McGrath really was worth $300,000 a year, or Chris Gayle $500,000, whether McGrath's great partner in crime Shane Warne (also retired) would add value on and off the field (Badale was pushing him as a potential captain), if, as a dashing opener, South Africa's Herschelle Gibbs was a busted flush. We discussed the danger of a total obsession with the big international stars. With a limit of four overseas players per team (on the field), the smart money would be on seizing the best Indian players, four of whom had to be under 22. With no English players declared available, Badale and his company were the sole English presence.

Manoj: Picking players for teams is one of the most enjoyable aspects of sport. Who should play, who should bat where, which combinations worked best. This was a discussion that every cricket fan has had on countless occasions. The difference was that this time it was for real. Seven days later I was going to have to make instant decisions about spending up to $5m on cricket players, which in reality was a $15m commitment, given that the contracts were for three years. We listed first, second and third choice options for each role in the team, an approach that we have subsequently adopted at every auction, extending that to five players per role with a fixed spend that we are willing to go up to. Commentators focus (naturally) on the value of a player but not sufficiently on the value of a player in a particular role, for a particular team. This is now especially important in Seasons 2 and 3, given the revised player contract terms, where players can be released annually.

I was keen on the use of data and analysis having read Michael Lewis's brilliant Moneyball. Statistics that are typically used to gauge players are often misleading. Analysis and research had to be a key element of the Rajasthan Royals, as we were always going to be at a spend disadvantage (given the budget that was approved at our ownership board), and given our chosen focus on building a profitable franchise within three to four years.

No one was quite sure what to expect as the auction approached. The night before, I was having a drink with Zubin Bharucha (who would eventually become our head of cricket) and Mike Watkinson, the Lancashire coach, at the Cricket Club of India. We were discussing the prospects for the next day, and we were then joined by the England superstar, Andrew Flintoff, who was doing some rehab in Mumbai. He scoffed at the auction. "I can't understand players prioritising playing for a few rupees over their international careers," he said. Ironically one of the first calls I got after IPL Season 1 was from Neil Fairbrother, Flintoff's agent, declaring his availability for Season 2!

Under the hammer

February 20th 2008 was the day that cricket was changed forever. Those 24 hours transformed players' lives, completely altered their priorities and perspectives. It gave a billion Indians hope and fascination and aspiration. It marginalised the world governing body – the ICC – and effectively elevated the domestic game above the international one. It changed the way people thought of, talked about and interpreted cricket. It made every national governing body recalibrate their goals and itineraries. It caused a huge stir in news agencies all over the world. It made cricket, temporarily, the most famous sport on the planet.

Manoj: In my mind, this was THE day that the IPL really arrived. No scene typifies the explosion in media interest better than the hordes of photographers and journalists who blocked the main staircase down to the Oberoi Hotel ballroom on the day of the IPL player auction. Our team, dressed in suits, struggled to get in. With the fashionably late arrival of Shah Rukh Khan and Preity Zinta, the show was ready to begin.

We sat at round tables in the ballroom. The table that you are given is quite important (this is now done the night before with lots), as you get different vantage points. We were at the back in the right corner – able to look over

Mumbai and Chennai, and with a very noisy Kolkata table next to us. We had created a dynamic auction model that allowed us to map other teams' spends as well as our own. We were ahead of the game at that early stage.

The players in every IPL auction are grouped into categories, generally the bigger names in the early groups, and then typically grouped by their skill – batsmen, wicketkeepers, spinners, fast bowlers, etc. Understanding the categories in which players are assigned is critical to auction strategies – as is understanding the likely pricing dynamics when a player is pulled out of the bag first in a category, versus last. If you are the last Indian fast bowler in a group of seven, and there are two to three franchises that need one and who have been outbid, then a player's price can sky-rocket dramatically.

First up in the auction was Shoaib Akhtar. Fifth was Shane Warne. No bids emerged as Richard Madley scanned the room. Just as he was about to declare the player unsold, we raised our paddle. Shane Warne. Sold to Team Jaipur. For his base price of $450,000. We had bought our first player in the IPL. Secretly I was nervous that no one else had bid. Next out was the biggest name of all the players in the auction – Mahendra Singh Dhoni. We knew he was going to be above our budget, so we sat back and watched the auction explode into life. $500k, $600k, $700k and then a million-dollar cricketer – Mumbai versus Bangalore versus Chennai – the biggest Indian families in open warfare – $1.1m, $1.3m and then finally $1.5m! We were shocked. We couldn't believe that Chennai had spent close to a third of their salary cap on one single player. How wrong we all were. Ultimately he was worth every dollar.

The first unsold player was the great Glenn McGrath – (he was later bought in the second round) there was a clear discount on retired players (from which we benefited with Warne). Our next big signing was the South African captain Graeme Smith – this was going to cause a stir, given his and Warne's much-publicised battles in the past. We benefited from some of the early 'spending frenzy' and 'auction ego' that nearly always occurs with the marquee players. Mumbai, for instance, spent 86% of their budget on five star players.

We stuck to our budgets, but not always our plans. We couldn't resist, and made mistakes. We bought Younis Khan and Justin Langer at low prices – even though we didn't need another top order overseas batsman – and they finished up playing one *game between them. I started to panic about our lack of international class Indian players – so we went all out for Mohammed Kaif and overpaid. We weren't just buying for one year, but for three years, so the sums of money were staggering. Late on there was a complaint from Kings XI that we had spent under the 'minimum spend threshold' (which had sensibly been placed there to ensure franchises created competitive teams). The claim was upheld by Modi, and we were fined. We had only spent $3m of our $5m budget, and the minimum spend allowed was $3.3m.*

There is no other experience in business quite like the IPL auction. Never would you sign up to legally enforceable contracts, committing to millions, with such a paucity of due diligence material. And never would you have to make so many split-second decisions, as you bid, stop bidding, and then re-bid to assemble a squad of 25 players. In reality, it was the most significant action an owner could make to influence the team's playing prospects.

There was blanket coverage in the Indian media, brimming with excitement about the first ever million-dollar cricketers, and word quickly spread around the world. 'SOLD! – The day cricket stars went under the hammer for a cool $42m' declared the *Daily Mail*. Modi had offered the players he'd signed the option of a base price or a fixed price – which he would guarantee – but he would also pocket the upside should the bid go higher. "Australia's Andrew Symonds chose the fixed price option," Modi recalls. "It was $100k. He was sold for $1.35m. He was crying. He only got $100k. All the rest of the money went to the BCCI." Some of the other price tags – like $800,000 for the Karnataka wicketkeeper Robin Uthappa (now a Royal, who had played a key role in India winning the T20 World Cup), were eye watering. "Just to add to all the controversy I encouraged activists to complain 'Look they are selling humans like cattle and sheep!' I encouraged people to boo me," Modi recalls.

A month after the auction India's U/19 team won their world cup. These players were suddenly highly sought-after. Modi announced an additional player draft to allocate them. Delhi got first pick. As they had already bought an array of batting talent including Virender Sehwag, Gautham Gambhir and AB de Villiers, they ignored the India U/19 captain – a certain Virat Kohli. They opted for the bowler Pradeep Sangwan instead. The Royals got fifth pick and, focusing on the value of all-rounders, plumped for the (then unknown) Ravi Jadeja.

The Royals also benefitted from having the biggest purse for the second player auction, given their miserly spending at the first one. There were many players who were not invited into the first auction, but who had specialist skills suited for the short form of the game. Two of the Royals' best purchases, Australia's Shane Watson and Pakistan's Sohail Tanvir, were made in that second auction.

While the auction drew howls of derision from many quarters, it was a brilliant innovation that addressed one of the key challenges in ensuring effective salary caps. It banished the role of agents (who earned over £200m in the English Premier League in 2019) minimising that value 'leakage' – and so ensuring maximum earnings for the players. It made player purchasing transparent. It also meant that there was one standard contract – so no lengthy debates and legal fees. Crucially, it prevented the richest owners buying up all the best players. They were shared around, and every three years most are given lot numbers and auctioned off again.

The first auction created huge excitement in the build-up to the tournament. Not only had it produced the first-ever million-dollar player (Dhoni) but it had also aroused some intriguing financial dynamics, with some star players attracting negligible bids and virtual unknowns going for astronomical sums. The young Indian all-rounder Irfan Pathan, for instance, was sold for $925,000, and his brother Yusuf for $425,000. And, because of that subsequent U/19s draft and Delhi opting for Pradeep Sangwan, the Royal Challengers Bangalore picked up Virat Kohli for just $50,000. Little did they know what a steal that was. It all created a fascinating dialogue in the lead up to the first match. The Royals felt confident with their mix of experience and youth. But the one thing that every Indian cricket expert agreed on before that inaugural season was that the Rajasthan Royals would finish last.

Manoj: While the auction generated interest, it was also a fundamental innovation in the design of the league. League design is critical not just for cricket, but for all sports. There are only two leagues in the world, in which all teams/ franchises are profitable – the NFL (American Football) and the IPL.

An Evaluation of Major Professional Sports Leagues

	NFL	MLB	Premier League	NBA	IPL
Fan Base Size	Low	Average	High	Above Average	High
Media/Digital Development	High	High	Above Average	High	Average
Player Spend Enforcement	High	Low	Very low	High	High
Player Purchasing Transparency	High	Average	Average	High	High
Calendar Exclusivity	Above Average	Above Average	High	Above Average	High
Relegation Security	High	High	Average	High	High
League Governance Evolution	Above Average	Average	Average	Above Average	Average
Ownership Model Sophistication	High	Above Average	Average	Above Average	Average

The only two professional sports leagues in the world, in which all franchises are profitable are the NFL and IPL

KEY: ◯ Very low ◔ Low ◑ Average ◕ Above Average ● High

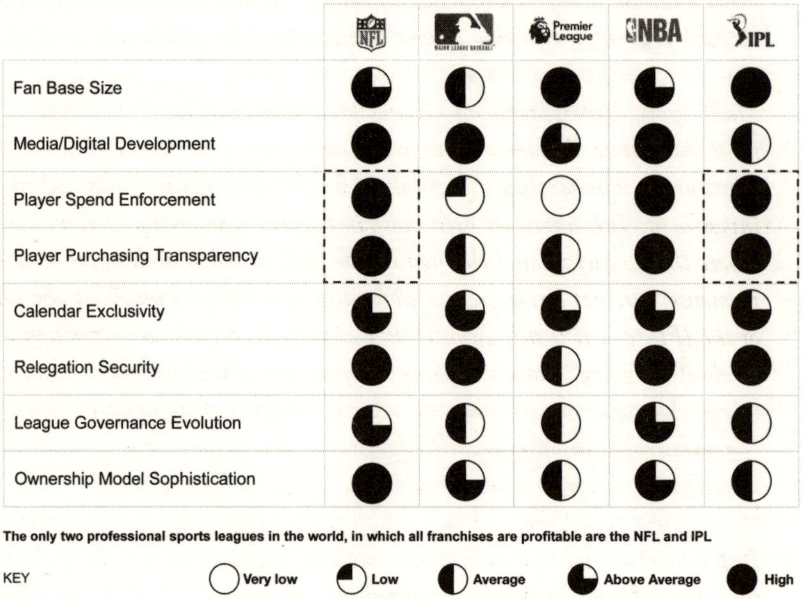

Fig. 4

While not conclusive, what the chart does highlight is the importance of salary caps and player auctions or drafts (to ensure the caps are not bypassed) as critical if commercial investment into a league is to be rewarded, and unpredictable season outcomes ensured.

League design in a post-Covid world

Manoj: The IPL was a new league, created under a new governance structure – which allowed for rapid, albeit highly concentrated, decision making. While already planned, its launch was accelerated to exploit India's T20 World Cup win. That level of agility is something that sports administrators across the world now need to attain, as we grapple with the coronavirus crisis. Rapid decision-making is a must. The IPL was not planned in detail, but certain critical 'anchors' were identified and focused on. The need for private investment, and the need for transparent player purchasing. Together, this would ensure the capital to invest, and the efficiency and innovation which private capital brings – while maximising the commercial value of the league through a focus on ensuring a 'level playing field' for player access.

Many sports have entered the era of professionalism with their players but retain amateur league structures and amateur governance structures. As sports professionalise these aspects, there is still huge potential to attract private investment. This has never been more important than in a post-Covid world, where the financial losses through league and match cancellations have been immense. Cricket has a great opportunity to grow and build on the success of the IPL, but it is still hamstrung by league and tournament design at all levels of the game. Too much money is spent on subsidizing forms of the game which should simply be amateur (although clearly there must be some form of reinvestment into the amateur game to ensure it grows). And there are too many games, with irrelevant outcomes.

In the brief period that coronavirus has hit, writing in May 2020, there has been more discussion than ever, about the economics of sport. Fans have realised the importance of live sports. Players have realised the importance of commercially attractive sport to their livelihoods. Teams have realised the importance of sponsorship and broadcast income to their ability to produce high quality competitive sport and make a profit. Governing bodies are reassessing their approach to private investment, and the importance of a level playing field in attracting that investment. As we adjust to the new normal, every league within cricket needs a reset with respect to aspects of league design. Cricket will need to consider rationalising both formats and teams, redesigning both schedules and tournaments.

Chapter 2

Creating Narratives

Inaugural IPL season was a brilliant opening chapter in a compelling story

Lights, camera, action

As the players assembled for the first IPL, everyone was intrigued to see how the theories of the new league would play out in practice. Could such a radical idea really work? Wasn't it all a bit contrived? How would a nation's sports fans feel about city-based teams created from scratch? Wasn't it all just a gimmick that would soon lose its fascination?

The marketing people were certainly giving it their all. The transformation of India was evident as soon as I arrived in Bangalore for the inaugural match. (I was the only English cricket journalist at the opening game, which tells you much about the attitude then towards the IPL in England). The wide, relatively organised streets of the city were punctuated by the usual huge hoardings advertising the latest Bollywood releases and fizzy drinks. But now they were augmented by vast, Tarantino-inspired images of moody-looking cricketers staring into the camera accompanied by the tag line "Be scared, be very scared!"

At Bangalore's leafy West End Hotel, I loitered with some of the players on the day of the first game, marvelling at the extent of Brendon McCullum's tattoos, how relaxed Jacques Kallis was, and the excitement exuded by many of the game's greats, including Shane Warne. Having recovered from the shock of their initial price tags (McCullum $700,000, Kallis $900,000 – more than four times what they earned in a year playing for their country) they weren't entirely sure what to expect of the tournament, since it featured some genuine talents but also a number of players, like Warne, who had retired from professional cricket. There was also the usual consternation among foreign players in India whether everything would actually 'work'.

The pre-match hype had been intense. The Indian public were bombarded by TV ads for weeks, Lalit Modi was on every chat show going, the IPL was all over the papers, and Bangalore was at fever pitch. Half of Bollywood seemed to have come to town. As night began to fall, I set off for the Chinnaswamy Stadium. It was bedlam on the roads. Everyone was honking and hooting. Being English I was preparing myself for a massive anti-climax.

It was anything but. The opening ceremony would have been a credit to any global sporting event – and like nothing cricket had ever seen. Thumping dance music whipped the 40,000 crowd into a frenzy as the cheerleaders of the Washington Redskins, imported specially for the occasion by Vijay Mallya, strutted their stuff – in the kind of skimpy, flesh-baring outfits that would once have been outlawed in India. There were rope acrobats and an incredible laser show through which eight abseilers brandishing the team flags descended. Finally, a cacophony of fireworks was launched from the roof of the stadium – the release of two months of intense build-up – the noise equivalent to 100,000 people clapping six inches from your face.

The eight tournament captains were introduced – seven legendary Indians and Warne. Sachin Tendulkar and MS Dhoni elicited huge ovations when they stepped up for their obligatory wave. But when the focus returned to the pitch-side stage and the sight of Shah Rukh Khan performing with a group of nubile dancers, the crowd really erupted.

Manoj: The integration of Bollywood with cricket was a masterstroke in the tournament's design – and one that I (as someone who had grown up in the UK), didn't fully appreciate until that evening. Within Bollywood, there are 'B listers', 'A listers', 'double A listers' and way above them all is Shah Rukh Khan, richer and more famous than Tom Cruise or Clint Eastwood – and adored by the entire country. He and Lalit had known each other since childhood, and there were few others within Indian cricket who would have convinced him to invest (and participate so actively) in the league. The profile that he and Preity Zinta provided as the tournament was launching was incalculable.

Finally, the match began. Obviously inspired by Michael Jackson's 'Beat It' resonating round the stadium just before the off, McCullum, the pocket dynamo from New Zealand, launched an incredible display of his own pyrotechnics. Batting for the visiting Kolkata Knight Riders, he treated the home bowlers with utter disdain. The 50 was raised after just four overs. He backed away and carved the ball over third man, clonked it beyond deep midwicket, and sliced it over the keeper's head. He went down on one knee and ramped a six over his left shoulder. It was a hot night and the cheerleaders, hired to jig about every time there was a boundary, were soon looking a little flushed. By the time McCullum had larruped his 10th six to go with nine fours, they were wearily waving their pompoms sitting down. He sailed past the T20 record score of 141 and ended the innings by jabbing a low full toss for his 13th six to finish a remarkable 158 not out (off just 73 balls and out of a total of 222-3.) Shah Rukh Khan, the Bollywood superstar owner, nodded his approval as McCullum left the arena. He could immediately see that his $700,000 outlay had been money well spent.

After McCullum's assault, the result was utterly inevitable. It was also irrelevant. The die had been cast. The tone had been set. Everyone could see the impact of this event would be felt far and wide. This was where cricket and mass entertainment finally met. On the way back to the hotel that night, I saw an IPL billboard featuring a bunch of players emblazoned across which was the slogan "We will shake your world." They certainly had. This was the arrival, in India, of 'sportainment'.

Modi was overjoyed. "You know when I started, we hadn't thought beyond the first game. I didn't know how it would all go. But then McCullum hit 158. I dedicated the IPL to him. That is when I knew the IPL had worked. It was shown on 110 channels in India."

Rewarding the victims

The great Indian batsman Rahul Dravid played in that first match at Bangalore for RCB, his home town (he did not join the Royals until 2011). Ten years on he reflected on the impact of the IPL's arrival.

"None of us knew what to expect. We knew it was big and obviously the number of requests I had for tickets proved it, but I thought, well maybe people will come for one or two games or even one season but how is the economics going to work out long term? Yes 40,000 people came to the first game but it made a huge loss. But the build-up and suddenly playing with different people from other countries and sharing a dressing room with them and practising with them was actually quite exciting, especially for me at the back end of my career.

"In that first game when McCullum started going, I could see there were so many of our team who had never experienced a crowd of 40,000 before and that kind of noise. They were like rabbits in headlights. The experience they've gained from those kind of experiences since has been great for our white ball cricket, so now when they come to an international game, they've done it, they've been there."

From a personal point of view, Dravid was excited by the sudden swell of T20 yet also conscious that a decade of hard labour in the Test arena – he, remember, is the man who faced more balls in Test cricket (31,258) than any other – was almost anathema to the next generation. "For me there was the challenge of learning to play a new game but also the realisation that you could suddenly become a hero in the space of ten balls. Or you could bowl one great over and you could be a superstar the next day. That was completely alien to my thinking. In Test cricket it took a long time to build a reputation, I struggled for years, it was a rite of passage. Here because of the hype and the drama you had guys who became celebrities overnight.

"Actually, I really liked that, because one of the things that always bothered me growing up in cricket was how few people actually made a living from the sport. I saw how so many players who played a bit of international cricket really struggled in their lives, and could barely make ends meet. I used to call them 'the victims of the great game of cricket'. They sacrificed everything in their careers and then they had nothing and didn't have the skills to prosper in the rest of their lives.

"So the IPL was great because it provided money for more people, more people benefited from it, there was the experience for a young Indian player to stay in a 5-star hotel. In the domestic Ranji Trophy you'd stay in a 3-star hotel and travel by train. Some of the Bangalore boys who played in the RCB side that first season had never even been inside the 5-star ITC hotel before. Now they were living in it for two months. The joy on their faces when they flew in a plane for the first time. That was really lovely to see."

Uncertain beginnings

The Rajasthan Royals played their first match the night after the Bangalore opener against the star-studded Delhi Daredevils, which included the swash-buckling Indian icon Virender Sehwag, the brilliant ambidextrous South African AB de Villiers and the great Australian pace bowler Glenn McGrath. The Royals were still missing key players like Graeme Smith, Sohail Tanvir and Younis Khan, so had a much weakened first team.

Manoj: We travelled up to Delhi from Bangalore and headed nervously to the Feroz Shah Kotla Stadium. The Delhi franchise, like RCB, had invested in an extraordinary pre-match exhibition and party. Akshay Kumar entered the stadium by zip wire, and a globally renowned BMX Bike Stunt group performed pre-match acrobats. The crowd were wild with excitement, the noise as deafening as the night before, and the Delhi team packed with stars. We were not expected to win, and our team sheet included several players that even the most knowledgeable Indian commentator would struggle to iden-tify. Indeed, one of the stars from our Cricket Star show in 2006, Dinesh Salunkhe, had made it into the starting 11. He had never even played for Bombay, his state side, and none of the commentators could even pronounce his name.

In readiness for the match, captain Warne had prepared a sheet of instruc-tions, with a title for each player: 'the leader of the pack', 'the cool finisher', and so on, and an outline of their specific roles. The plans were meticulous. But stage fright or general confusion caused them to immediately unravel from the moment the umpires took the field. The two openers went to the wrong ends. The Royals made a limp 129 and were thumped by nine wick-ets. The portents for the team were not good. The misery was compounded by the Royals cheerleaders – flown in from Moldova – being clueless about cricket and continually celebrating the wrong things, jumping up and down to celebrate as the Royals lost wicket after wicket.

Sitting in one of the hospitality boxes at the Feroz Kotla I was struck by the amazing transformation at a venue which, ten years before, was more of a compound than a cricket ground with dilapidated buildings. Now the ground was built up on all sides with glistening, impressive stands, a smart pavilion and VIP seating areas. The stadium was populated by a happy throng of baseball-capped, replica-shirted supporters, eating popcorn and drinking beer – a cinema-type crowd – men and women, families and groups of lads and girls. There was not a sarong or a saree in sight. The marketing men had excelled themselves.

Manoj: I felt sick after the first match. Friends who'd come out for the game tried some reassuring words, but there really were no positives. Suresh, the co-owner, sent me a text which simply read: 'What rubbish have you bought?!' There was no after-match party for us, just a four-hour debrief with Warne and the coaches. They were all in a state of shock, and anyone other than Warne would surely have been racked with some of the same self-doubt that kept me up all night. He, at least, seemed even more determined to figure out the most effective 11 and how to get the slightly overawed young Indian nucleus to perform. He was still talking at 4am.

The launch of the IPL could not have gone better. The media management – with controversy after controversy (from deliberate non-issuance of media passes, to the 'rights and wrongs' of scantily clad cheerleaders, to astronomic player costs, to the negative commentary about the IPL auction) all ensured 24/7 coverage. It had all of the elements of the best reality TV and more, but I had a sick feeling that this could be a long and very public six weeks of humiliation.

There was no time to reflect. Life in the IPL moves faster than MS Dhoni's wrists. After 48 hours the Royals were playing their first home game in Jaipur against Preity Zinta's Kings XI. And, in spite of the challenge of converting a modest stadium into a modern entertainment venue that would win over the local population, the RR owners knew that success on the field was not just the best way but really the only way to attract serious support.

Manoj: Getting our home stadium ready for the tournament was relatively straightforward, as we had a good relationship with the Rajasthan Cricket Association – who have generally been a good partner to the franchise. It was the state association who effectively licenses BCCI to use the ground, who along with their operational teams sub-license to the IPL franchise for a sum that has ranged from $30,000 to $100,000 a game. For the state association, this was fantastic income, but managing the state associations, who were used to being in total control of major matches, was a tricky assignment. Ticket allocations, especially the all-important 'free' tickets were of huge importance in India. Managing ticket allocation is a crucial skill to ensure smooth running of matches in India. It is not just about 'free', but who gets what seats. Most of our high-end hospitality passes were quickly gone to a combination of government officials, friends of the state association, and, of course, the Jaipur Royalty. One of the ultimate ironies in India is that the people who can afford tickets are generally affronted if they have to pay!

On the marketing front we had slightly missed the point on the particular brand of tournament that the IPL was cultivating. It had already become a unique mix of Bollywood entertainment, celebrity razzmatazz, and a bit of cricket. But our entertainment budgets weren't in the same league as other franchises. Frugality was etched into our plan from the very start, perhaps too extremely. (On the first game our single firework took off in the middle of the first over just behind the bowler's arm!) It did have the one desired effect, of ensuring the players were under no illusion that they were here to play cricket, and if you are as focused as we were on building value in a franchise then we knew all that really mattered was how we performed on the field.

It was the genius of Warne that made that desire a reality. He had reinvented the art of leg spin in Test cricket in the 1990s. Now he was the inspiration for its burgeoning value in the shortest format. He instinctively knew how valuable a bowler who could turn the ball both ways to marauding batsmen could be, and his brilliance engineered victory in that first home game. He also recognised the rare talent of their cheap pick from the Indian U/19 draft – Ravi Jadeja.

"The more we saw of him – the way he moved in the field, the athleticism, the swagger – the more we thought 'we've got something here'," Warne says in his autobiography *No Spin*. Contradicting the thoughts of local coaches who believed Jadeja was a 'bit of a spinner who bats at nine', Warne said "This guy can do it for us in the top four or five. He can come in after the first six-over powerplay and take down the spinners." And he was regularly proved right.

The height of unpredictability

A remarkable final over in the Royals' subsequent match with Deccan Chargers (now called Sunrisers Hyderabad) transformed their season. The Chargers had a star-lit top order of Adam Gilchrist, VVS Laxman, Shahid 'Boom Boom' Afridi, Andrew Symonds and Rohit Sharma. A world class demolition unit. They crushed the Royals bowlers into submission, making 214-5. Symonds supplied a 47-ball hundred. At that point only one similar total had been successfully chased in the five-year history of T20.

Now fortified by South Africa's incredible hulk Graeme Smith (who arrived only hours before the game), and the unknown Yusuf Pathan, the Royals had slashed, scythed and scrambled their way to 198-7 after 19 overs. Seventeen were needed from the final over. Warne was at the non-striker's end.

Manoj: So, after 39 overs of cricket, chasing one of the highest T20 scores in history, it had come down to the last over. It seemed almost inevitable that the ball had been given to the most expensive international player in Season 1 of the IPL, Andrew Symonds. With 14 needed from four balls, Warne was on strike. I was back in London watching the game on Setanta Sports with my wife Katie and the kids. My daughter Asha asked "Can Warnie bat?" "No," was my curt response. He carted the next three deliveries for 4,6,4 and we had won with a ball to spare. One of Warne's mantras as captain was "We can win from anywhere..." And he had just proved it. He had also shown extraordinary leadership, and from that moment our young team believed everything the captain said. And that was the moment the Rajasthan Royals truly arrived in the IPL. Everyone loves an underdog – and that quickly became our brand positioning.

Three games later we were top of the table and stayed there until the playoffs.

Gossip was already rife with how other owners were bestowing gifts and par-ties on their teams, whereas our only investment had been to ask Kingfisher (one of our sponsors) to throw a disco after each home win. The night we beat Chennai Super Kings, I got a call from our match-winning Pakistani fast bowler Sohail Tanvir (the 2008 tournament's leading wicket-taker) asking if I was pleased, to which I obviously said yes. He asked how I would express my thanks, and I nervously said let's meet for breakfast. I asked Warne to join us. Tanvir explained that 'where he came from' great performances were rewarded with gifts, to which Warne duly responded, "Yes mate, but we are a team, no individual prizes – but I will make an exception," and he produced a used cricket ball from his bag (which he claimed was the match ball), then signed it, gave it him, and went back to bed. Warne's man-management skills were certainly different!

He was one of only three IPL captains who had never played in T20 interna-tionals, but his cricketing acumen was extraordinary. He set the tone on the field, with outstanding performances. So many of his wickets were the opposi-tion's star players. His captaincy was a combination of meticulous planning and gut instinct. He was also surprisingly strict off the field. Punctuality was, and is, a huge issue for him. He hated anyone being late for a team meeting or a team departure, which Ravi Jadeja habitually was. So, the bus left for the ground without him. And he was made to walk part-way back to the hotel after train-ing in 40-degree heat. Punctuality was excellent after that – until the final.

However, there were many other factors to explain our success. You cannot thrive in an IPL without consistent performances from your 'big' players. Graeme Smith and Shane Watson, who would win the tournament's most valuable player (MVP), were massive. The statistics hid other contributions they made, setting an example off the field, and providing a huge physical presence at the wicket – which in the hustle and bustle (and ferocious sledg-ing) that typified our games was important for our younger Indian players, such as Swapnil and Jadeja. Yusuf Pathan became a national superstar, with his incredible six-hitting ability. Sid Trivedi was to become a Royals legend. We were willing as a franchise to give non-established players a chance, some-thing that has been a deliberate part of our strategy from day one. Weaving together such a combination of cultures, ages and experience levels was also a credit to our coaching leadership team of Darren Berry and Jeremy Snape (whose appointment was the only early battle that I had with Warne).

A fairytale ending

The 2008 tournament built to a crescendo in late May with the inaugural IPL final between the originally unfancied Rajasthan Royals and MS Dhoni's confident Chennai Super Kings at the DY Patil stadium in Navi Mumbai. A 10,000 strong melee surrounded the Royal's hotel as the coach departed for the stadium, again without Jadeja who had missed it. He was given a lift to the ground by Mark Onyett (a partner of Badale's) and his friends.

The stadium was crammed with 55,000 riveted fans all yelling their heads off. The city – in fact the whole country – had come to a standstill as everyone sought out a TV to follow the drama. Bollywood, India's giant movie industry, had ground to a halt. Every employee had pulled a sickie. The match featured lots of errors and swung wildly one way then back the other. Eventually the last over arrived with the outcome still in the balance. Four months of franchise creation and player accumulation, of brand cultivation and sponsorship nego-tiation, of team building and strategic thinking and endlessly criss-crossing the Indian subcontinent had come down to this. Six balls to make history.

Rajasthan Royals needed eight runs for a famous victory over the much more fancied Chennai Super Kings. The mercurial Warne was again at the wicket partnered by the Pakistani left-armer Tanvir: two artful bowlers now need-ing to be composed batsmen. It is one of the beauties of cricket that the severest pressure is often applied to the least able. They faced the bowling of Chennai's crafty, experienced finisher Lakshmipathy Balaji.

Eight runs to win off six balls became three required off two. Tanvir flicked a full toss to long leg and they scampered a couple. The final delivery. One run to win. With $2m for the winning team it was then the most lucrative ball in cricket history.

Manoj: I looked around the stadium packed full of screaming fans. Indians chanting the names of domestic and foreign players who had become heroes in a tournament launched less than four months ago, playing for teams created less than three months ago. It was an incredible sight, even in a country famed for its cricketing passion. My focus switched back to the cricket. A deafening silence returned as Balaji began his run up.

The ball is short and somehow Tanvir scoops it wide of mid-on. Warne is already halfway up the wicket. Bedlam. We've won! I raise my arms aloft, then hug everyone, first my wife, then my parents, then my sister, and then my best friend and business partner, Charles, and finally Suresh Chellaram and Ranjit Barthakur, my partners in this Royals adventure. As we descend onto the pitch to congratulate the players, my first words to Charles – partly tongue in cheek and partly to prove that I wasn't getting completely carried away are – "It's probably time to sell it!"

A decade on, after a rollercoaster ride of success and failure and reward and penalty and ecstasy and exasperation, that might have been an astute commercial judgement. But it would have denied those who ran the Royals a decade of invaluable experience in how to establish and evolve a highly successful sporting business. Much of that experience – the clever ideas and elementary mistakes and valuable learnings – are in this book.

Manoj: Part by design, and part by accident in that first season we applied many of the most important lessons in building a winning culture in a franchise. Leadership is absolutely vital and, with Warne, we had a natural. Motivation is key at all levels. Warne had a point to prove – the best captain Australia never had. Many of our coaching leaders, like Jeremy Snape – whom I got to know at Leicestershire, and Darren Berry – were outside the mainstream system. They brought new thinking, and were unsung heroes. The use of pretty basic data had given us a small edge and this was an area we would continue to invest in. However, we were slow to learn in many areas. We didn't work enough with our sponsors. We hadn't yet applied the Indian formula of Bollywood plus cricket. We were slow to build ancillary revenues. And we were too narrowly focused with our stakeholder management. As is often the case with start-up businesses, we were too sensitive to cost, and didn't invest in some of the right areas. But it was an amazing start to our journey.

It was an amazing start to the IPL, full stop. It had a seismic effect on the game and its players worldwide. Was it great planning or beginners' luck? Probably a bit of both. But as the cliché goes, it's harder to stay at the top than it is to get there in the first place. The Royals were soon to discover that.

But the formula of 'creating stories' in and around the IPL was omnipresent and turned the whole affair into a six-week soap opera. Modi had set out to dominate all aspects of the media, and he overachieved. Sports bodies, run by former players and bureaucrats, rarely have genuine marketers and entrepreneurs designing tournaments. They are often too long, under promoted, and under invested – especially in the area of creating the narratives that capture the public's imagination.

Well-funded sports like boxing spend significantly on pre-fight build up, and the development of the characters that enter the ring. Other sports bodies don't see it as their responsibility. The great tournaments and most memorable leagues have brilliant, unexpected narratives – the performance of the home Japan team in the 2019 Rugby World Cup, the Leicester Premier League winning side in 2016, the Kansas City Chiefs winning their first Super Bowl in 50 years in 2020. The Royals – the least fancied team – winning the inaugural IPL, and off the last ball, was in that category. You can't design and predict these stories. That's what makes live sport so precious – its ability to create 'impossible to script' narratives. Broadening the number and reach of those narratives is a key task for sport's marketing professionals – especially as the competition for those eyeballs intensifies.

Post-Covid 'narratives'

Manoj: During Covid-induced lockdowns we have all spent hours watching the future of entertainment through streaming platforms like Netflix and Amazon Prime. However, for all of their billions of investment into content production, people still miss live sports. Indeed, the criticality of live sports to traditional broadcast channels has been brought into sharp focus – and it is not just because of the unpredictable narratives created by the games themselves, it is also the large volume of narratives (and content) that each game creates. To sports fans, television pundits expounding on history or holidays is a poor substitute for pundits describing a brilliant boundary catch, an aggressive tackle, a powerful scrum or a blistering serve.

The IPL founders created narratives around every aspect of cricket – the design, the off-field entertainment, the owners, the finances, and they were focused on ensuring that each and every game would have its 'own narrative' by ensuring balanced teams. Sport is entertainment, and entertainment is about creating and telling stories. In a deep recession, where competition for fan spend and sponsor spend will increase, the ability to create, market and embrace differentiated narratives will be crucial for survival. Cricket must broaden its appeal, and this means creating broader narratives, that encompass far more than just the game – including the event, the pre- and post-game entertainment, the characters, and the dialogue about the running of the game. All aspects of the game have the potential to create a good story.

Chapter 3
Building Valuable Media Rights

How media companies maximise and
recoup their vast outlay on sports

Hot stocks

Investing large sums in a sports franchise carries a high degree of risk. But now is as good a time as any to buy a major team. Why? Because the broadcast and digital media rights to the major sports leagues continue to spiral upwards. Television networks are running out of mass-audience content – especially as the vast majority of content is viewed on-demand or as 'catch up' with consumers skipping or ignoring the advertising. Live sports still deliver high ad revenue. TV stations are now paying 60% more to screen major NFL games than they were five years ago. There has been a 250% escalation in the value of the NBA rights. Formula One is now followed in 240 countries, with each race getting 7m unique users across its digital presence, and 500m fans registered. The pattern is the same everywhere. The table below shows how the TV rights to the English Premier League have increased since its foundation (a 300% increase from 2010 to 2016, though there has been some levelling off recently).

EPL Media Rights

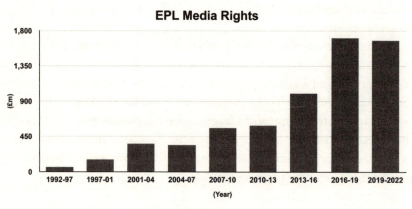

Fig. 5

The first IPL TV deal was $1bn for ten years (to Sony). The most recent one is $2.5bn for five years (to Star). A 400% increase pro rata. Every broadcast chief knows that a major sporting event is more likely to deliver a mass audience than a soap or a reality show. With the technology behemoths like Apple, Amazon, Netflix and Facebook now parking their wagons close to, or inside, the stadiums, the rates will go ever higher. One of the most fascinating aspects of the most recent (2016) IPL rights auction was the participation of Facebook – bidding $600m for the digital rights alone. It is inevitable that the major owners of sports rights will change over the coming years, and the smart media companies need to start thinking 'clever consortia' rather than simply 'how much?' Amazon's recent acquisition of specific NFL rights is a sign of the future.

Sports rights and team ownership are the hot stocks of the 21st century. It has been boom time. A key driver of franchise attractiveness relates to how much of this broadcast revenue is passed on to the franchises, therefore the owners. Around 60% of the central TV revenue the NFL earns is shared among the teams (who get roughly $250m each). It is a similar ratio in other leagues (50% of broadcast revenue in the English Premier League is shared, for instance). The fact that 80% of IPL's broadcast income (reduced over time to 40%) was going to be passed on to the franchises in the initial stages of the tournament was one of the main lures of outside investment.

Cricket had never really hooked big investors before. But such was the compelling, and financially attractive, nature of the IPL prospectus, that the richest man in India was tempted. The wealth of industrialist Mukesh Ambani, the son of a wool trader, had, in October 2007, risen above that of Bill Gates. His willing participation in the IPL was an important catalyst that helped persuade other major business figures to invest. Yet such wealthy franchises could easily buy up the 20 best cricketers, have the next 20 best on permanent standby and a private plane on call to fly them wherever was required. Such exceptional purchasing power is not good for the long-term dynamic and financial attractiveness of a league. Media rights are maximised through balanced competition – a level playing field. Especially in the initial stages of a new tournament, competitiveness is the name of the game. Uncertainty of outcome is a key driver of fan demand.

The player auction and the player salary cap were therefore fundamental in restricting the ability of the wealthiest to automatically be the best. The auction was transparent, removing the opportunity for a rich owner to 'bid' $100,000 for a player while also offering him a huge private incentive to sign. Failure to abide by the financial guidelines is increasingly penalised by sports' governing bodies. Consistent flouting of the £7m salary cap, by whatever means, was the reason Saracens rugby club were relegated from the premiership in late 2019. They had effectively circumvented the cap by co-investing with star players, instrumental in them clinching three premiership titles and two European cups in five years. Premiership bosses correctly understood how damaging that was to the competitiveness, and therefore value, of the league.

The IPL salary cap was initially set at $5m per team (it has now risen to $12m), an approximate 50% of the annual TV rights income for each franchise. There is also a minimum spend (75% of the total), which ensures that franchises have competitive teams, and don't simply short-term profit maximise at the expense of performance. This all leads to the potential for unpredictable outcomes, therefore perpetual interest. The greater the number of close contests, the more broadcasters will ultimately be induced to pay for the rights to a league. In the 2019 IPL season 30% of the matches were decided in the last over.

Manoj: The design of the IPL always had maximisation of media rights at the core of its business model. Being founded by an entertainment industry entrepreneur was crucial in this regard. The initial acquisition of star players was the key to starting the virtuous cycle of 'media rights' economics. The obsession with controversial headlines ensured that everyone had heard about the IPL before it had started. It was on the front pages, middle pages and back pages.

However, the hardest aspect, especially with the constant competitive pressure from owners, is to ensure a level playing field between teams – so that any team can win any game. This is where so many leagues go wrong. Ultimately, an unbalanced playing field will reduce the overall value of a league's media rights. Most people in the UK pay their Sky and BT Sport subscriptions for the games between the big teams. The IPL's focus on transparent player purchase was the 'magic' to ensuring effective salary caps, unpredictable outcomes and guaranteeing the long-term media rights value, which in turn allows players and investors to derive maximum return for their efforts. The way to maintain media value of a sports league is well summarised by the graphic below.

The "Virtuous Cycle" of League "Media Rights" Value

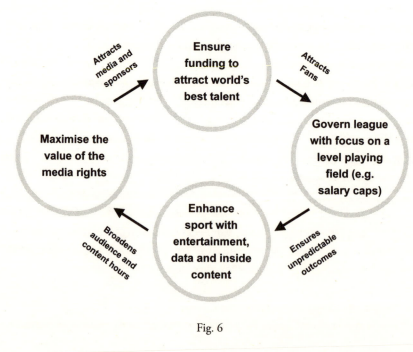

Fig. 6

The effect of the salary cap

Is there a correlation between the competitiveness of a sports league and the rigorous enforcement of a salary cap? It looks like there is. The NFL has had a strict salary cap in force since the 1990s (in 2018 it was $177m). Since the millennium 17 teams have featured in the Super Bowl (i.e. the final.) In Major League Baseball there is no salary cap but a 'competitive advantage tax' is levied on teams exceeding the agreed threshold spend on players. The result is 12 different teams winning the World Series since 2000 (although the biggest spenders, Boston Red Sox, have won it four times, as we'll see later.)

Contrast that with European football leagues which have no salary cap. In the English Premier League since the millennium, 13 of the 19 titles (68%) have been won by either Manchester United (8) or Chelsea (5) – and only five teams have won it overall, with Leicester's 2016 success a serious outlier. The situation is even worse in Spain, where since 2004 Barcelona or Real Madrid have won 14 of the 15 La Liga titles. You can't call that a 'league'. It's a duopoly.

Without the long history of La Liga or the English football league, the IPL could not afford to be dominated by one or two teams, and it is not. Five of the eight current franchises have won the tournament, and only one of the ten teams who have regularly competed – Delhi Capitals (formerly Daredevils) has failed to make the final. The salary cap has been highly effective. The rollercoaster ride of many of the teams in the diagram below emphasises that.

The Finishing Position of All IPL Teams (2008-2019)

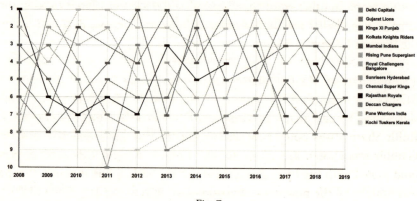

Fig. 7

Keeping the lid on

It is often said that football is the alimentary canal of sport: what goes in one end comes straight out the other. Premier League salaries are astronomical not to say crippling. Manchester City's wage bill (in 2019–20) was £260m. Manchester United's was the highest at £332m. But these clubs have huge revenues from broadcast and sponsorship so could comfortably cope. It is mostly the struggling clubs like Stoke, Sunderland and Swansea who spend the highest proportion of their income on players' salaries (in some cases over 75%) You can see how hugely they depend on the broadcast income by staying in the Premier League (anything between £80m and £120m).

The auction and salary cap were very important for IPL owners. No one had to fork out more than $5m on players in each of the first three years. The system also nullified the ability of players' agents to hike up salaries for their most sought-after players. Nevertheless, the initial guaranteed broadcast and central sponsorship income (around $10m per team per year) still hauled a cricketer's income up to unprecedented levels. Before the IPL, the top earning cricketers from England and Australia were earning on average £250,000, and the Indians were at about the same level (heftily topped up with endorsements) but most other international players took home a basic salary of £100,000 or less. A select few stars therefore earned £10,000 a week, but no more. In other words, the highest paid cricketers earned roughly the same as a footballer playing for teams in League One, two divisions below the Premier League.

The purchase of MS Dhoni and Australia's Andrew Symonds for around $1.5m each in the first IPL auction (2008) had already raised the bar considerably. The next major auction in 2011 created the first $2m cricketers. Rohit Sharma was bought for that figure by Mumbai Indians, Gautham Gambir was chosen as captain for the Kolkata Knight Riders for $2.4m (and joined with big hitting Yusuf Pathan for $2.1m) and Robin Uthappa was bought by the new Pune Warriors team also for $2.1m. Then in 2015 Yuvraj Singh was snapped up by Delhi Daredevils for a record breaking $2.5m. Given that the competition lasts a maximum of seven weeks, that works out at $320,000 a week. Or around $150,000 a match. The largest salaries have actually been commanded by the retained players (each team is allowed to retain five players after every three-year cycle) – and few will know what Virat Kohli is paid by RCB – as the retention discussions are bilateral and outside the auction (and the cap).

The new competition catapulted cricketers' earnings to the level of elite Premier League footballers. And not just the star players either. The unusual nature of the auction system, leaving some franchises suddenly short of players with a specific skill – left arm fast bowlers for instance, or experts at the 'death' of a T20 innings – created some strange outliers. There was Irfan Pathan, for example, not in the Indian one-day team, whose steady left arm seamers and late-order hitting ability, gave him a $1.9m price tag. Or another left arm paceman, Englishman Tymal Mills, unable to play anything other than the shortest form because of a chronic back complaint, who went to the Royal Challengers Bangalore for $1.8m in 2017.

Manoj: Although, when comparing price tags for players in the IPL it is important to note that the dynamics are very different between a year one (of a three-year cycle) auction and years two and three. In year one, teams are buying upwards of 20 players and have to balance their spend accordingly. In *years two or three, teams may simply be targeting two or three players, and so sums can be astronomical – e.g. Kieron Pollard went for well over $1.5m in IPL3 and Ben Stokes for $2.1m in 2017.*

It began in 2008 as it was meant to go on, with the Royals, the cheapest franchise who spent the least amount on players winning the inaugural competition. They made good use of modest resources and the value of their franchise instantly soared. But they understood the vital value of maintaining the salary cap and ensured that message was broadcast loud and clear at the team owners' first get together at the super-luxurious Mandarin Oriental in Bangkok.

Manoj: Differences emerged at the first owners' workshop on issues such as the right level of the player salary cap. We (the Royals) were at one end of the spectrum, wanting it as low as possible (but at a level which would still attract the world's best players). Others wanted it as high as possible. Another contentious issue was player retention. The Chennai Super Kings were happy with their squad and wanted unlimited retention, and yet there were teams like Delhi who wanted all players resubmitted to the auction every three years. Both points of view had merit. Retention was important to allow teams to build identities, which are often inextricably linked between franchise and star players. Equally, anything that would start to eat at the effectiveness of the salary cap would be disastrous for franchise profitability, and ultimately value.

The concept that was developed for Season 4 whereby teams could retain up to five players, but at a cost that was then deducted from their auction purse seemed a sensible compromise. Fundamentally, teams will always look for an edge to get an advantage. In this case, because uncapped players were not included in the auction, the pay levels of young unknowns shot up irrationally, with stories of flats, cars, jobs for the family being offered to a large number of young Indian talent. That has partially been solved by including all players in the auction – but the issue of incentivising young talent development still needs addressing. The hardest part of maintaining the virtuous cycle of media rights is getting the owners to work together – especially the more powerful ones.

Less is more

In 2019 America's NFL had eight of the 20 most valuable sports franchises in the world, and the league's teams have an average value of $2.86bn, up 11% on the previous year. There are three main reasons the NFL is such a phenomenon. First, collaborative owners who form part of a collective association and work together for the good of the whole enterprise. Second, unpredictable outcomes. The stringent enforcement of the salary cap and the effectiveness of the draft system has enabled 12 different teams to win the Superbowl since the Millennium. That continues to drive up the media value.

A third asset is the small number of games – in relation to baseball (MLB) or basketball (NBA), anyway. The regular NFL season consists of just 16 matches per team over a 17-week period (as opposed to 162 in baseball and 82 in basketball). So with just eight home matches per franchise, the games have 'rarity value'. The lead-up to each match builds anticipation. By game day hometown expectation is at fever pitch. This drives allegiance and further enhances individual franchise value through burgeoning media rights. Currently the NFL earns more than $5bn a year from broadcast revenue.

The same is true of the IPL. Five different teams won the title in the first six years (as the team's finishing positions table on page 50 shows). That excites each franchise (and their owners) as well as the nation as a whole. It is a dynamic situation. And each team plays just 14 matches before the playoffs – seven at home and seven away. Each game is a major event. Like a mini festival. The rarity value creates tremendous opportunity to build anticipation for each match through advertising and promotion and media content which in turn enriches expectation and allegiance. Much attention is focused in the week before a match on creating an audible buzz, interviewing local cricket-loving celebrities, whetting public appetites. This is another common denominator linking the only two major sports leagues in which every franchise is profitable.

Such was the impact the tournament made in its first year that it easily survived being forced to relocate to South Africa in its second season

– because of the Indian government elections at home. The teams' images and styles had already been established and the TV audience unaffected by where the games were actually taking place.

Broadening the audience

Because of the time a cricket match takes and its essential unfathomability, the sport has endured a perennial struggle to retain its audience. Football, for example, is simpler and shorter and generally not played during working hours. It is also cheaper to cover (fewer commentators/cameras/production staff required). As a result, a degree of responsibility has always rested with broadcasters to keep cricket interesting and relevant. The Indian TV stations covering the IPL have succeeded brilliantly here where many others have failed. They were motivated, as much as anything, by how much they had spent acquiring the rights. The more expensive an asset is, the harder you'll work to promote it. Squeezing astronomical sums out of broadcasters for cricket coverage was just one of Lalit Modi's key transformative moves.

In the mid-2000s – pre IPL – Sony had the rights to all domestic international cricket shown in India in a deal negotiated by Modi on behalf of the BCCI. They brought more of an entertainment feel to it, condensing exciting moments into short packages sponsored by individual companies and creating a 'wraparound' highlights show *Extra Innings* before and after the live coverage. They also introduced female presenters like the Indian soap star Mandira Bedi (the first female presenter was Ruby Bhatia) who added a touch of glamour to the programmes. The CEO of Sony, NP Singh, explains the philosophy behind the shows.

"We brought female anchors into our coverage of the 2003 World Cup. We wanted to make cricket more inclusive, entertaining and engaging and that worked really well. We continued to do that for all our cricket content. We were used to starting the whole show an hour early, with our anchors and our experts, and with the IPL we knew we wanted them and our band and our performers to create that whole atmosphere of festivity before the match."

That approach put Sony into pole position to cover the first IPL, though the guarantee of an extraordinary $1bn for the first ten years of the league undoubtedly clinched the deal. The Bollywood connection – in terms of the ownership of the teams – chimed perfectly with their demonstrable intent to make the game more appealing to families and women as well as men. Andrew Wildblood, the IMG executive who, with Modi, was an architect of the IPL, explains their rationale.

"In the early 2000s India was still broadly speaking a one-television-household country. The television, crucially, was controlled by the woman of the house. She had remote-control power which meant that men could not see even the day-night one-day internationals because the women were watching more traditional entertainment programmes.

"India has a history of soap operas that run for years. We figured out that we had to work on the idea of the IPL catering to all genders and age groups and that is what brought the Bollywood element in. We needed to create a tournament not to compete with Test match cricket but to compete with what else you might do at that time of night in India.

"The way we did that was to create a tournament in the manner of a soap opera in so much as it was on every night; if you had not seen it the night before you were not in the conversation by the office water cooler the following day. It was something that you had to have an opinion on and it was something that would dominate the country for the period of time it was happening.

"If you look at crowds in India before IPL came along you will see hardly any women at the ground. IPL crowds now contain a lot of women. It has almost become like a summer event. It is something good to be seen at and be part of. Everybody wants to go to Wimbledon in the UK. Everyone wants to go to the IPL in India."

IPL Viewership by Gender

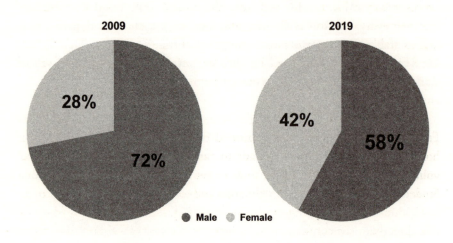

Fig. 8

This couldn't have happened without a very smart marketing campaign. Sony were intent on producing, in NP Singh's words, "The greatest entertainment extravaganza ever." They worked with agencies to create 'Manoranjan ka baap'.

"Manoranjan is 'entertainment' and baap is 'dad'. We were projecting the IPL as the 'big dad' of entertainment. The storyline of the promo is about a lady who has got twin boys – one is called Mano, the other Ranjan. Their father has gone missing for several years. Everyone keeps asking 'When will Mano and Ranjan's dad come back?' When the IPL got announced, we said 'this is the dad of Mano-Ranjan. He's back… forget about everything in life. Sit in front of the TV and you'll get hugely entertained.'

"And that's what the IPL did. It delivered on that promise. From a viewership perspective it was a huge runaway success. That innings in the first match from Brendon McCullum set the tone for the entire IPL. In Season 1 our average ratings were 4.9% [of viewers] for that whole season. That is huge for a brand-new domestic league. Soaps got more – say 7–8% – but for the IPL to get almost 5% throughout the first season of a new cricket tournament was amazing. And the final was around 10%."

There is no doubt that Sony's approach ramped up the entertainment level. The matches were lively enough, but when you factored in sweeping shots of an ecstatic crowd frantically waving at the camera, Bollywood stars displaying their every emotion as the play unfolded, cheerleaders doing their thing and excitable commentators exclaiming "Ohhh that's HUGE, that's OUTA HERE!" as a ball sailed into the night's sky and bounced on the roof of the stand, or "That one should have an air hostess on it!" it was hard not to be engaged.

From the moment Ravi Shastri opened proceedings by growling "'Tayaar hoh Mumbai party Karne?!" – ready to party Mumbai?! – to get the crowd going, the coverage used all the tools to get the viewer closer to the action. Spidercam whooshed around the players and sometimes dived down to their level, almost eavesdropping on their conversations, players were mic'd up to talk directly to the commentators/viewers, in the case of AB de Villiers even as he was actually taking the ball behind the stumps. Graphics showed the monumental distances the players were hitting the ball (often over 100m) and there were explosive sound effects added to slow motions of big hits. There was more melodrama than in a Bollywood movie – and that's saying something. A match was a total assault on your senses. It's what the Indians call 'tamasha' – loosely defined as something joyful and fun.

Appointment to view

The most fundamental thing of all was the timing. An IPL match started at 8pm prompt – probably just as many Indian families were gathering for their evening meal – and was done, in theory, by just before bedtime (though lately the finishes have often been after midnight). Essentially it took care of your evening's entertainment, and there was something for everyone – the colossal hitting for the men, the emotion and posturing of the players (and celebrities) and the music and dancing for the women – like Dwayne Bravo's hip thrusting every time he took a catch – and the brilliant fielding and general excitement for the kids. It was beautifully packaged family entertainment on *every night at the same time* for six weeks, virtually uninterrupted. It becomes addictive.

This has been a historic problem with England's T20 league, and sport more generally. Sky have tried to create 'appointments to view' with football – the 4pm big match on a Sunday, or Monday night football – but the fragmentation of soccer across multiple channels makes it harder. This is what the organisers of England's new tournament The Hundred hope will be transformed, with a match beginning at the same time every night through the height of summer, weather permitting of course. (One fundamental advantage the IPL has is that the average evening temperature in most of India in April is a perfect and reliable 25 degrees and it is generally dry.)

"The 8pm start for the IPL was great,' says Sony's Singh. "The 4pm start on weekdays wasn't as good. Playing under lights – even on TV it looks beautiful. The colourful attires of the players, the cheerleaders, our hosts and anchors on ground, all that helped us to build up to a crescendo. We showed Bollywood stars on the ground enjoying the game and we were even interacting with them. That helped the viewer understand that those celebrities were just like normal people – enjoying the game of cricket.

"Viewing habits have really changed. In the 1990s community viewing in the market was huge. They didn't have a TV in their own homes so they'd watch it together in a tea-shop or a community space. Now, they watch it in their homes. The IPL is viewed together with the family. It has brought families together. It has given them a reason to all come and sit together at 8pm and watch TV. It's become a family-and-friends viewing opportunity in prime time. One other development has been bars and pubs advertising 'watch IPL live for 300Rs and a beer' and attracting business that way. It was a bit of a nightmare because it was our signal being pirated without any payment to us. But we figured it was ok because at least people were watching our product." It was, in fact, subliminally energising the Indian economy.

Having had initial doubts about the viability of the whole thing, the Indian great Rahul Dravid soon realised how important the 'appointment to view' aspect was.

"At the end of that first Season I could see it was going to be incredible. I just had to see the reaction of my own friends. They'd say 'Look we know you Rahul, we want to watch you play, we know when the RCB games are on. Other than that, we do not know who is playing who. But it doesn't matter.

We know that when we get home from work at 8 o'clock there's a match. And my wife and I will get a drink and our dinner and we will sit down in front of the TV and the cricket is on. And we know that we can connect with somebody there. When the World Cup is on, I'd watch India of course. But when South Africa is playing New Zealand or something there's nothing in it for us. But in the IPL either I'm watching a Dhoni, or I'm watching a Virat, or Chris Gayle, or some local kid that I can connect with and it's brilliant entertainment 8 til 11.'

"The timing was an absolute masterstroke," Dravid continues. "Although now I wonder if it shouldn't start at 7pm because matches are finishing really late, the kids aren't going to sleep. They might need to pull the timing back a little bit." Alternatively, they could erect a countdown-style clock to ensure an innings is completed on time. If it is not, the bowling team loses a fielder for the remaining overs. There is all manner of entertainment possibility there.

Extending the reach

One of the most tantalising aspects of live cricket for broadcasters is its commercial potential. "Cricket is very good for advertisers," says Sony's NP Singh, "because there are so many natural breaks – between overs, wicket-breaks, strategic timeouts. And people keep watching through those breaks as they're mostly short. Viewer retention is very high. In football there are no gaps for ads except at half time and then people go and make some tea or take a short viewing break. In the first year of the IPL we did not cover our costs. We never expected to. But after 4.9% viewer share in Season 1, Season 2 became really hot. There was huge interest. It had established itself as a really strong brand. Gradually over time the ad returns got better, and in the end, we made a decent profit. Not incredible but reasonable."

Whatever 'reasonable' is, the returns were obviously sufficient for Sony's arch-rivals Star to bid five times more (pro rata) in 2017 for the IPL rights. Their new $2.5bn five-year deal (2018–2022) is a superb combination of investment and expansion. The enormous outlay has prompted them to make significant upgrades to the way the game is broadcast to reach the maximum number of people. In an era when viewers have almost bound-less choices about what they watch, tailor-made programming is increasingly attractive. It gives a show a more personal feel. So, Star have introduced bespoke, segmented coverage for India's hugely diverse regions.

"We realised that although the IPL was popular in India, there were some sections of the community that were not properly engaged in it," says Star Sports Executive Vice President, Sanjog Gupta. "One of the reasons for that was language and style. For so many Indians their first language is their local dialect and cricket was only being broadcast in English and Hindi. A lot of people in the southern states for instance, or West Bengal, felt excluded. There was definitely a desire for us to communicate with them in their local language and perhaps in a different tone too, so they could call the tourna-ment 'My Premier League' rather than 'the Indian Premier League'."

Within Star's multi-storey tower in Lower Parel, Mumbai, there are eight separate studios, each with their own production gallery. They use these for other sports too, like the Pro Kabaddi League, styled on the IPL and which is now the second most watched sport in India. For either IPL or kabaddi coverage, there are a pair of host presenters in each of several studios – each with different layouts and backdrops – speaking in one of India's numerous regional dialects. The live pictures from the game are fed into the main pro-duction unit and then filtered into the different studios with specific graph-ics. Local experts from the different regions sit in commentary booths adding their words to the pictures in the local language. So, each region has its own bespoke coverage.

"For the IPL the English-language coverage was quite colourful," says Gupta, "but for instance in Tamil we made it more sporty-analytical with different graphics styles. We broadcast the 2019 IPL final on 17 channels in eight different languages. There were 113 cricket commentators scattered about somewhere in this building." The IPL is giving ex-players greater opportuni-ties as well as current ones. The audience for the 2019 final was estimated at 600m viewers.

The coverage is very interactive. Borrowing from American sports, there has been a growing trend in cricket to mic-up the players and interact with them when the game is on, and, more recently, to utilise the stump microphones for a more inclusive feel. It really does get the viewer closer to the action – another example of cricket being ahead of other sports in TV innovations. In Australia recently, Fox Sports even occasionally muted the commentators for an over to allow the viewer to listen in to the conversation round the bat. Much of what is said on the field is pretty inane, but in a Test match against India, Australian captain Tim Paine was heard baiting the youthful Indian wicketkeeper Rishabh Pant with a suggestion that he could join his Hobart Hurricanes team for the Big Bash League. "Do you babysit?" Paine asked as the ball was fed back to the bowler. "I can take my wife to the movies while you watch the kids." This was genuinely funny and prompted a subsequent Instagram photo of Pant holding Paine's kids at a players' reception. It went viral. But Pant was the real winner, getting multiple endorsements for baby products!

To further titillate the casual cricket fan, Star marketed some IPL matches differently. Week 3 was 'rivalry week' for instance, featuring the two most historically successful teams – Mumbai Indians versus Chennai Super Kings – or identifying individual rivalries like Virat Kohli against MS Dhoni or Chris Gayle against his West Indian compatriot Dwayne Bravo. And, mirroring the success of Sky TV's Super Sunday premier league output, Star introduced their own Super Sunday version for the IPL. "The idea was to lighten the coverage, give it a more day-out-with-the-family feel, make it a bit more entertainment based," adds Gupta.

Crucially every match was covered, live. So it was a continuous narrative. Committed fans never missed a ball. But, like a TV soap opera, you could also join the story halfway through. "Our real challenge now is to find a way of getting the kids more interested,' Gupta reflects. "We have found particularly that children under the age of 15 don't engage as deeply as the rest of the community." Largely as a result of the smartphone's boundless capabilities, teenagers now have the concentration span of a gnat. The genius who can reverse that development will probably make even more money than Steve Jobs.

Sponsors' delight

Here's a prediction: the cost of broadcast rights for cricket will escalate further. The sport offers television companies such a range of opportunities to recoup their initial outlay through the vast array of advertising spaces and breaks. The stumps for a start. Central to the game. The area behind the wicket where the wicketkeeper stands. Always in shot. The boundary rope – now more of a triangular cushion – perfect for a logo. The boundary fence. The scoreboard, the big screen, the sightscreen, which alternates between being pure black (or white) when the bowling is from that end and carrying a huge sponsor's logo when it is not. In the IPL there is a VIP seating zone in a prominent position in the stand which is sponsored. As are the team dugouts (KFC Big Buckets). There are so many 'properties' to put your company name on.

Then there are the natural – and artificial – pauses in play which can be ownable or used to promote a product. The wicket breaks, of course, the drinks intervals, the change of innings break, the umpire reviews and run-out adjudications when all eyes are on the big screen. The strategic timeout, where teams have a few minutes to reset – a clever addition that creates an additional commercial opportunity (it is branded the CEAT strategic timeout) – but also has a player value (to consult with coaches or teammates) and gives the competition a USP. It is all excellent punctuation in the overall story. Short. Sentences. Have. More. Impact.

But that is not all. That is not even the half of it. Cricket is essentially lots of individual incidents joined together as a match. As the players say about T20 – 'every ball is an event'. You've got potentially 240 in one game. Groups of them can be packaged together. Sponsors love them. The Yes Bank Maximums – "Finishes with a Dhoni straight six," says the TV director in your ear. The Fabulous Fours "brought to you by Suzuki." The Samsung Classic Catches ("One minute ten left, finishes with 'take a bow Glenn Maxwell!'"). The Ultratech Cements Monster Hit ("Three different angles, and a 108m distance graphic").

A post-match review show featuring endless amounts of these packages lasts the best part of an hour – with inevitable ad breaks of course. As a pundit you hardly get to say anything and, in a way, you hardly need to. The tightly edited clips tell the story. The viewers love these bite-sized cricket snacks and they work superbly on YouTube too. Again, it is to cricket's eternal benefit that there are so many different elements to the game that can be grouped together to tell a separate story – misfields for instance, or individual wicket celebrations. Companies are even starting to sponsor crowd catches. Kia motors offered £1000 to any spectator who took a clean catch in the crowd during a televised T20 match in England. It cost them £12,000 in the high scoring match between Surrey and Middlesex at the Kia Oval in 2018 (all of which, naturally, is insured, so the only cost is the premiums).

And because there is a natural pause in the action after every ball, they can fill the screen with graphics and messages – what they call 'bugs' or 'banners' or 'crawlers' and L-shaped graphics that shrink the live picture into half the screen with a sponsor's logo or message displayed round it – and the viewer who is used to the tempo of cricket – basically one delivery every 30 seconds – won't miss a ball. You get into the rhythm of it and know subconsciously when to look up from your iPad or smartphone. Second-screening (watching the TV while surfing the net on your phone or tablet) is now a huge phenomenon. There's a whole brand-new source of revenue (see Chapter 8 – Embracing the Digital Revolution).

Then, of course, there are the players' outfits. Cricket is actually a great sport to sponsor for one basic reason. "Cricketers are stationary for longer than footballers," says Ravi Chauhan, a sponsorship evaluation expert with Neilson Sports. "When they are standing at the crease or in the field, or getting ready to bowl, it is easier to read the company logos on the shirts. Therefore, the exposure is better."

Placing a company name on a shirt is a precise art, with a vast amount of research going into the optimum size, colour and positioning. "There are 1000 analysts monitoring sports sponsorship in our Bangalore office, using image detection technology and AI to measure exposure, visibility and penetration," Chauhan says. "Obviously the initial colour of the shirt is important to help the sponsor's logo stand out. Striped or multicoloured shirts are generally ineffective, bold, solid colours are better. Position-wise, front of shirt or left shoulder (for a right-handed batsman) are best for the logo. And use the maximum space allowed. It's amazing but some sponsors don't use the whole permissible area."

Chennai Super Kings got this right at the outset with their choice of bright yellow, which stands out almost luminously at night (as do their fans). That is one reason they are the IPL's most distinctive brand. The Royals have belatedly taken the bold colour option with their all-pink strip which has made a significant difference to their recognisability. They are also one of the first to enlist a global (rather than national or local) sponsor. For the next IPL season the Royals shirts will be emblazoned with Expo 2020 (or 2021) Dubai.

"The IPL has tremendous scale and reach [a potential TV audience of 700m], it is short and intense and it is a fantastic night-time spectacle. Logos show up better under floodlights," Chauhan says. "It is now ranked in the top five sports sponsorships in the world. Ad rates have tripled and the title sponsorship has quadrupled. The IPL gives you a lot of bang for your sponsorship buck." Most franchises now sell their main shirt sponsorship for between $3m and $5m.

Sponsoring an IPL team offers a multitude of opportunities. There are airline partners to fly the players around, hotel-group associations, 'pouring' partners at the stadium (e.g. Pepsi), transport and even fashion partners. Each of these sponsors will get branding and receive tickets, hospitality opportunities and access to certain players in return. The latter is a major advantage as some of the big stars are otherwise unattainable. Away from the game India's Virat Kohli's day rate to endorse a commercial product is an eye-popping $700,000. But during the IPL his team sponsors will have some (effectively free) time to use Kohli built into their contract.

"Sponsoring an IPL franchise has really helped some smaller brands get exposure," says Arshad Shawl, the founder of Alliance Advertising. "An association with a franchise – a sponsorship tie-up or product placement like a car or a motorbike on the outfield or some special hospitality for their clients is so much cheaper than a national advertising campaign. [The current TV ad rates for the IPL are $14,000 for a 10 sec slot.] It's a great way of getting a leading player as a brand ambassador too. The stats say that the return on investment is much higher for cricket than other sports. Maybe one reason is clients tend to stay with cricket for five to ten years instead of dipping in and out."

There has been increasing integration between teams and sponsors lately, and a blurring of the lines between obvious advertising and subtler methods. The Kingfisher brand, sponsors of the Royal Challengers Bangalore, presented its products as a sort of post-match harmoniser after the stress and intensity of the game. 'Divided by teams, united by Kingfisher' was the slogan, trading on the image of IPL teams as the ultimate after-match party hosts. They also developed a series of short, sharp adverts dubbed the Kingfisher Indian Prank League featuring well known cricketers like Kohli and Gayle playing jokes on each other – jumping out from a bush dressed in a bear costume, or appearing from under a silver salver through a hole in a restaurant table. Although they sound slightly naff, they appealed to a younger Indian audience desperate to get a closer acquaintance with their cricketing heroes.

Manoj: The approach taken by many Indian sponsors is still to see the IPL as a media buy, rather than a partnership or a business activation tool. When you look at the smartest global sponsors, they generally invest three to five times their sponsorship spend on 'activation' (supporting activities built around the rights that they acquire). Standard Chartered's sponsorship of Liverpool is a great example, spending three times their multimillion pound shirt sponsorship on activities that grow value, ranging from exclusive client activation events, to deep digital integration, to partnering on summer tours to Asia. Indian sponsors typically leave their purchase decisions too late, valuing only the TV time, and not the opportunity to create deep fan integrations and activations.

The other intriguing development is the growing involvement in the IPL of women's brands. Fifteen years ago, the majority of the spectators at Indian cricket matches were male. Women found the environment too intimidating and uncomfortable. The liberation of females in Indian society, the improvement in stadiums and facilities, the Bollywood factor, the cheerleaders and the general entertainment at a match that doesn't last all day has lured women by the million to watch or follow an IPL match. It has become cool to sit with your girlfriends in the Sachin Tendulkar stand at the Wankhede Stadium clad in a Mumbai Indians shirt. The cameras pan across lines of attractive young women in capped-sleeve T-shirts and jeans waving their '4' placards. As we've seen television viewing data reveals that now 42% of the TV audience at an IPL match are women.

This has led to the first sponsors of a male contest by a (mainly) female product. On the 2019 Kings XI shirt above and to the right of the Kent water purifiers logo is 'Lotus Herbals' – a selection of shampoos and cosmetics. The sight of Chris Gayle, monster hitter, sporting a woman's beauty brand across his right pectoral is quite something to behold. This is the definition of disruptive advertising. Or, as one ad executive put it, "A hard-core female brand on an alpha male chest." Sales of Lotus Herbals SPF 15 moisturiser were up 20% since they decided to sponsor an IPL team. It is a hugely important development for the game. It properly validates it for women. The IPL is officially gender neutral. And that opens a whole new world for the business of cricket. Maybe one day we'll have the L'Oreal Timeout, "Because you're worth it."

Basically cricket – in India especially – has become an animated billboard. As a sport that takes up a lot of space, people and time, it needs to be. That said, there is still infinitely more scope for sponsorship. And this will keep driving the media rights through the roof, to the great satisfaction of players and stakeholders.

Broadcasting in a post-Covid world

Manoj: In business, there is nothing quite like the threat of job losses, or pay cuts, to focus the mind on who pays the bills. In sport, it is all about the value of media rights, which are recouped through advertising and sponsor spend. In the short term, these income streams will come under huge pressure, although for sports like the IPL that have locked in long-term deals, that impact will be lessened.

Broadcasting costs will also be challenged. The broadcasting challenge of live sport is now immense, having to experiment with tighter camera angles, CGI-friendly productions of fans, increasing player access during the game, more ref-mics, even robot fans (used in Chinese basketball). Major investment is being made into integrating fan noise from the home into the TV production.

However, Covid lockdown has accelerated the switch in consumer behaviour away from the traditional TV broadcasters to the internet (Over the Top

– OTT) platforms. This trend is irreversible, which makes live sports absolutely crucial to the survival of traditional broadcasters. Live sports are also critical to the continuing share growth of OTT platforms. This is why investment in sport has never been so attractive. But as many of the traditional TV players disappear, and we see more Big Tech consolidation, multiple sports are competing for an ever more concentrated pool of spend.

Leagues and franchises must work together to invest and build value in those rights, to command the highest values and protect the financial viability of their sports. For the bigger leagues, that might even extend to investment and creation of their own OTT platforms. Salary caps are a non-negotiable as they drive unpredictable outcomes in every game. Not only do they ensure a level playing field, but they create suspense, drama and edge-of-the-seat excitement.

Clever marketing ensures viewers make an appointment to view. Fans love access to more than the game. The most dynamic organisations will provide viewing experiences segmented by audience type, and ultimately personalised. And they will work with broadcast partners to create the most entertaining viewer experiences. Sport's governing bodies will need to include and embrace more visionary broadcast brains.

A radical transformation is on the broadcast horizon, encompassing how we view, what we view and ultimately, who controls what we view. Sport will not escape this revolution.

Chapter 4
Star Alignment

The science of identifying and enhancing
skills to produce the best sport

Surprise signings

It is not the best players that win sport's leagues. It is the best *selected, developed and managed* players that secure trophies. An assemblage of highly ranked stars is no guarantee of results. Manchester United fans have been acutely aware of that recently. Identifying, nurturing and harnessing the players' skills is the key to success. That produces the best teams, and the best sport. One of the big enticements of the IPL for the world's top cricketers is obviously the money, but the tournament's attraction has also grown with the opportunity to play with (and against) the elite players from other countries, to work alongside the most forward-thinking coaches and to share new ideas and strategies. The IPL is a cricketing brainstorm. It is a sporting version of one of those annual tech conferences in Silicon Valley.

The assemblage of all this playing and coaching talent (and the prizemoney available) pushed every team harder to find winning formulas. It provoked innovation. They looked deeper into the game to seek marginal gains. Cricket – always a game of numbers – was, for the first time, making proper use of analytics. The Royals were ground-breakers in this area. They were disruptors. In the first few years of the IPL they constantly brought in unknown players or sprung surprises. It was all based on clever thinking and smart analysis.

On 7 May 2013, for instance, the Royals were playing Delhi Daredevils in Jaipur. The ground was packed and the match was littered with international stars: Rahul Dravid, Virender Sehwag, David Warner, Mahela Jayawardene,

Shane Watson and the towering Morne Morkel to name a few. Limbering up alongside them before the match was a short, squat middle-aged Indian. It was assumed by some that he was an owner's or sponsor's brother or he had won some kind of prize.

But a few minutes later the 'prize-winner' took the field with the Royals and after the six-over powerplay, the captain Dravid asked him to bowl. The not out batsmen were Australia's Warner and Sri Lanka's Jayawardene, two of the best batsmen in the world. Undeterred the unknown player fizzed down some respectable leg breaks. He conceded just five singles in his first over. It was only then that the commentators discovered that he was 42-year-old Praveen Tambe from Mumbai. Their lack of knowledge was to be excused. Tambe had never played a first-class game, or even a T20 inter-state match. He had no professional playing record of any kind. The highest standard he had experienced was the Dr DY Patil Cup, a corporate T20 competition for banks and oil companies and government organisations in Mumbai.

Tambe bowled his four overs for 30 runs, and no wickets. Nothing special. But in fact he had done exactly what was required. He had bowled straight, brisk, non-bouncing leg breaks and been hard to hit for boundaries. He had kept the scoring rate to a moderate 7.5 an over in the notorious middle overs when teams look to accelerate, and helped keep the Daredevils to a modest 154-4 which the Royals easily overtook to win by nine wickets.

So who was he, and how did he get here? Zubin Bharucha, the Rajasthan Royals coach, who at that time was delving more deeply into statistics and analytics than most other coaches, explains. "We wanted to carry on the leg-spin tradition we had started with Shane Warne. We based it on data. We analysed the lengths that were hardest to hit and what type of leg spinner would be most effective. We were looking for a leggie who could bowl in Jaipur – a very different pitch to Mumbai or Chennai – we wanted someone who could be skiddy and bowl a certain length and was short in stature. We looked everywhere to find someone who fitted that description. Eventually we discovered a 42-year-old playing club cricket in Mumbai. He played at the club – Mumbai's DY Patil – where we held trials. That was Tambe. We took him to Jaipur to see how he'd go on that black soil and it was perfect. He bowled just where we indicated, and because there's not much bounce he's hard to hit."

On the day of his third appearance, I was working in the UK as a studio pundit on the IPL for ITV. No one knew Tambe but I had heard of him from Manoj. "He's a 42-year-old leggie from Mumbai who skids the ball through and is hard to get underneath," I said. "He will probably bowl early in the middle overs." The other pundits – England's Michael Vaughan and Paul Collingwood – looked at me quizzically, wondering how I could possibly know all that from 6000 miles away and why a team would be so prescriptive with their bowling plans. But that is how the Royals operated, (and most other T20 teams were beginning to follow suit). Sure enough Tambe bowled overs 7, 9 and 11, was hard to hit for boundaries and briefly I was afforded clairvoyancy status.

"He ended up being Dravid's talisman," says Bharucha. "When he wanted a wicket, he went to Tambe. By the time people worked out how to play him we had qualified for the IPL playoffs and he had taken us to the semi-final of the Champions League [against Chennai Super Kings in Jaipur in which he took 3-10]. What you were seeing there was the playing out of a numbers game that we had been following for the previous two or three years."

Cricket's best kept secret

The source of these 'numbers' is fascinating. It is not some glitzy, hi-tech block in downtown Mumbai but an unprepossessing-looking two-storey unit above a Domino's pizza franchise on a main road just along from Chennai's Marina Beach. The cluster of pizza delivery bikes – a strong indicator of India's burgeoning middle class – are nestled together under a tree outside. This is the headquarters of Kadamba Technologies, a sports analytics company set up by software engineer Rajesh Aravamudhan who began by supplying data to ProZone – the player-movement charts used by football teams. Upstairs in a modest open plan office, a large team of video analysts – what they refer to as coders – sit in front of TV screens showing cricket matches from around the world. Some are watching a one-day international between India and West Indies – there are two coders per game for major matches to maximise accuracy and detail – another is monitoring a live Australian state game, others are viewing reruns of India's recent one-day series in England. There's also a screen showing the Pakistan v New Zealand Test series.

At one desk a technician shows me various slow motions of the South African leg spinner Imran Tahir's leg breaks and googlies, highlighting minute differences in grip and action for the various deliveries. Another video analyst is putting the finishing touches to a complicated-looking graphic about England's Joe Root. It contains wagon-wheel score-charts and ideal field settings labelled 'when new' and 'once set' (tailored to Root's preferred methods of scoring early in an innings compared with later on) and some advice about where to bowl to Root at different stages of a one-day innings. Staff monitor, record and analyse every ball of every professional (both domestic and international) match in the world and store it all on giant databases. Within seconds they can call up virtually any ball from any game played in the last half dozen years. This is the Big Brother of cricket.

Bharucha first began using Kadamba's services for the Royals in 2009 – sourcing players from afar, helping to plan strategies for the auction and advising on certain match tactics. They noticed, for instance, that Sachin Tendulkar, who opened for Mumbai Indians, liked pace on the ball early on and was usually more successful against bowlers he was familiar with, because he knew what to expect and could plan for it. They challenged his meticulous preparation by opening the bowling with a batsman, Ashok Menaria, who bowled only occasional spin. He got Tendulkar out immediately. They worked out that the best way to counter Lasith Malinga's brilliant death bowling was to go right back on the stumps and that he was much less effective against left handers or if you went down the pitch to disrupt his method. They were always armed with intriguing statistics which allowed seemingly ordinary players to perform above themselves.

When Rahul Dravid was made Royals' captain, he was interested to find out where all this information was coming from. So Bharucha took him to Chennai to meet the Kadamba team. "Rahul was amazed. He said "This is the best kept secret in Indian cricket. And I want it to stay that way!"

A few weeks before an auction a group of analysts seconded to the Royals would sit round the table, each 'representing' a different IPL franchise having studied their bidding patterns from previous years and assessed their playing requirements. Then they'd simulate the auction, going through a range of possibilities and permutations, often all day and for several days in a row. Every detail and price was meticulously recorded.

"The way we prepared for auctions was unbelievable," Dravid recalls. "We were ahead of the curve. After the simulations we would predict the prices that players would go for. We'd rarely be more than 10% out. We got the odd one wrong – I mean you can't account for someone like Vijay Mallya suddenly going berserk and buying Yuvraj Singh for 14 crores [well over $2m]. That was an impulse buy. But I still have an old notebook with the simulation numbers and they matched almost exactly what came out of the auction. At the Royals we decided we couldn't afford the top players, so we'd go shopping much lower down the list. But we got great value because we knew really accurately what players were actually worth."

The Royals won ten IPL games in 2013 energised by the unearthing of relatively unknown talents like Tambe, Sanju Samson and West Indian Kevon Cooper – bought in the auction for a bargain $50,000. With Shane Watson's power and Dravid's sublime skills and astute leadership, they quickly qualified for the playoffs. They got within a whisker of the 2013 final, only losing a closely-fought semi-final to the eventual winners, the expensively assembled Mumbai Indians, with one ball to spare.

Manoj: That 2013 team was the closest we have got to emulating the heroics of 2008. What was so pleasing was how many within that team were new discoveries, or players who had been discarded by other teams. The work by our analytics team also fundamentally changed the roles that certain players were asked to adopt, and the roles that we paid most money for. It is not always easy to get players to buy into the new roles. Batsmen, in particular, all want to bat in the top three, but boundary hitters at five and six are as valuable, even though they don't always appear in the leading run scorer charts. Brad Hodge came into the Royals squad as a star batsman batting in the top three in the Big Bash. However, when our team looked at the data, it showed that he struggled against spin in the middle overs (and we had Shane Watson up front). So the team convinced him that his ability to hit sixes against the fast bowler would be better served in the last few overs. Hence, we kept holding him back and he won several crucial games. Eventually, a decade after he thought his international career was over, he was picked by Australia to play the finisher role in their T20 side.

Wedded to the advantages of microscopic analysis and making the most of marginal gains, the Royals continued to pluck virtual obscurities from auctions – like

India's Karun Nair ($100,000) who went on to score a triple hundred against England in a test match in Chennai. Ajinkya Rahane who had been bought in a trade from Mumbai Indians at his base price ($50K), who at the time was known for his sedate test match style batting, but transformed at the Royals and went on to score two T20 hundreds in the IPL. An ageing Brad Hogg ($100k) who delivered tremendous results through the middle overs. There was Sid Trivedi at his base price ($50K) who went on to become one of the longest serving Royals, along with Shane Watson ($100k). Shreyas Gopal at base price ($50K) who is currently the leading leg spinner in the team. Riyan Parag at his base price ($50K) who is currently the star attraction with the bat in the middle and end overs. Rahul Dravid with an average T20 record to show at RCB but who came into his own at the top of the order with the bat for the Royals. Then he had the fortitude to immerse himself into the study of the data, and critically, apply it to the considerable benefit of the franchise in winning games during that period. The aforementioned Tambe ($25K) – and having missed the playoffs only on run rate in 2014, the Royals qualified for them again in 2015 – despite Dravid's retirement – before perishing at the hands of the brilliant AB de Villiers in the finals 'eliminator' against Royal Challengers Bangalore.

RCB failed to make the final and have always flattered to deceive, outlaying millions on star names without calculating how they can form an effective team and have still never won the IPL. Whereas, through scrupulous spending and meticulous analysis of specific skills and requirements – employing an advanced version of *Moneyball* metrics – the Royals have continued to outperform some of their more glamorous rivals. With Kadamba's help they have proved that data is the modern performance-enhancer, the legal version of anabolic steroids. It has made them the most successful IPL franchise at unearthing unknown talent and enhancing that talent's material worth (i.e. financial value) over time, as the graph below illustrates.

Manoj: That period from 2013–15 is when we felt, as a franchise, that we had really sorted our playing, analyst and coaching structures. We had the right balance among the leadership. We had a competitive team, and we were constantly unearthing new talent. The following chart was built by one of the major global technology funds that wanted to invest in the Royals in 2019. They analysed the purchase price of every player in every squad, in every auction, and looked at how that value developed over time (by looking at the player's subsequent auction prices, and trade prices). We came top. It was like having your homework marked after twelve years.'

Player Value Creation

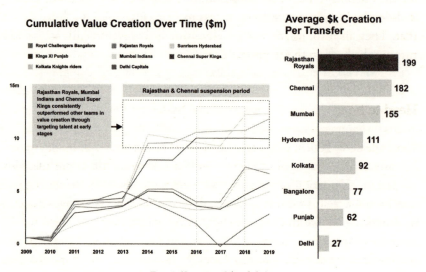

Fig. 9 (Source : Silverlake)

Though other teams have gradually cottoned on, and the Royals' scientific advantages have been reduced or been relied upon too heavily, they are still often ahead of the game. Rajesh Aravamudhan, Kadamba's boss, plays me a clip of the 2018 IPL auction on his laptop. It shows the teams' officials bidding for Ben Stokes. The bidding bounces around the room between the Kings XI and Mumbai Indians. At 11 crore [$1.4m] it stalls. It seems like Kings XI have secured him. Then almost at the last second the Royals raise their paddle. It catches the other teams by surprise. There is one more bid but the Royals get him for 12.5 crore [$1.8m.] Rajesh smiles. "He was within our budget," he says.

As well as categorising and assessing individual players, Kadamba analyse general trends too. "There's lots of focus on the number of dot balls (balls which yield no run) batsmen consume," Aravamudhan says. "Dot balls are a myth. It's the team that hits the most boundaries that win T20 matches. Dot balls and ones are a kind of 'minus' for the batting side, but boundaries are the key to winning." And that, in this business, is what it's all about. T20 and the IPL have ushered in the era of Spreadsheet Cricket.

It is vital that high performance, together with tight finishes, are maintained for the ongoing value of the league and its world-class reputation. Finding and developing players perfectly suited to particular roles is a huge part of that. They, in turn, use the data to fine-tune their specific skills so they can turn up the heat on their opponent.

Head to head

Until the early 2000s, data played little part in cricket selection or strategy. It was a science-free zone. Generic averages were monitored, but there was no precise calculation of when a person batted or bowled, or who against and how successful he was in particular situations. Players were chosen – or dropped – on whims and hunches. There was seldom any video footage available of specific dismissals or bowling spells and no graphics of batsmen's scoring areas or bowlers' pitching zones. In fact the absence of specific analysis was true for most sports, outside baseball anyway.

The advent of Hawkeye changed all that. It was originally a TV tool invented for cricket coverage, its use in other sports like tennis and football came later. Soon the England camp were getting their own feed of it. In 2009, six years after the publication of *Moneyball*, England hired a real analyst – Cambridge maths graduate Nathan Leamon – to properly process the data and inject it into team strategy. He began with simple block graphs of an opposing batsman's strong and weak areas – Shane Watson's are illustrated below. For the bowler, green are the spots to focus on and red the zones to avoid. The numbers relate to Watson's average and strike rate if the ball is in that specific area. Watson's batting average against England steadily declined as the bowlers gradually applied this data to their approach. It also offered guidance as to which bowler would be best suited to dismiss him.

Batsman 'Hot Spot' Analysis

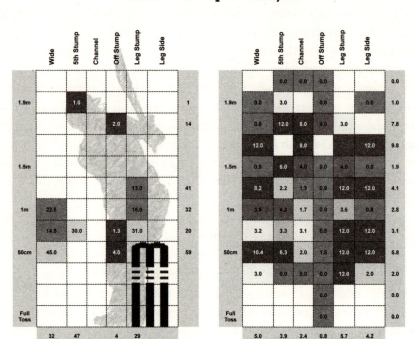

AVERAGE   RUNRATE

Fig. 10

Carefully researched 'match-ups' – a particular bowler who has a good record against an exceptional batsman – potentially pushes both players to their limits, heightening the contest. It is a duel to the death. It could go either way. That is the beauty, fascination and inherent power of sport. In the IPL, identifying these match-ups through analytics and data are all an intrinsic part of each team's preparation now.

On the morning of the Royals' match against the Super Kings in Chennai in 2019 for instance, the analytics team sit and plan the strategies with the Royals' bowlers in the team hotel. The team analyst Panish Shetty, pulls up on his laptop a graphic of Shane Watson (now with CSK) – a more advanced version of the illustration above. It shows his strike rate in individual areas illustrating all the balls he has scored off in recent tournaments. Each one of those balls can be clicked on to reveal a video clip of that actual delivery.

They have identified that he is less effective against 'tight lines' (balls at his body) and also if the delivery is below stump height. There are some simple reminders of where to bowl alongside the graphic. A bowlers' aid to confront the seemingly ageless MS Dhoni is a complex wagon-wheel that identifies his most productive area (deep midwicket), and his least (through cover). The plan for the Royals quicks will be to bowl a combination of 'bouncers, hard length deliveries and wide yorkers'. Although the plans for Watson work in the match and he is dismissed early, Dhoni's presence and the feverish crowd support appears to intimidate the Royals bowlers who are also hampered by a wet ball. The Master Finisher smashes 28 off the final over of the CSK innings to post a match-winning score. The best laid plans and all that…

This high level of analysis and monitoring has a major impact on individual performance. The players are stimulated to find new ways to succeed (e.g. the seemingly ageless Dhoni). It is the source of all the amazing new shots and deliveries. The IPL has accelerated innovation. The great American philanthropist John Paul Getty, the man who financed the Mound Stand at Lord's, always said he preferred cricket to baseball for its 360-degree potential. The batsmen have delivered on that front with their daring scoops and ramp shots and switch hits and power drives. The bowlers have responded with clever variations, decoys and strategies – the short, crafty leg-spinner Tambe for instance – challenging the batsmen to find a different route to the boundary. The fielding agility has been astonishing with acrobatic relay-catches on the boundary edge now commonplace. The end product is a dynamic game that is mutating faster than the X-Men.

Manoj: There will always be aberrations and anomalies in sport, many of them inexplicable, but the more carefully planned and prepared these teams and players are, the greater the likelihood of a high level of competition and therefore an unpredictable outcome. These innovations are undoubtedly working in the IPL. In the 2019 season over 30% of the matches went to the last over (the highest ratio in the 12 editions of the tournament) and the final was decided on the very last ball. It was an outcome only exceeded, of course, by the 2019 World Cup final which was a tie and required a super over to decide the winner. That is what you'd call producing the best sport.

Predictive analysis

Increasingly IPL teams have taken their player-data processing to another level. Seeking anything to achieve marginal gains they have begun utilising the artificial intelligence of companies like the one I visited in West London that predicts outcomes in a match, from an individual ball to an overall result. They aim to predict which permutations of players will work best in various scenarios and evaluate and separate the ones who have that winning mentality from the ones who don't.

This information is derived from a bank of triple-layered computer screens. One of these is displaying a pentagon which statistically represents players' batting methodologies, depicting the probability of various outcomes. There are five parameters: the likelihood of getting out off a delivery, of playing out a dot ball, of scoring a single, a two or a boundary. Eoin Morgan and Ben Stokes are contrasted (see below). So on any given ball Eoin Morgan is more likely than Stokes to get out, but there is also an increasing probability that Morgan will manipulate at least a single. His pentagon is skewed more towards scoring options. This makes them varyingly effective for different roles.

Batsman Scoring Analysis

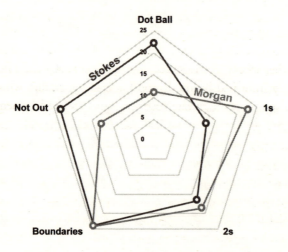

Fig. 11

The analysts are inputting data and experimenting with different team line ups. The computer can calculate from all the simulations what impact a selected player can have when he is entered into a preferred 11. This is quantified as 'runs added' (or lost) to the team with that player. They can work out for instance that substituting Jos Buttler for a mid-ranking IPL opening batsman in Indian conditions would gain an average team 8.2 runs per innings. This equates to increasing the team's win percentage by approximately 12%, a significant margin. That is why Buttler is so feared.

Originally this kind of data was mainly used in the auction process or pre-match to work out which individual players or combinations would add the most value to a franchise. But they are beginning to be employed to assess ideal batting line ups in different conditions and situations, right up to who is the most likely batsman from a choice of three to score the 12 runs required off the last over, or which bowler has most consistently held their nerve in critical, ten-to-win situations. CricViz, a data analytics service launched by the aforementioned Nathan Leamon, which also includes the predictive WinViz element, is now a ubiquitous aid to T20 teams' planning and preparation. The coach's hunch will gradually be eclipsed by the machine's intelligence. There is also clear potential for misuse of this data by gaming firms, so it needs to be regulated.

Mind over matter

The work that all these team analysts do primarily looks at the physical, and statistical properties of players and teams. And of course it has become common in other sports. For instance, football and rugby team head coaches are immediately informed by the laptop-brandishing trainer when a certain player's sprint speeds or heart-rate recovery times (relayed by sensors in the player's shirt) are declining. He will be substituted if possible, restoring the intensity of competition on the field. Barcelona FC were pioneers in this area, driving the players to extremes in training three days before a match, then employing a 'tapering strategy' – easing off the physical levels closer to match-day but honing the tactical and technical readiness of the players so they were fit and super sharp for the big game. England's rugby coach Eddie Jones has been using a similar system known as 'tactical periodisation' – training players to identify, and increase their intensity at, key phases of the game.

But the intense pressure of these high-octane sporting encounters, and the high stakes, can compromise a sportsman's skills and focus. At moments of almost unbearable tension some rise to the occasion, others crumple unexpectedly. Think of Ben Stokes conceding four successive sixes in the last over of the T20 World Cup final in 2016 as an example. (And yet at such critical moments with the bat he has been immense.)

Hence recently there has been a greater focus on psychological profiling of players, especially in the IPL. The Rajasthan Royals' player appraisals evaluate how often a batsman has taken the responsibility of securing victory in a run-chase or a bowler has defended 15 to win off an over, revealing how they handle pressure. Regularly seeing the team over the line gets an extra mark on their report card (see column two in the actual example below).

Overall Mental Fitness

Ability to singlehandedly change the course of the match - if the player does this more than twice he gets a 4, for doing it once he gets a 3	Ability to take the team to victory - if the player displays this more than twice he gets a 4, for doing it once he gets a 3	Ability to perform under pressure	Ability to remain calm and composed in tight situations	Ability to pull out games under the oppositions nose - if the player displays this more than twice he gets a 4, for doing it once he gets a 3	Ability to be a big game performer	Ability to take charge of a situation in the middle - if the player displays this more than twice he gets a 4, for doing it once he gets a 3
2	2	3	4	2	4	2

Scale to use if no specific data is available

1 - Unsatisfactory   2 - Needs improvements   3 - Effective   4 - Excellent   5 - Outstanding

Fig. 12

Manoj: Similar to the growing demands on senior management in business, there will be an increasing emphasis on a player's mental agility. Their ability to change their play. Their ability to respond to different situations. Their ability to flex where they bat in a line up. Their ability to bowl variations.

Their ability to react to variations. Mental agility will increasingly become a critical selection criteria – especially for long tournaments with varied challenges and conditions.

Sitting in the red-roofed clubhouse of Bombay Gymkhana looking across the famous Azad Maidan, an expanse of 22 interconnected cricket pitches framed by the grand Victorian buildings of the University and the Law Courts, the Royals' T20 guru Zubin Bharucha indicates the pitch where the Royals conduct specific scenarios to monitor a player's mentality and effective decision-making. "We are trying to breed fearless, unselfish players not fazed by pressure or future worries," he says, "so we create actual match situations – 36 to win off three overs for instance – simulating them as best as we can."

It is hard to truly replicate the pressure of a match with 40,000 fans screaming their heads off and spidercam swooping down low between balls to remind you that a few hundred million might be watching on telly, but muscle-memory from practising these situations reduces the stress. "One 17-year-old Mumbai kid we were trialling was amazing. He knew no one. The environment was completely new. Scouts were watching. Huge pressure. First ball of the trial he walks right across his stumps and flicks a straight ball over fine leg for four. Boom! Second ball he backs away and smacks it over cover. Boom, four more! Completely uninhibited. That's the future right there. That's the mindset that you want." That player, Yash Jaiswal, lived in the groundsman's tent at the Maidan in his teens and could not get a first-class game in 2018, so the Royals could not buy him in the auction. They had to wait until 2019, after which he played for India in the U/19 World Cup and was the player of the tournament scoring 400 runs. He is sure to make his Royals debut soon. He is potentially another major Royals discovery.

The emergence of a player like Jaiswal encapsulates cricket's rapid changes in the 21st century. The game they're playing now is unrecognisable from 20 years ago. There have been three distinct phases of development. You could call the first ten years the fitness decade. The physical prowess of players received so much more emphasis once teams began employing full-time trainers in the early 2000s. The yo-yo tests and the fat-pinching callipers were out in force. Some cricketers became as fit as Olympians. The years from 2010 onwards will be regarded as the data decade. All professional teams now employ various analysts to package video highlights and make sense of statistics.

The next ten years might be called the mindset decade. Increasing focus will be placed on the player's brain, uncovering its ability to make good decisions under pressure and assessing how that decision-making can be improved. Cricketers essential skills will be tested in the laboratory as much as on the field. To that end the Royals selected a psychologist, Paddy Upton, to take charge of the team in 2019. "Teams are all looking at similar data, we're equally well prepared for matches," he says. "But those matches are won and lost in key moments. That boils down to the mental side. We can practise for everything in cricket except recreating that high-pressure moment. It's early days but I think I have found what the neurophysiology is of that panic or choking moment. It's effectively a fight or flight response. We have found a way of recreating that, en masse, just in the team room. You might call it neuro-hacking. I can have 25 players in the team room and they get into a highly stressed mental and physical stress situation simply by holding their breath. I can watch all of them and if any of them comes out of this state I know they have succumbed to their body and their brain. They learn how to zone out and override the stress signals from the brain and the body. You can do it in the swimming pool too. Already the players are reporting some amazing responses."

It was an ingenious idea which did not meet with everyone's approval. And for various, complex reasons, the Royals had such an up and down season when Upton trialled these measures they rarely got close enough in games to exploit their ability to handle those pressure moments. But it is undoubtedly a sign that the next stage of player development might well be as much in the laboratory as in the nets.

Manoj: Analysis into the personalities of players is not simply related to their individual performance. It is also about how they fit within a particular team and culture. There is a lot of time off during tournaments, and players that can positively impact an environment, or actively teach and mentor younger players, and who are happy being part of a squad – not selected in the playing XI – are hugely valuable. We were particularly excited to add an experienced Indian player like Robin Uthappa to the squad this year – who has the experience both to perform and to influence our very young, but exciting, domestic talents. As in business, one or two sources of negative energy can damage overall team performance, but one or two inspirational, collaborative players can transform a boardroom or a dugout. How leaders integrate players from multiple cultures will be critical as more star players emerge from smaller towns and cities across India. It can never just be about performance statistics.

The management of inequality

The colossal investment in the IPL – from owners and media organisations – unsurprisingly excites the best cricketers in the world. They understand the cricketing – as well as financial – benefit of taking part in this annual festival of the game. They know it is a fantastic opportunity to broaden their skills and knowledge of the game through working with some of the elite players and coaches as well as playing in front of huge crowds and dealing with numerous pressure situations. National teams benefit as well as individuals. The upskilling of England players like Kevin Pietersen, Eoin Morgan and Paul Collingwood undoubtedly helped them win the ICC World T20 in 2010. Six of the triumphant team had IPL experience.

Naturally, the handsome potential earnings are also a major attraction (although English players have to compensate their counties for the percentage of the season they miss. Sam Billings earned less than £10,000 when he played for Delhi, for instance, as he had to pay most of his IPL salary back to Kent). The lucrative salaries were a wonderful development for some hard-working but largely unheralded cricketers. It transformed many Indian players' lives. Irfan and Yusuf Pathan, for instance, who were brought up living in one room in a mosque in Vadodara, where their father worked as a muezzin. They learnt to play cricket in a dark, neglected area of the mosque which people believed was haunted. They couldn't afford cricket boots or kit. But they were spotted at a local club, graduated to colts cricket and finished up playing for Baroda. Both got selected for Indian one-day teams in the mid-2000s but it was the IPL that made them. After seven years of consistent performances in the tournament they were rich enough to build their family a multi-storey mansion in a smart district of their home city. It is one of many rags to riches stories emanating from the IPL.

IPL – Top 10 Auction Buys

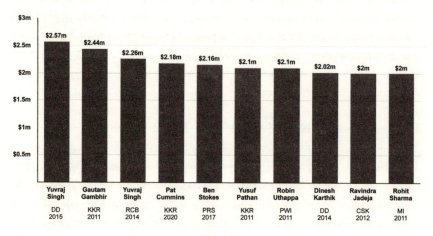

Fig. 13

Such an influx of cash does, however, cause issues, particularly around inequality. Almost every IPL team has some team members on a salary (based on auction price) of $50,000 and some others on twenty times that. It is the nature of modern sport that there will be big discrepancies. It happens in all leagues. It is something you have to deal with as a player, and is an incentive to do better and prove your worth.

What is not so easy to handle is the wild variations in purchase price of individual players from year to year caused, as we've seen, by the unusual nature and strategies of the auction process. This requires careful handling. Take the example of the stylish Indian batsman Ajinkya Rahane, for instance, who the Rajasthan Royals bought for $1.2m one year, but purchased for a bargain $600,000 in a subsequent auction (the auction price sets the player's salary).

Ranjit Barthakur, executive chairman and local figurehead of the Royals, explains how the franchise dealt with these sorts of anomalies. "The fact is at least 30% of players feel underinvested in. We try to be sympathetic but our approach was to say 'If you were given more in an auction than you think you deserve, would you give it back?' With Rahane we also said 'look if we make the playoffs, we'll give you a bonus and make up the difference' and we did. What we do ensure is that every player is treated equally. The daily allowance is the same, the food in the hotel is all laid out buffet style so you can choose what and when you eat, duties to sponsors are evenly shared out, all the hotel rooms are the same size and standard, except for the captain. We try to emphasise the importance of being a team, we are all in this together. We also try to be transparent as employers and attempt to illustrate that the players are not being exploited." The IPL is where capitalism and socialism meet.

Manoj: Managing player egos is one of the hardest aspects of running a sports franchise. It's much harder than running a normal business. Nothing prepares you for the world of sportsperson management. The bigger they are, the more complex the challenge. To achieve what they have, they are naturally self-focused (and in some cases selfish). This creates a very particular dynamic to manage. They are used to having everything organised for them, so small logistical issues can often become overbearing. They are away from home a lot (especially cricketers), so taking a family perspective on each player is important. There are massive differences in maturity, especially amongst the younger Indian players. And when it comes to money, you've got to accept that sportspeople, when they perform, are the first people to tell you they should be paid more.

Players are extraordinarily myopic in their perceptions of their value. One player came to me in the lift and he said, "Sir, sir you're only paying me 50 lakhs [$70,000] and last year you were paying me 2 crore [$280,000.]" And I said "I'm sure you didn't mean to say that. I'm sure you meant to say 'Sir thank you for trusting me again even though no one else was interested.'" The auction exacerbates it, of course. It's so public.

The beauty of the auction is that a player gets paid what the market feels that player is worth. That said, players will often expect the owner to compensate the player if they get a low price. They are obsessed with comparisons. In 11 years, I have never had a cricketer come up to me and feel bad about being paid too much.

There are a few players that have demonstrated at least some awareness and responsibility regarding the sums that they earn in a country with so much *poverty. Ben Stokes is one. He donated $100,000 to help with victims of the Rajasthan sandstorms and child slavery trafficking. There are 60m people in Rajasthan – 110m if you include neighbouring states with no IPL team. Over a third of them earn less than a dollar a day. We have a real responsibility to perform for these people and be sensitive to what we're earning. Players and franchises are only earning what they do because of those people's passion for cricket. That generates the colossal TV rights.*

We try to be fair and transparent with players. We have a bonus system. We have performance-based incentives. We'll give someone who's paid a lower salary a disproportionately high bonus if we do well. I think over time when players understand that, then you build a deeper, more constructive relationship with them.

Stokes not only donated a large sum, but also expressed an interest in seeing what his money had paid for. During the 2019 IPL he spent an afternoon visiting a rehabilitation home in Jaipur for victims of child slavery. He met children who had worked 15-hour days in appalling conditions. Nearly all of them had suffered from malnutrition. Many had been physically abused. One stared at him in wide-eyed admiration and asked "How do you manage?" referring to his ability to bat and bowl so successfully. He simply responded, "How do *you* manage?" His visit captivated a room full of abused kids and raised considerable awareness for their plight and others like them.

The question of course arises, what is the right amount of player revenue from a sport's league? It is a perennial debate. The owners say that without them there would be no team, and the players say that without them there would be no sport. It wouldn't be a professional sports team unless there were at least a third of the players moaning about pay. In fact it is probably no different to any business. It's just that in sport a league or tournament's income is so much more public.

If you look at the statistics for other leagues that have been around a lot longer than the IPL, there is a small variation in the percentage of turnover distributed as player wages. In Major League Baseball it is 61% (the highest), the others – NFL, NBA and NHL are around 58%. The English Premier League is slightly lower – at around 56% wages as percentage of turnover. Currently in the IPL, players receive between 30 and 50% of team revenue (Franchise revenues vary between $30m and $50m a season – and the players' salaries are capped at $12m, although this doesn't account for the higher salaries paid to retained players). Given that for the first ten years, few of the franchises made any sort of consistent profit, at present the wage share-out seems reasonably fair. Now that the media rights are rising, it will be fascinating to see how the new salary-cap level settles over the coming years. The people who take the financial risk deserve a return. Yet that won't stop the arguments.

Manoj: For years we have said that increasing salary caps has little impact on a team's ability to acquire a player. It is all about relative spend, and how much you rate a player relative to others, when you have effective caps. All you do by increasing salary caps is transfer returns from the league to the players. If you increase the salary cap of $12m to $14m does that increase my chance to get Rohit Sharma? No, you've just increased the market price for Rohit Sharma. All you have to decide is what percentage of your salary cap you spend on a particular player. That's what Chennai did so brilliantly in that first year. I never thought anybody would spend even 20% on one player. Chennai spent 35% on Dhoni. Worth every penny. We got it wrong. We spent too much money on back-up players. We had Younis Khan ($300,000) sitting on the bench. I had to encourage Justin Langer ($75,000) to stay at Middlesex because he wasn't going to play.

Managing player costs is a key aspect to franchise ownership. The auction helped massively, and the limited role for agents has been a major positive. But there are also always teams and owners for whom finance is more accessible. Mumbai Indians became the IPL's Manchester City. Keen to establish early dominance, they were very active in off-season trading. They have also historically paid significantly for marquee players. All of the franchises have evolved their approaches – welcoming shorter contracts, tightening non-payment for injury unavailability, supporting the extension of the auction to include uncapped players. English players have always had a 'discount' because of concerns about their availability – especially at the tournament's later stages. What we have seen more recently is a hike in the amount paid to young players, which will bring with it new problems. The IPL has not fully cracked the challenges of player cost inflation, but has applied many principles, which other leagues could borrow.

There is no doubt that cricketers' bank balances, and abilities, have been seriously enhanced by appearing in the IPL. But the high stakes do ramp up the stress levels. It is an individual sport within a team game. Each member has both singular and collective responsibilities. That is cricket's special ingredient. So, it is the franchise that manages their individuals most adeptly that will prevail. It all adds to the melodrama.

Post Covid star alignment

Manoj: The complex challenges of player management will not get any easier post Covid, but what will change will be what we deem to be acceptable earnings for the top stars. Capitalism, free markets and survival of the fittest have been the dominant mantras of the last 40 years, but Covid has highlighted inequalities across society in a starker fashion than ever before – whether through the increasing likelihood of death by virtue of being poor, or the low salaries paid to frontline care and health workers, or the reaction of high earners to pay cuts. Sport stars have had mixed reviews and mixed performances during Covid. In football, we have seen the best and worst of the superstar pay mentality. But fundamentally, the issue is created through poor design of salary structures, the tolerance of excessive agent influence (where in some cases it is unclear who runs the clubs or indeed decides what is best for the players), non-transparent buying processes for players, and a 'win at all costs' mentality of many private owners.

The arrival of analysts, in the post-Moneyball era, has meant better decision-making and more accurate reflections of value for players. It has also led to much higher-quality skills development and competition – improving the quality of the sport. Within cricket this has created a much more watchable end product, with the next stage being greater integration of day and information into the game.

Professional sport has to have the profit motive in its franchises and rights holders, but the distribution of that profit across the sport is also critical. Stars must, and should, get their fair share, but aligning their incentives more to those of the league and team economics (as the US does by linking player salaries to media rights), is perhaps the way to build fairer and greater alignment.

Capping salaries ensures that the negative side-effects (parents choosing football academies over a broad-based education for their children) are avoided and also ensures the commercial viability of all parts of the sport. That said there is no water-tight model to ensure this, and an event like the IPL has leakages (with retained players).

It is not just sport that needs to face these realities but society as a whole – whether it is the amounts paid to leaders in industry, banking or fund management. The world needs a reset as to what appropriate incomes are for different jobs. This only comes from having more 'stars' in our governments and regulatory structures. Within sport, getting that star alignment will be even more important in a post-Covid world, to maintain the commercial opportunities for stars of the future.

Chapter 5

Building Tribes

The principles of creating fan engagement

That's entertainment

One of the most remarkable aspects of the IPL is how eight hurriedly cobbled-together teams conjured out of a neglected domestic circuit were suddenly able to elicit passionate support and fill stadiums with over 40,000 adoring fans.

> *Manoj: While considering investment into the IPL I was quite sceptical about how quickly franchises would build fan followings. India was a country obsessed with its own cricket superstars, and the idea that they would support foreign players against these stars seemed unlikely to me in 2008. We were quickly proved wrong. I remember the Mumbai crowd chanting 'Watson, Watson' as he [Shane Watson] bowled hostile, body-threatening deliveries at two Indian icons – Virender Sehwag and Gautam Gambhir – in our inaugural season semi-final. That, for me, was a defining moment.*

The teams engendered an immediate following, borrowing ideas and methodologies from some of the world's most established sports brands. According to *Forbes*, the six most valuable sports franchises in the world in 2019 were the NFL's Dallas Cowboys (top for the fourth year running), baseball's New York Yankees, Real Madrid, Barcelona, basketball's New York Knicks and Manchester United. All, apart from United, are worth over $4bn. In comparison the most successful IPL franchises currently have a value of between $300m and $400m.

The billion-dollar teams above have all had the benefit of at least a 50-year head start on any of the franchises in the IPL. But that is not the only reason they are so valuable. It is also not just related to success on the field (although heavily influenced by it). Manchester United have won more major league titles than any other English football team. Real Madrid and Barcelona hold a permanent duopoly over La Liga. Off the field investments also contribute to value. Buoyed by a successful history, the Dallas Cowboys retain a massive brand value, in spite of a lack of recent success. They haven't won the Super Bowl since 1996 and have failed to even reach the playoffs in the last five seasons. And the immediately recognisable New York Yankees have won only two MLB World Series in the 21st century, the last in 2009.

Winning on the field isn't the only route to creating an attractive sports brand. What you do *off* it is also important. Lalit Modi was instrumental in the early stages of this. "It came from the football World Cup," he said. "I used to attend them with Shah Rukh Khan. He was an old schoolfriend. Their after-show parties were flamboyant. I set out to copy the best. That's how I created the hoopla round the IPL. I hired the best DJs. The players weren't able to go out of the hotel (because of the crowds). So I booked the whole hotel and staged the parties there." The post-match entertainment helped to give the IPL an identity – not universally felt to be a positive one. (Modi, the ultimate ringmaster, made the parties into a media 'property' and sold the rights to a broadcaster.)

Many surveys have been conducted on what factors govern attraction and loyalty to a sports team. Three fundamentals stand out:

- entertainment value
- group affiliation
- authenticity

The first of these, **entertainment**, is logical. If you're going to spend your hard-earned cash watching a sport, you want to be stimulated and uplifted, even if your team lose. A lively end-to-end game which ends in defeat is ultimately preferable to a dull 0-0 draw with barely a shot on goal (unless of course that draw secures a playoff spot or staves off relegation). The most popular teams play with a certain style, a panache, that excites their fans and gains an admiring reputation. They are entertaining and people want to be associated with them. There's an audible buzz. That means investing in at least some glamorous, glitzy players rather than just ones who will necessarily guarantee results. Real Madrid's 'galactico policy' is a case in point, hiring the likes of Luis Figo, Zinedine Zidane, Ronaldo and David Beckham in the early 2000s. It boosted the club's profile overseas as much as it did at home.

Manchester United always had a culture of hiring exciting, charismatic players too – a legacy that began with George Best in the late 1960s through to Eric Cantona in the 1990s and Cristiano Ronaldo in 2006. It was not always a guarantee of Premier League points but it gave the team a visible style and ambition to entertain. The disgruntlement felt by many United fans who watched the stuttering 2018 team fashioned by José Mourinho wasn't so much because of the disappointing results as the lack of adventure in their play. And evidence the passionate following that Jurgen Klopp (at Liverpool) and Pep Guardiola (at Manchester City) now achieve with their forms of beautiful free flowing football. Winning is the sugar coating.

In the IPL the Royal Challengers Bangalore adhere most closely to the 'galacticos' policy. They make a point of investing in the biggest, most exciting names in T20 cricket like Virat Kohli, AB de Villiers and Chris Gayle and they strut their stuff in their 40,000-seater Chinnaswamy Stadium which is always packed to the rafters. They have maintained a fervent, loyal, local support despite never having won the tournament.

Similarly, Chennai Super Kings have consistently retained their charismatic, iconic players year after year – MS Dhoni, Suresh Raina, Dwayne Bravo and Ravi Jadeja. They exude style as well as quality and have focused on player and team consistency more than any other franchise. It was the disagreements over player retention policy that initially led to the battle between the BCCI powerhouses, Lalit Modi and Narayanaswami Srinivasan. Despite their suspension from the competition at the same time as Rajasthan Royals, CSK remain one of the most popular franchises in the IPL with one of the highest brand values. The decibel levels when Dhoni comes out to bat in Chennai are bone-shaking.

Building a brand with less lavish resources than those available to some franchises, the Rajasthan Royals realised from the outset that, having not purchased the big names, they needed some stardust. Hence the signing of Shane Warne, despite his retirement from international cricket, as captain. As one of *Wisden's* five greatest cricketers of the 20th century, he gave the team credibility, presence and a playing ethos that married flair and imagination with fun. He explained his overriding philosophy was to "create an environment where everyone is treated equally and encouraged to express themselves. Ideally, the players buy into an aggressive style of play and learn the value of taking risks in order to win… Lastly it's really important to enjoy playing, to have fun out there."

Manoj : We owe some of the credit of the selection of Warne to Ravi Krishnan, our vice chairman in Season 1, who was at school with him in Melbourne. Ravi was convinced he was still hugely motivated to play in the IPL, even though he had retired. Right at the outset of the IPL Warne was insistent that we had to have a 'brand' of cricket that we wanted to play. For him, it was always about attacking, trying to take wickets, score boundaries, and being fearless. This fitted well with the heritage of Rajasthan, and we quickly became popular. No other player had a bigger impact on the success of the IPL in the early years than Shane Warne. Equally, no other tournament could have been better designed for Shane Warne. Commentators often use the phrase 'box office' for certain sportsmen – those that entertain, those that keep people in their seats – Warne was the definition.

CSK have built a very strong identity. They have focused on winning and have an incredible record. They have built a deep relationship with Dhoni, their leader since Season 1. They chose a distinctive colour – yellow. They used Indian cheerleaders and Indian fan entertainment – the CSK drums. They have tapped into their Tamil identity. They have invested in local leagues. And so they now have a fervent, cricket-mad home base, where we always seem to lose!

The Royals traded on their underdogs' tag. They weren't a team brimming with stars, but they became respected for making the most of limited resources, nurturing young, unheard-of players, instigating unexpected 'plays' and scrapping to the death. It was a David v Goliath sort of scenario that everyone can identify with, encapsulated in that first 2008 final. Over time the Royals found that even if they weren't everybody's number-one team outside the state of Rajasthan, they were most people's second favourite team and that, in a country of a billion potential cricket fans, is not a bad place to be. To this day, the Royals have an emotional connect with fans across the subcontinent – and an association with unearthing new talent, performing beyond expectations, and everyone in India still knows the sounds of their year one anthem – 'Halla Bol!' (a war cry, literally translated as 'Raise Your Voice!').

The house that Jerry built

Entertainment doesn't have to be provided just on the field of play. Most English people you meet who've attended a major sporting event in the US exclaim about the outstanding experience, from when their entry ticket is scanned at the start to the final whistle/claxon/hooter several hours later. US sports stadia are at the forefront of providing the total experience, as Damian Dexter, an award-winning sports TV producer and regular at many sporting venues in Britain, discovered. "I took my wife and teenage sons to a Toronto Blue Jays game," he says. "From the moment they sang the national anthems before the match until leaving the stadium at the end, the entertainment was relentless. It was so slick and coordinated. Every time a new batter came to the mound the announcer would big him up and then his stats would appear on one of the big screens and a highlights package of his best hits would appear on another and then they'd show a pitcher on one screen and the ball would fly horizontally across another and be shown being whacked into the crowd on a third. Everything built to a crescendo and there was a countdown and the crowd were totally engaged as the pitcher wound up. It was fantastic. We all loved it."

Dallas Cowboys take this exceptional in-house experience to extremes. The giant AT&T stadium complete with retractable roof, built by owner Jerry Jones at a cost of $1.4bn in 2009, has the largest HD TV screen in the world, measuring 50m across suspended from the centre. It's like a great airship above the arena displaying enormous close-ups of the play, accompanied by giant speakers. Escalators whisk spectators to various viewing levels or swanky merchandise outlets, mobile apps guide them to their luxury arm-chairs, there are numerous categories of seating. It is all climate-controlled. You can see your face in the washroom floors. Everything is bigger and better and smarter than at any other venue. Everyone is treated like a VIP. The Cowboys generate more than $100m a year from their luxury suites. It should be called the OTT stadium not the AT&T.

Yet a fan does not feel alienated from the action. That is key. Peter Griffiths, an IMG executive who helped design the IPL and has been working on the NFL for four years, identifies an optimum distance between the players and the spectators. "Nine feet from the LED boards to the edge of the pitch is ideal. That way the players have enough safe space to overrun the line but they are not too far from the crowd. Any further and the play seems more remote. Cricket sometimes takes the boundaries in too far so that the players are a long way from their fans. The players need to be able to interact with their audience and sign autographs or pose for selfies." He has created a con-sultancy business specialising in how to engage sports fans. It's called Nine Feat! The new Tottenham Hotspur stadium conforms to this ideal spec. The front row of spectators is aproximately eight metres from the touchline. They were 18 metres away in their temporary home at Wembley stadium.

Starting from a considerably lower base than the NFL or EPL teams, the Royals worked on creating a much simpler, though still special, experience in their Jaipur stadium. A major disadvantage with all IPL stadia is that the franchises don't own them, but just rent them for the days of the home matches. They can't construct permanent installations, shops, interactive tours of the ground or a sky walk hanging from the roof which is what you get at Tottenham's new stadium.

Manoj: The in-stadium experience at the IPL is still a long way behind inter-national standards. I took my family to a Florida Panthers ice hockey game in America a few years ago. I was driving down the highway, still 40 minutes away from the stadium when my phone bleeps with a message asking "Would you like to park normally or VIP?" They are starting to take my money before I've even arrived. Then it asks if I want to order pizza and fast-check into the stadium. It was really eye-opening. I haven't even got into the stadium and I'm $150 down. That's not including the tickets. But it was all painless.

Maybe they are charging you $7 for a coke that would normally cost you $2 but it's brought straight to your seat. You're not missing any of the action. None of it felt like I was over paying, just receiving high quality service. I was grateful. It was pure entertainment. But we can't do any of this in India at present because we don't own the stadiums. They are leased from the state associations who are in total control. We would love to build a stadium for Rajasthan – something which the state and the country can be proud of. However, seven home games do not justify a $300m construction, so the key will be other uses – shopping malls, retail parks, etc. Key to this will be the development of 5G artificial playing surfaces, with drop-in wickets. This will be a major innovation in a game that can be so weather-affected, but even more importantly it will create a multi-use dimension to cricket stadia, which will transform the economics for stadium investment.'

A good recent example of how hamstrung an IPL franchise can be by their stadia is provided at the M.A. Chidambaram facility in Chennai. Through 2019 a third of the ground was empty for Super Kings games because the Chennai municipal authority declared that there was a gap of only six metres between four of the newly built stands. For safety reasons, the gap should be eight metres. So those stands were cordoned off, depriving the franchise of 12,000 tickets per match – about £150,000 – for five years.

Raghu Iyer was the Royals' chief executive from Season 4 to 8, and was heavily focused on the customer experience to garner loyalty. "Our grounds used to be terrible. People sitting in the baking sun on concrete slabs behind barbed wire. There were regular lathi (baton) charges from the police. Jaipur's quite a small, low stadium but we dressed up areas of seating and created various levels of hospitality. They'd never had that in Jaipur before. Also, we added to the roadside-type food and brought in things like proper popcorn or burgers, as well as chaat and samosas – we gave it a cinema-type experience. Even at a basic food stall we made sure the guy serving wore white gloves. They were simple, affordable improvements but they worked."

Iyer was not alone in recognising a major deficiency in the fan experience at Indian cricket matches. He says "Ladies' toilets. They were horrible, if they existed at all. It was hardly surprising that 95% of the people attending cricket were men. To get the families in we realised we had to attract the women. They are the people who run the home and make the family decisions. We placed a major emphasis on providing plenty of decent women's toilets." This is reminiscent of Arsenal's (and David Dein's) focus on the same issue in the early stages of the Premier League.

One of the most dramatic changes in the cricket demographic in India has been the presence of women. Mothers, wives, sisters, aunts, grandmothers, often groups of teenage girls or working women enjoy a night out at the IPL. They are attracted by the unthreatening atmosphere and the lively ambience, the exciting game, the hygienic surroundings, the latest Bollywood songs on the PA and the cheerleaders dancing to them. It is like a night out at the movies, only better. This is an extravaganza and now they are actually in the same arena as stars like Preity Zinta or Shah Rukh Khan. There they are clapping and cheering (or dejected at the loss of a wicket), looking really quite normal. It is aspirational. It is a water cooler moment. Something to tell your work colleagues when you are gathered around one the next day.

When a Bollywood star – Shilpa Shetty (winner of the UK's *Celebrity Big Brother*) – and her husband, Raj Kundra, expressed an interest in buying a share in the Royals, the IPL's 2008 champions, the franchise welcomed their approach. With the Royals lacking a showbiz element, it made total business sense. It upped the glamour quotient, it would attract more families, and capture more media value.

One of the greatest achievements of IPL Season 1 was that a high proportion of fan attendance were women and children. By the 2016 tournament 42% of the TV audience for an IPL game were female. This not only broadens the addressable consumer base, but also transforms the rights value to sponsors – which in turn drives up the value of media rights. "The music, colourful jerseys, close encounters, different international players playing as a team, it's an amazing vibe that seems more like a festival," said a female fan from Mumbai. "The IPL tends to have a fun version of rivalry between friends as there are different supporters from the same area, watching the same match at the same time," said her friend Neha Dey. "Another factor that I enjoy is celebrity spotting at the matches, especially if you are sitting next to the dugout." This is what has led to the female-cosmetic sponsorships.

Total engagement

Group affiliation strengthens the bond to a sports brand. Finding other people who share your passion is a validation, a point of reference, a common denominator. It creates a feeling of identity and belonging. They form a community and develop an interaction. They meet up at matches and establish societies and wear replica shirts. They become a tribe. Through this collective bonding their sense of loyalty becomes increasingly embedded (in the case of many English football clubs it becomes a lifetime sentence). Sports-team affiliation is much more powerful than consumer loyalty to, say, cars or fashion labels, even among women. The key is to get them young, when they are impressionable, and that was why the targeting of families at the IPL – largely through women (i.e. mothers) was so important.

Starting a franchise from scratch and creating that affiliation is a challenge. Again, having a playing style – an ethos – is fundamental to create a USP. The Royals underdog status and ability to be more than the sum of their parts really resonated with their community. Their initial 'sell' was Shane Warne and his ability to get the most from limited resources, and this platform was one that Rahul Dravid was able to take to another level – especially with respect to the young Indian talent.

Manoj: The 'underdogs' tag even stuck with us as champions. When we launched the unknown left-arm fast bowler Kamran Khan in South Africa in 2009 – there was huge excitement across the Indian media. There was universal acclaim when Warne backed the youngster to bowl to Chris Gayle and Brendon McCullum in the IPL's first-ever super over in 2009. The truth was that the strategy of reliance on unknown talent started to run its course in 2010 – but it did make for some memorable moments, and the Royals have been a powerful platform for so many young players. You need matchwinners for such a short tournament, and we kept our budget-first strategy for too long – focusing on clever buys rather than an overall team spend that would allow us to compete to win the tournament.

The Royals continue to comb the country – especially the local state – for hidden talents (4000 aspirants turned up hoping to join the Rajasthan Colts in late 2018). It engages and excites the community. They can identify with 'one of theirs' that made it big – for instance Rajasthan-bred Ashok Menaria lit up 2010, and briefly looked like the next Ravi Jadeja (although they missed the Rajasthan-born Chahar brothers who were snapped up by other franchises). Another example is Sanju Samson, who hails from the cricketing outpost of Kerala but who attended one of Rajasthan's trials aged 17 and made an instant impression on Rahul Dravid. Within a few months he was carting Australia's fearsome fast bowler Mitchell Johnson about and smacking South Africa's equally ferocious Dale Steyn into the crowd. In his sixth season with the Royals he is now one of India's brightest stars having become the youngest player (aged 24) to record two IPL hundreds.

Nurturing and retaining young, locally-bred players has been one of the pillars on which the great sporting brands like Manchester United and Barcelona have maintained their reputations. It gives them a core identity. United's famous 'class of 92' team – featuring home grown players like Ryan Giggs, Paul Scholes, the Neville brothers and David Beckham – won eight premier league titles. In that time, they topped the EPL in starting appearances for home grown talent. Barcelona have La Masia (the farmhouse), an academy holding 300 players – many from the local community – regarded as the best in the world. Having produced Lionel Messi, Xavi and Andres Iniesta, and four others who were part of Barca's UEFA Champions League triumph in 2011 (the core of the Spanish team that won the 2010 World Cup), it is a justifiable boast.

These training systems reinforce traditional club values which encourage further allegiance and affiliation. They generate local pride and a buzz around the city when these players are in the local newspapers or seen around. This is the essence of 'clubbability' creating the feeling that everybody – players, coaches, parents, employees, colleges, sports associations, fans – have contributed in part to the success of the whole. Manchester United forged the idea of 'One United' in 2003 and that and a distinctive style of attacking play is an alluring combination.

Manoj: One of the design failures of the IPL has been the lack of incentive to continue to invest in and develop young talent. If teams were able to hold on to players whom they gave debuts to, for three to five years, then you would see teams investing much more ambitiously into talent-spotting and academy development. We have partnered with Zubin Bharucha, our head of cricket, into a private academy in Nagpur. It will allow us to work all year round with young players. We have made a major investment in creating state of the art facilities, building a school for young people, and creating a self-sustaining business – where touring teams from all over the world visit. It is also a great place to experiment with our innovations.

At the moment some franchises keep game-ready young talent on the benches – simply to stop other franchises from accessing them. Or they stop young players going to other teams' trials, or simply breaking existing contracts with teams. We had a young player try to leave after Season 2 when another franchise offered his family 30-year job contracts. He signed with them while under contract with us. The penalty was a year's suspension for the player which hurt us much more than it hurt him. This was Ravi Jadeja, who has become one of India's finest all-rounders.

The real deal

None of the IPL franchises had the benefit of a football club's rich history so were establishing these allegiances from zero. Like many teams, the Royals gave away tickets to get the ball rolling. The trouble is in India complimentary passes to major cricket matches are like golden tickets to life – confirming instant status and privilege. The early trickle of requests for freebies soon becomes a flood. (Complimentary tickets were also a vital way of winning and maintaining allegiances with the local officials.) In fact, such was the success and burgeoning reputation of the Royals franchise that one member of the operations team was threatened at gun point over free pass allocation. Such is the desperation for upward mobility and to be seen in the 'right places' in India. The IPL gatherings are an important event in many respects.

Free tickets are all very well, but if the product is substandard, they are worthless. The **authenticity** of a contest is vital to generate a substantial following. People will turn up to exhibition games occasionally, but to retain serious support it has to mean something and the team must be selected on merit. There were stories in the early years of the IPL of officials interfering by engineering their sons or nephews into the squads – a historic legacy of a state association system where such favours are expected. Shane Warne was very clear on this at the outset of the Royals' journey. When one such player was proposed to him, he said "We've sifted the best 16 cricketers from 50 you gave us. We've chosen the very best. Making a change will betray their trust, set us back and compromise our chances. If he has to be in the 16, he takes my spot because I ain't in it." Warne got his way. Not only the players but the public would have seen through it if he had conceded. The whole enterprise would have been devalued.

Manoj: Ahead of, and during every IPL auction, we will get calls asking us to buy a particular player, "He is a good boy, just give him a chance" they say. Sometimes they are desperate. The status afforded to a player, simply by virtue of being in an IPL squad, is enormous. While teams may have been willing to consider compromises on squad selection in the past, the stakes have always been too high for the selection of the playing eleven as everyone wants to win.

The prominent brand strategist Robert Passikoff talks about the importance of "the game being real and meaningful" – a proper contest in other words. If it is not, for whatever reason – because it is an exhibition or a benefit match or someone is not there on merit – it is harder to take seriously and therefore build loyalty. The sequence of Legends Exhibition matches between Warne's Warriors and Sachin's Blasters staged in baseball stadiums in America in 2015 and featuring a collection of retired players lasted only one series. Interest would have been hard to sustain.

The Royals fans were not best pleased after a week of the 2019 season as their beloved team had badly lost their first three matches. They had also witnessed the ruthless 'Mankadding' of Buttler – run out at the bowler's end by Kings XI skipper Ravichandran Ashwin while feigning to deliver the ball. Outside England Mankadding is very much part of cricket now. Buttler, a privately educated, self-effacing Englishman having his wicket effectively stolen by the wily, opportunistic Ashwin is a symbol of the way India grabbed the English creation that was T20 and made off with the spoils. English cricket was caught napping. India set the rules. You might call it 'reverse colonialism.' That and the usual global attention on the IPL every April and May is incontrovertible proof that India is the new Home of Cricket.

Intriguingly there were also political and financial dimensions to Ashwin's actions. As a player who was temporarily out of favour with the Indian national side he needed to make a statement that still emphasised his significance and impact. Otherwise his value to an IPL franchise – effectively his share price – would continue to decrease. That is his future. He chose a soft target – Buttler – for his ambitions – as a Royals colleague said, "Like shooting Bambi". Would he have done the same if Virat Kohli had been the non-striker? Not likely. His brand value would have plummeted. It is a classic example of where business and sport collide.

The authenticity of the IPL is one of the reasons it has been so successful. Even in the first exploratory year all the players gave it their utmost. Only Jacques Kallis turned up relatively out of condition. But seeing the intensity of the contests, he was as fit as a butcher's dog the following season. The high salaries and the lucrative prize money are only part of the inducement. The competitiveness of the players and their inherent pride is the spur to higher achievement. You could see that writ large in the 2019 tournament. Teams prepared assiduously. They practiced for hours before matches. Watching David Warner and Jonny Bairstow smashing runs and haring up and down the wicket for Sunrisers on a sultry evening in Hyderabad egged on by 55,000 screaming fans, most dressed in Sunrisers' orange, felt like watching an Olympic event. International calibre fast bowlers like Ben Stokes and Jofra Archer were whizzing balls down with all their might to try and inhibit them. They were challenging one other. It's infectious. It leads to unpredictable outcomes. That makes for compelling viewing. And satisfied customers.

Manoj: People are now beginning to understand the value of sports franchises, but no one really explains how you build that value. Over the years, we developed our own view of a virtuous circle of building franchise value. We were fortunate to have early on-field success, but in the subsequent years we got complacent and we didn't invest in that on-field performance – relying too much on the distinctive brand of the 'underdogs' from year one. When we combined on-field performance with that brand – investing properly in superstars alongside young talent, as we did in Seasons 5 to 8, we performed well. That builds the emotional connect with fans, which drives engagement.

The "Virtuous Cycle" of Building Franchise Value

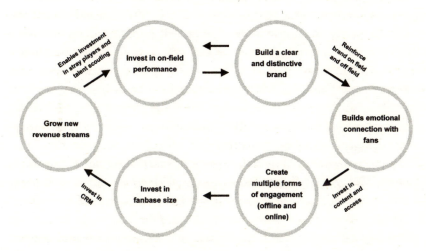

Fig. 14

We could have avoided a lot of mistakes if someone had given this chart to me 12 years ago. Even now, we have much to do – investments in CRM (customer relationship platforms), digital content and stadium experience being the obvious big areas. There is one major weakness of the IPL, which is the relatively short period of engagement that a seven-week tournament allows a franchise.

The importance of tribes post Covid

Manoj: We all want to belong to something, and Covid has forced us to re-evaluate our sense of community. Community causes and institutions inspired and drove the first sports clubs, and that heritage and that link is critical – even in a world of franchise sport. Fans need a sense of ownership, whether financial or emotional, and without this they will disengage. A disengaged fan base greatly reduces the value of a franchise.

So what franchises and brands stand for, what they do for their communities, how they engage their fans and how they invest in those tribes will be as important in the new normal. We will be entering a period of greater localism, less travel, more appreciation of community. Sports franchises, clubs and leagues should seize these opportunities. The franchises and brands that develop a longer-term distinctive identity, that welcome fans into the tribe, engage them with unique access and experiences, and reinforce that with a strong collective sense of social purpose, will be the winners. Post Covid that social purpose will become even more important.

There may also be an unbundling of tribal value, as fans' obsession with super-stars determine their franchise loyalty. Was it the marketing strategies of RCB that created their brand identity or the presence of Gayle, de Villiers, and of course, Virat Kohli? This interplay between the franchises and their superstars will also define success in building tribes. CSK, KKR and MI have done it superbly. We were slow to recognise the value of the Indian superstar, but, as in business, the truly great brands define an ethos and culture and then pick players that fit – not the other way round. Those truly great brands aim for sustained success over short-term wins.

Chapter 6
Beware the Fix

Betting is intertwined with sport, but its
corrupting tentacles are ruinous

Banged to rights

With smart use of data, a well-balanced side, and, under the calm leadership
of Rahul Dravid, an enterprising attitude, the Rajasthan Royals were top of
the IPL table in May 2013. Then calamity struck. Three Royals players – the
extrovert Indian fast bowler Sreesanth and two less well-known team members – Ankeet Chavan and Ajit Chandila – were arrested after an away game
versus Mumbai Indians and subsequently charged with spot-fixing. Chandila,
a steady spinner who often bowled in the powerplay, had conceded 14 off his
second over that night with some ill-directed deliveries. A leading Australian
player, who was ill in bed, remembers watching the game and thinking there
was something suspicious about the over at the time. "He was generally so
accurate and him losing his line like that was odd. It didn't look right."

*Manoj: I was watching the game back home in London. I thought nothing of
our defeat. We had just lost to our main title challengers away from home in a
close match. What was to suspect? We were having a brilliant season. We had
a captain, Rahul Dravid, of the highest integrity. We had a brilliant team
dynamic with a solid coaching and support staff set up. And then I woke up on
Friday morning to 16 missed calls from Raghu Iyer, our chief executive. On
returning the call I heard the dreaded words, "Three of our players have been
arrested for spot-fixing, and one is currently behind Mumbai police bars."*

It was a devastating moment not just for the Royals but for the IPL too.
That hard-earned authenticity was suddenly in tatters. The team fragmented

almost instantly and people began to question the validity of the tournament. How many other uncovered examples of this were there? Who else was involved? Was that victory last week real? Is everything rigged? Players were combing their memories for whom they had spoken to and met in the team hotel.

Manoj: The story was wall-to-wall in India. The press were hounding every player, every staff member, and we had no idea how to deal with it. We were completely unprepared. Our squad had to leave Mumbai immediately for a game against Hyderabad a few days later. We got beaten heavily. I set up a conference call with the coach Paddy Upton, Rahul Dravid the captain and Shane Watson. It was a very fractious conversation. There was a lot of emotion flying around. Dravid said – "Manoj you've got to get here. There's a lot of stuff on TV every hour. Players are being called in for questioning." Factions had formed in the team. There were Australians in one corner, West Indians in another, Indians in another. Mistrust everywhere. [Australia's] Brad Hodge had apparently thrown a bottle against the team room wall. I flew to Jaipur and when I got there it was like someone had died. Everything had unravelled. I had a meeting with the team at the Jai Mahal Palace hotel – normally an oasis of calm. There was lots of aggression. "What are you going to do to stop our names being sullied?" the players demanded. It was febrile. There was lots of hostility and anxiety – players worried about parties they'd been to or gifts they'd accepted. The whole team spirit we'd spent weeks building up was destroyed.

We had still made the playoffs and had to pull together to play the Eliminator in Delhi. Paddy Upton had a plan: a simple day of team building with no cricket. It started with a poem under everybody's door, Rudyard Kipling's 'The Looking Glass'. "It's all about not looking at other people just being able to look yourself in the mirror." Then everyone including me was put into groups to make videos about life with the Royals for an imaginary sponsor. We watched them together. They were absolutely hilarious. I still remember Brad Hogg being filmed doing some weightlifting in a gym in women's underwear. It provided a release, made everyone forget about cricket, put everything in perspective and brought everyone back together. The next day we won the Eliminator at the last gasp (Hodge hit two sixes off the last over to win it). The team deserved it for what they had been through the previous four days.

It was almost as good as winning the trophy in the first year, but in a different sort of way. We were hugging each other in front of 40,000 people. I've never seen so many players and staff crying.

Dravid, captain of the Royals, says this episode was a vital wake-up call to the league. "It was a huge shock. We had given these young boys so much opportunity, a chance to play, we'd put so much effort into them and then they got sucked up with this match-fixing. It was so disappointing. That something like that could happen so close to me and I'd not know anything about it was a huge eye-opener. I had heard that stuff like this happens, but I always thought it happened somewhere else. We thought we were in control of the situation. It makes you realise that in this, you're not. These players are only with us for say eight weeks. The rest of the time – say 44 weeks of the year – they're in their home towns meeting so many different people, building different relationships you have absolutely no control over. It made everyone realise we have to put better processes in place: security managers, anti-corruption units. Sometimes I feel bad because the game has become so policed, and the joy of playing a sport you love has been lost somewhat. But we can't go back. It's like after 9/11, so many things changed at airports. It was depressing what happened, but hopefully some good has come out of it."

An ancient pastime

Having won the 2013 Eliminator, the Royals lost the play-off Qualifier to Mumbai Indians thereby missing out on their second final. They had survived with their dignity intact. Just. The arrests had, however, completely undermined the IPL's credibility. There was a kind of 'I always thought it was dodgy' sentiment about the tournament and prominent members of the English cricket establishment, who had been sceptical about the IPL all along, were quick to comment.

'Caught out: Indian Premier League scandal' yelled the *Financial Times*. 'IPL rocked by new match-fixing allegations' exclaimed the *Daily Telegraph*. One leading English cricket writer suggested the IPL had always been a "hotbed of fixing."

Ironically cricket actually began as a vehicle for gambling. In England. The first organised games in the early 1700s were mainly arranged by rich aristocrats who would assemble teams of professionals and their friends and wager relatively large sums (at least £200) on the result. The temptation to fix matches was overpowering. There is written evidence of many games being manipulated by dodgy umpiring, inaccurate scoring or captains on-the-make rigging results. The portrait of one famous culprit, Lord Frederick Beauclerk, used to hang in the Lord's pavilion.

Because the game is made up of so many mini events – balls, overs, individual innings, partnerships etc, it is a perfect sport for betting. A T20 innings is regarded basically as 120 individual 'events' (deliveries) and grouped in passages of play (e.g. powerplay overs) so it was bound to attract the gambling community. Globally, an astonishing $750m is bet on every IPL game – and that is just the wagers that are known about – making each IPL tournament worth at least $30bn to the gambling industry. The mind boggles as to how much would be wagered if gambling in India were legalised.

So how does the system work? A news report in the *Times of India* in April 2019 offers a clue. "A few hours ahead of the IPL match in Jaipur on Tuesday police arrested 15 persons for allegedly betting on matches," it announced. "Police seized 82 mobile phones, six laptops, three internet dongles, and four television sets and Rs 54,000 in cash. They also had one register of bets which ran into ten lakhs of rupees. ($15,000). The 15 arrested are natives of Jodhpur, Nagaur and Bikaner. They were staying at two flats on Ajmer highway in Jaipur."

There are at least 100,000 bookmakers in India. The network is vast, from the big syndicates right down to local operators. They might just be a simple shop or a back office in a side-street in a nondescript Indian town. Many are in Mumbai's crowded suburbs. Inside the 'office' a couple of bookies take bets on one of a number of mobile phones – everything is recorded. Each local bookie might have 200 clients, each using nicknames, all recommended by someone they know. It's like a large, intricate social network.

Each customer bets on credit with the local bookie. They are also paid in credit. It is based on trust. No cash transactions occur (except once or twice a year when balances are settled). Betting prices are governed by a major international exchange with which the largest bookies – usually based outside India – will have multiple accounts. The prices are relayed on mobile phones by a 'commentator' monitoring the major exchange. The prices vary according to how much money is being placed. It's a bit like the old British tic-tac system at race meetings.

The betting has now moved to mobile apps, which make it easier and quicker. Every ball you can see the odds with a click on your smartphone, and then place the bet. Money is settled after every match, or on a weekly basis. This part is still done physically – there are no online transactions. You can only get access to the app through a referral from an existing client or contact, as the payment is still reliant on trust.

The temptations for fixers and their accomplices are obvious. Many tales of suspected match-fixing emanated from the IPL in that unstable period between 2010 and 2016. English players told various stories of bowlers who had obviously been paid to bowl deliberately badly in powerplay overs or batsmen who got out in mysterious circumstances. There are several incidents and bizarre moments in T20 games – and players become easily suspicious.

The rumblings of spot-fixing and illegal activity have been persistent in the smaller leagues. Just before the start of a match in the first edition of the Afghanistan Premier League in October 2018 one team captain approached the well-known overseas star of the opposition. "You'll win the match today," the Afghanistan-born captain said matter-of-factly to the star who reported this comment back to his team. The prediction was right. Even though the overseas player's team were chasing a relatively high score, they got home in the last over.

Manoj: There are lots of worrying stories from players and coaches, who participate in the smaller leagues. Certain competitions have already been discredited, and many of the best players have chosen not to play in them. The smaller leagues have an important purpose and must be encouraged. However, they need regulation and investment support for their anti-corruption teams – or the stories, and dubious incidents, will damage the credibility of the whole game.

Despite the deterrents of life bans for convicted match-fixers and the work of the ICC anti-corruption unit (ACU), the stories still surface from the less lucrative leagues. The problem is the huge discrepancies in players' salaries from league to league, and even within leagues themselves, as well as the vast amounts being bet on cricket.

The incidences of players rigging actual outcomes of matches has been substantially reduced by the work of the ACU. Players have to compulsorily hand in their phones and devices before they enter a dressing room at the beginning of a match, and at the IPL a BCCI-appointed security officer is assigned to every team. But the head of the ACU Alex Marshall says they need to continue to be vigilant.

"The corrupters have changed tack and they go after coaches and support staff rather than players," Marshall says. "It's a better route for the corrupters. These staff have regular contact with players and are party to valuable information like team line-ups and batting orders. In trying to persuade cricketers to manipulate all or part of a match (rarely all), there are a set of tried and tested methods. There is usually a monetary offer made to induce the participant into carrying out the fix. The player might be compromised through a sexual encounter. The approach may come from a trusted acquaintance. Ex-international players, coaches, analysts and administrators have all featured in recent investigations.

"In the case of a recent corrupt approach made to Sarfraz Ahmed (the Pakistan captain), the approach came via a net-bowling manager he had known professionally and personally for a decade. The corrupters might offer their informant $10,000 – $20,000 for regular information. That means quite a lot to the lower paid employees in a team. There are so many vulnerable people in cricket – they will even target U/19 internationals or women's cricket. The more televised events there are the more people there are in an unregulated environment. In some cases, there have been corrupters buying into franchises. [The ICC declared the 2017 Ajman Allstars event in UAE corrupt partly for this reason.] The problem we have is that in some countries it is not a crime to fix matches or bribe players. But the players are getting much better at finding and reporting approaches."

The ACU are much more vigilant and have started flushing out some big names. Sri Lanka's former captain Sanath Jayasuriya was recently banned for two years from associations with cricket after refusing to cooperate with various enquiries, and a similar fate befell Bangladesh's top player Shakib Al Hasan for failing to report corrupt approaches. There are rumours of other famous names that the ACU are closing in on. Slowly but surely they are cleansing the game.

Manoj: One of the biggest threats to a sport, and cricket in particular, is spot-fixing and match-fixing. The moment that happens to a sport it loses authenticity. It takes years to recover. In some parts of rural India there used to be a perception that the IPL was just a money-making machine for the rich and the whole thing is rigged. I've heard that from taxi drivers. The moment that perception becomes broad-based, you're finished. It has taken us several years to recover from our players' spot-fixing. We were executing everything that the league had suggested, but now we have tried to go even further, investing in our own security blanket around the team to do as much as possible to safeguard the players. We have a former chief inspector of Mumbai police who works with us year round, and travels with the squad throughout the tournament. We have CCTV monitoring across our team floors, and in public areas of the hotels. We do extensive player briefings. However much a franchise does, players and support staff can be enticed, so a hardening of legal and criminal sanctions is still needed. It needs to be treated in a similar way to the hardening of laws around 'insider trading' in financial institutions.

A conflict of interest

The underlying issue is that the gambling industry and sport are blood brothers. They are joined at the hip. Look at English football. Stoke City played a home match against Middlesbrough in the English Football League in October 2018. Stoke are sponsored by Bet365 and play at the Bet365 stadium (the company was founded in Stoke by the Coates family who are directors of the football club). Middlesbrough are sponsored by an online casino 32Red. The competition's official name is the EFL Sky Bet Championship. Some 27 out of the 44 clubs in the Premier League and the Championship feature a

111

betting company on their shirts. This is just if you were in any doubt about the influence of gambling on sport. And we haven't even mentioned the 95% of ad breaks during English football matches that contain a gambling advert (although recent laws in the UK have a ban on in-game ads). Over the pond in the NFL there has been a major spike in casino sponsors with Caesar's Entertainment becoming the league's first-ever 'Official Casino Partner'. There will be a surge of sponsorship interest now that gambling on sports has been legalised in the US. Betting companies are tripping over each other to market themselves through sport.

The mistrust of betting is prevalent across the US because of historic concerns about Mafia involvement. The Supreme Court's recent decision has opened up the sports betting market. Peter Jackson, chief executive of Flutter, which owns Betfair, describes the opening up of the US as "the most exciting development since the arrival of online betting." A combination of population size and the passion for sport could make it one of the most lucrative sports betting markets in the world. Now legal in 14 states, five others have legislation pending. Estimates for the size of the potential market vary wildly. Some value the market at over $8bn in revenue in a few years. If the American Gaming Association's $150bn estimate for the illegal sports betting market is accurate, it could be even larger.

Manoj: American sports are long and produce lots of data. The potential for bets on details like the speed of a baseball pitch or the number of yards gained in football are multiple. The popularity of in-play betting (called 'prop bets' in the US) has grown fast. But there are divisions between the sports owners and gambling companies. The league and teams argue that they produce the sport and should share in the proceeds – in effect getting royalties. Casino operators argue that by offering sports betting they are encouraging even more people to watch games, and that drives the value of their digital and media rights.

There's no escape from gaming's expansion – even in India. On the giant screen in Hyderabad for the 2019 Sunrisers against Royals IPL match is a slick advert for Dream11, a rapidly growing Indian daily fantasy game operation. Its headquarters nestle in central Mumbai among the high-rise banks, media companies and stockbrokers of Lower Parel. The company was begun around the time of the launch of the IPL in 2008 by two 22-year-old graduates who were fans of English football's Fantasy League and thought they could do the same for cricket in India.

Dream11 allows you to pick a team before a match starts and nominate which players will perform the best. Based on their outcomes you are allocated points and get a rank at the end of the match. If you've entered with money your winnings are paid out according to your ranking and after a service fee has been deducted. Legally, this is not regarded as gambling but a 'game of skill' according to the Indian courts, because you are judging players on current form and past performance. In 2019 Dream11 had 53m users and was growing past 100m at the time of writing, already making it the first billion-dollar gaming company created in India.

Manoj: India remains one of the largest remaining sports gaming and gambling opportunities in the world. The 'game of skill' distinction, borrowed from other countries, is being tested constantly. It has to be a question of when, not if, sports gambling ultimately becomes legalised within India. There have been numerous calls for gambling to be legalised – from politicians to players to industry. (In 2018 the Federation of Indian Industry called for legalisation, pointing out the loss of 19000 Crore Rupees in Tax for the government.)

Dream11 are described as a 'sports company' and intend to diversify into selling sports analytics. The company's success is just the tip of the iceberg for the gaming industry. The fantasy sports business is set to grow by five times in India in the next two years as companies develop social gaming apps, and sports simulators will enter this market too.

Perhaps the ultimate effect of that will be to not only grow gaming but accelerate the legalisation gambling in India. The 'game of skill' distinction is a complex one, and one that will be tested by many companies over the coming years. Accredited betting companies could be regulated to act on strange activity, as they do in the UK, and punters who mysteriously seem to be consistently and phenomenally successful will have their accounts terminated. And hopefully cricket's association with the 'fixers' will be removed.

Gambling in a PC World

Manoj: As the world tumbles into recession, and consumer spend collapses in most areas, the list of industries which remain resilient include gambling and gaming. In fact, during 'lockdown' gambling and gaming companies have witnessed prolific growth. As sport looks to maintain existing sources of income, and indeed develop new ones, its uneasy relationship with gaming will not only continue, it will grow. Humans will always want to bet, and particularly on sport. The challenge for the authorities is not to prevent it, but to control it. The way to do that is to engage with the industry and regulate it tightly. Regulators are rarely smarter than the industry participants, and so collaboration is key.

Within India, cricket is dominated by illegal gambling, controlled by members of the underworld who often operate outside India. It is the single biggest threat to the game, and the Covid-induced recession will compound the problem. The authorities must work with government to create a clear legal framework where the game can benefit, governments can benefit (through capturing that lost tax income), industry players can be strongly regulated and most importantly fans and players can be protected. Even then, people will inevitably cheat, and here much tougher legislation and punishment is needed. While franchises must be held accountable, must follow the right processes, ensure the right player education and monitoring, they will never be able to cut it out completely, without much stronger sanctions for players.

However, post-Covid gaming and gambling revenues will be critical for the game's growth, so while we must 'beware of the fix', we must also engage with the ethical parts of the industry.

Chapter 7
Keeping Law and Order

The importance of strong, impartial sports governance

Rule-breakers – allegedly

Sport's governance isn't the sexiest of topics, but two major stories have brought the subject into sharp focus within Europe recently. In November 2019 Saracens rugby club – English Premier League champions and European Cup winners in three of the previous four seasons – were fined £5.4m, docked 35 points and relegated by Premiership Rugby for violating salary cap rules. They had effectively lured high-profile players to the club, skirting the salary cap by entering into investment ventures with them, including paying a very large quantum for one player's 'image rights'. Two months later on 15 February 2020, Manchester City, Premier League champions in successive seasons, were fined £25m and banned from European competitions for two years for failing to adhere to UEFA's financial fair play rules. The club's Abu Dhabi owners had allegedly paid extra money (therefore buying power) into its coffers while camouflaging it as sponsorship income.

Despite the pleas from the two clubs' officers (and supporters) the judgments were met with widespread approval. At last a governing body was rigorously applying the financial rules and standing up for itself rather than being hoodwinked, bribed or bullied by powerful clubs or wealthy owners. They had recognised the importance of maintaining a level playing field, knowing that is the best way to keep a league competitive, entice more fans and ultimately retain its value.

Manoj: Business has consistently learnt that when large profit is created quickly, the role of the regulator becomes critical. We have seen that recently in both the banking and technology sectors. Without regulation there will also be players within the industry that chase profit at the expense of the customer. With astronomical sums at stake and big players in the market, sport is now no different. Major sports leagues have long since outgrown amateur governing structures.

Sometimes a sport needs a scandal, a controversy, to establish the right governance framework and personnel. Or in the case of the IPL, multiple scandals. It began in 2010 with Lalit Modi himself perhaps wielding too much power and influence, allegedly bypassing the governing council in decision-making, awarding contracts without transparency, amongst other alleged misdemeanours. The charge sheet was long and complex. Effectively he was being forced out by powerful internal rivals. One of Modi's chief 'crimes' was the presence of his family members in two franchises – Kings XI Punjab and Rajasthan Royals (even though regulation had been passed by the BCCI in 2007 allowing family members to have economic interests in the franchises). This was used as justification to expel the teams from the competition. BCCI served a notice of termination, which was duly contested.

Manoj: The stated reason for our termination related to unapproved changes in the transfer of ownership of our Indian subsidiary. The speculation suggested a desire to remove any investors with a connection to Lalit Modi. We had Suresh Chellaram – his brother in law.

Mukesh Ambani was a big help. He said you've got to challenge this. He introduced me to one of the three great heroes of the Rajasthan Royals. The first one was Shane Warne, the second Rahul Dravid. The third is Harish Salve, one of the very top lawyers in India. The very best lawyers in India are not only ridiculously expensive, but they are inaccessible to most people. Mukesh put me in contact, and I had to convince Harish to represent us, even though we were paying. His father was an old president of the BCCI. He said "My dad would hate this injustice. We're going to win this."

In the end the judgment came through, after an arbitration presided over by one of India's most senior and respected Supreme Court Judges – Justice Srikrishna – confirming that the termination was completely baseless. Without the help and support of Mukesh Ambani, introducing us to Harish Salve, we would have struggled in a complex legal system. The Royals might have been a three-year story. That would have made the league un-investable, because of the ease of a business being terminated. The verdict increased the value of all the franchises.

In many years of doing business in the UK, we had naturally been used to having to engage lawyers. However, we had no idea how important your legal preparedness was in India. It is very easy for almost anyone to serve up public interest litigations (PILs), which need constant monitoring. And the local state politics can also present a multitude of complexities. When business people talk about the challenges of 'business in India', the complexity of the law and the politics are high on the list. Harish Salve (and Rohan Shah) have been important members of our off-field team. We never expected that legal fees would be our second largest expense item after player costs!

At the same time as our termination, we were served with a $20m fine from the ED (Enforcement Directorate – the Indian agency responsible for enforcement of foreign exchange regulations). The fine related to alleged infringements at the time of our company formation. This was the one issue that could have impacted our business outside India. Such violations are (rightly) tracked by all global agencies, so this was particularly stressful. In reality, as was later pronounced and declared by the Appellate Tribunal – the ED's own appeal function, the alleged violations were technical, pro-cedural and venial in nature, it did not cause any loss to the Indian gov-ernment and therefore the fine was completely disproportionate. Thankfully, we had kept the BCCI fully informed, but we had not sufficiently invested in our legal teams. The speed of the tournament set up in season one – from franchise award to first ball in 70 days – was also a factor, as well as our lack of Indian operating entities. India is continuously getting easier as a place for foreign investors to do business, but investment in strong legal and tax support remains an essential lesson.

The reformation

Modi was subsequently expelled from the BCCI in 2010 and retreated to London, but both Kings XI and Royals were reinstated before the next tournament. Shakily, the IPL recovered its composure. Yet not long after, in 2013, there was more controversy. The dust had barely settled from the three Royals players being charged with spot-fixing when Gurunath Meiyappan, tightly involved with the Chennai Super Kings, was voice-recorded dealing with an illegal bookmaker, and he was heavily implicated in spot-fixing activity. To complicate matters further, Meiyappan was the son-in-law of N. Srinivasan (then the BCCI chief and leader of Indian Cements). Shortly afterwards, Delhi police broke the news that Raj Kundra, husband of Shilpa Shetty and the Royals 10% shareholder, had admitted betting during IPL games (there was never any allegation of spot-fixing). Despite Kundra's declarations of his innocence, and CSK'S protestations that Meiyappan was merely an 'enthusiast' and not actually a CSK official, the scandal escalated. After refusals to resign as BCCI chief, Srinivasan was forced to step aside, at least temporarily. After the player spot-fixing scandal, this was another hammer blow to the Royals.

The BCCI committee, led by the late Arun Jaitley, subsequently cleared the culprits of any wrongdoing. But the Bombay High Court intervened. The Supreme Court was summoned to instigate a fresh probe. The BCCI was analysed and interrogated by the top legal counsels in India. Kundra and Meiyappan were suspended immediately.

More judges and committees were assembled by the Supreme Court to decide the penalties and initiate substantial changes in the BCCI. The Royals sent Manoj Badale and Rahul Dravid, along with former Attorney General, Mr. Ashok Desai. They met Justice Rajendra Mal Lodha and his colleagues in Delhi.

Manoj: It was another traumatic period. We felt that we might lose the franchise again – but also felt that we were not being given a chance to put our side of the story. The media was baying for change at the BCCI. We were rapidly becoming collateral damage. We asked for an opportunity to meet the Chief Justice panel, believing that if Rahul Dravid and I could get in front of them, then they might understand how we were the victims – not the miscreants.

We pleaded for 15 minutes at one of their sessions. Although they were impressed by Rahul, one of the judges expressed sympathy for the fact that he had to play on the same side as Sachin Tendulkar. He said, somewhat bizarrely, 'You would have otherwise been a famous star'! Another judge challenged me, questioning whether I was the lead owner, as he had never seen me on television! It was clear that their minds were made up, and it was simply a question of what punishment and how severe.

Here was a franchise owner, Raj Kundra, alleged to have done something illegal, and expressly against the franchise contract. But I'd say, show me the instances in corporate history of someone who has a 10% share in a company, and is alleged to have done something wrong, and yet 100% of the company is suspended from trading for a substantial time. It felt unfair to penalise the whole franchise for the alleged, not proven, actions of a minority shareholder.

It was a protracted affair. Finally, in July 2015 Justice Lodha delivered the verdict. The Royals and CSK were to be suspended from the IPL for two years (and temporarily replaced by Rising Pune Supergiant and Gujarat Lions). Srinivasan, having presented the ICC World Cup trophy at the final in Melbourne as ICC's first chairman, was barred from contesting BCCI elections. There was also to be major reform of the BCCI, with regular elections of state association heads, proper accountability of subsidies given to each state and a general attempt to professionalise the game's administration. The Supreme Court ultimately overruled the BCCI. Its intervention prevented the IPL from potential implosion.

Manoj: The Lodha reforms were quite broad in their remit. Supreme court judges were well placed to rule on some issues such as transparency, concentration of power, Indian legislature, supervision of the game. There were a lot of useful recommendations, and the intervention of the courts in the running of a sport was a major turning point in the evolution of Indian cricket, and within sport more generally.

The following table illustrates the areas on which the Lodha Committee were asked to make recommendations. It shows those recommendations, and the status of their adoption (in 2019) by the BCCI. There are still significant differences between the BCCI and the Supreme Court on many of the reforms, and the level of intervention of the courts in the running of cricket within India. That said, it has been a fascinating debate around who the ultimate regulators are, and to whom the governing body of cricket is ultimately accountable. India will not be the only country that is forced to evaluate these issues. As the size and influence of the sports industry grows, so will the debates about the need for more accountability – either from the courts or the government.

119

Lodha Reforms Summary

#	Category	Details
1	**Structure**	**PURPOSE** • Increase overall transparency • Establish a level playing field between states **KEY RECOMMENDATIONS** • Removal of "Affiliate" member status, leaving only Associate (non-voting) and Full (voting) • Full membership for all states; only one vote per state; removal of zones (President now elected by all states instead of rotational basis) • Non-state members shall be non-voting Associate members • Transparency of BCCI funds distributions to members **STATUS** "One state one vote" and non-voting membership for non-state entities will not be applied
2	**Governance**	**PURPOSE** • Decrease concentration of power in certain BCCI sections • Address lack of experience of certain office bearers • Address lack of representation of players and women • Introduce a limit on tenure **KEY RECOMMENDATIONS** • Replacement of BCCI Working Committee • Revamp of IPL Governing Council • IPL committees and commissions should comprise members nominated by the Ombudsman, Ethics Officer, and CEO • Restriction on office bearers including age (max 70 years old) and other offices **STATUS** • Apex council to be appointed only after upcoming BCCI elections • Initial term limit extended from to 6 yrs • Age limit only for office bearers but not state representatives and committee members
3	**Management**	**PURPOSE** Ensure greater professionalism in BCCI management **KEY RECOMMENDATIONS** • Appointment of a CEO • Reduction of the number of BCCI committees to only two committees ((i) Senior Tournaments and Tours and (ii) Fixtures & Technical) **STATUS** • CEO appointed • Committees suspended until CoA steps down
4	**Players**	**PURPOSE** Safeguard players' interests **KEY RECOMMENDATIONS** • Creation of a players' association (current and formers) • Compulsory registration for player agents **STATUS** Formation of player's association still pending
5	**Conflict of Interest**	**PURPOSE** Define types of conflict of interests to be administered by the Ethics Officer **KEY RECOMMENDATIONS** **Mandatory disclosure of circumstances potentially leading to a conflict of interests, including:** • Direct/indirect associations or arrangements with associates or family members • Simultaneous holding of multiple roles potentially conflicting • Commercial relationships with third parties **STATUS** • Accepted in principle but Ethics Officer not appointed yet
6	**External Oversight**	**PURPOSE** Ensure an external supervision of BCCI's function, especially from a conflicts resolution, governance and ethics perspective **KEY RECOMMENDATIONS** • Introduction of an Ombudsman • Introduction of an Ethics Officer • Introduction of an Electoral Officer **STATUS** Accepted in principle but no appointments have been made so far (expectation that they will be made by end of 2019)
7	**Commercial**	**PURPOSE** Restrict advertising **KEY RECOMMENDATIONS** Certain restrictions on the number and timing of commercial advertisements during test matches and ODIs **STATUS** Rejected by Supreme Court
8	**Others**	**PURPOSE** Propose changes to the Indian legislature with regards to cricket mediatisation and betting **KEY RECOMMENDATIONS** • Reclassification of BCCI under the Right to Information Act, making it subject to information requests from the public re-its decision-making • Legalisation of betting subject to certain safeguards (incl. a regulatory watchdog, a registration system, strict rules to ensure player transparency and strict penal sanctions for offenders) **STATUS** • RTI classification under judicial review • No action taken on betting legalization

Fig. 15

Breaking up the cartels

The above is a good case study for sport. It focuses on a number of key issues. Obviously, sports need governing bodies but who are they answerable to? In the first era of professional sport, this wasn't as important as it is now with the amount of money and the level of power involved. The larger (and richer) the sport, the more likely there will be powerful people in the ruling body. Ruling bodies afford a status and influence. And because many of them are accustomed to electing each other it can become a self-perpetuating private fiefdom. In America the NFL is effectively owned by the league's teams – creating a group 'monopoly'.

Look at the controversies that have bedevilled organisations like FIFA, the IOC, the IAAF, even the FIA. They took years to unravel. Sepp Blatter was general secretary of FIFA from 1981, and despite regular accusations of financial impropriety was president from 1998 until his eventual deposal in 2015. Bernie Ecclestone was the immoveable supremo of Formula 1 for 19 years. Sports governors can be impregnable. Arguably, the lack of transparent and impartial governorship nearly derailed the IPL and undermined its status and credibility.

Ultimately, there needs to be a higher authority monitoring the governors. But who? A sequence of police forces and law courts supplied the answer in India – an unwieldy, labyrinthine arrangement. You don't really want to be relying on the legal system to oversee sports bodies. That ultimately is not going to ensure efficient or effective governance. The FA might like to think they are the ultimate arbiters in English football, but they have limited influence over the Premier League. Even governments have struggled to regulate sport, appointing external regulatory bodies, or instigating reviews and inquiries through their sports ministries. However, it generally yields little more than comment; they have limited ability to censure associations.

Manoj: Sport is no different to any other major industry. It needs effective regulation. There is a danger when regulators under invest in their leadership teams and there is also a danger when they have no accountability. This topic will grow in importance, as the significance of sport grows, and as the financial power vested in these regulators increases. It is also exacerbated by the profile and the media visibility of any such debates – as evidenced by cricket-obsessed India. At a minimum, a good starting point is to drastically improve transparency by increasing the reporting requirements of such bodies. When boards are generating income streams of hundreds of millions of dollars, the people for whom the sport exists for – fans and players (past and prsesent) – should expect a level of visibility and transparency (and possibly even influence) into how that money is spent.

The UEFA president, Aleksander Čeferin, recently raised an important issue while posting record $15bn revenue results. When asked what he felt about the organisation's commercial success, he said, "It all depends on what we do with that success. Our primary objective is to protect, promote and develop football across Europe. Our power is worthless unless it incorporates the notion of purpose over profit."

Private money

Private ownership is an increasing feature of major sports. There must be strict rules governing their activities and interests. Should there be a suitability rating for prospective owners? Can they own more than one team? How do you assess and measure any conflicts of interest?

It is too easy to abuse your power for personal (or family) benefit. This undermines the integrity of a sport. Its reputation is diminished. It is no surprise that the image of the IPL was seriously tarnished by the scandals of 2010, 2013 and 2015. Everyone suffered. Owners, players, administrators, supporters. Cricket itself was in the doghouse. In a hugely competitive sports and leisure market, the advent of T20 had galvanised worldwide interest in cricket. The scandals within the IPL were jeopardising it again.

Back in 2011, there were strong feelings (especially from the ruling Indian National Congress government of the time) that the IPL had got 'too big for its boots' and was now careering around in a wanton, unregulated fashion. Reflecting the fragility of India's expanding bubble – a number of financial scandals had been uncovered in the industrial, technology and property sectors – the IPL was suddenly looking in a rickety state. One new franchise

– Kochi – was cancelled due to an internal shareholding dispute between the co-owners (Kochi won the arbitration but still await their bank guarantee). Another – Hyderabad – was terminated after its holding company went bankrupt. (NB: ICICI who mortgaged the franchise, is currently in arbitration with BCCI over claims that the holding company could not be terminated as the franchise belonged to them). Sahara went almost as quickly as it came, with the promoter Subrata Roy, ending up in a civil jail for a while – however they are also in arbitration with BCCI. There were rumours of others in financial trouble, and corruption stories were rife. This was a critical moment in the IPL's evolution.

Manoj: This was also a critical moment in the IPL's evolution, but also in India's evolution. The IPL was fast becoming a microcosm of the challenges of doing business in India. For years, foreign direct investment into India had been slow. Historic concerns had included political stability, concerns about corruption and the risk of retrospective legislation.

The IPL was ground-breaking – one of India's most significant domestically created 'products' that had attracted foreign investment and international renown. It was globally visible. As the factions within the governing councils battled, the future of the tournament looked fragile, which was impacting India's global reputation. The IPL was fast becoming a bellwether for the investment environment in India.

The intervention of the Supreme Court and the Lodha reforms were important to restore confidence. It provided a new framework for future governance. A new constitution established. The Interim Committee of Administrators (CoA) would oversee the introduction of two governing councils (elected by the 36 Indian state associations) with limited terms of office and greater transparency. There would also be a number of professional appointments – including an ombudsman and an ethics officer – to resolve internal disputes and conflicts and ensure fair elections. This interim model had strengths and weaknesses and has recently faced many challenges. This chapter is far from complete.

Manoj: The Lodha reforms were painful – especially for our franchise. I was unsure if we would recover from a suspension, and whether the new franchises were really temporary. Only the intervention of the Supreme Court would abate the media – who were demanding change at the BCCI. Ultimately, you cannot have a sport (or indeed any business) run by the courts, but it does highlight the importance of strong balanced regulation when the financial stakes are so high.

Problems arise when the role of regulators becomes confused. Cricket boards should focus on scheduling, growing participation, protecting the fan, driving a social agenda and setting the rules (and determining the punishments when those rules are broken). When regulators start to do things that private operators can do more efficiently, or indeed raise investment for, then outcomes will be less optimal.

Private ownership is essential to drive investment and innovation. However, there needs to be a broader debate about what type of private ownership – and with what checks and balances. Ownership that is simply based on ability to pay, will have challenges. And too many sports league owner groups, especially in the US, simply look like 'Billionaire Clubs'. There is a much broader debate to have around the optimum private ownership structure – and in particular, fan representation and protection. Community investment in the ownership structure is important, and lessons from the original structure of many soccer clubs in the UK, and more recently, lessons from the Bundesliga, could perhaps be applied.

Sports leagues need independent regulators, and to avoid conflicts of interest – an initial problem in the IPL. It is not a problem exclusive to cricket. Sport needs to create a much clearer framework for the accountability and responsibility of the various participants. Governments have to have a stronger role to ensure ultimate accountability, with legislative consequences for issues such as spot or match-fixing. The governing bodies need to be free of commercial conflicts. Franchises need to have representation with the regulators, but they should not be the regulators. Importantly, regulators need high quality and diverse leadership teams and boards.

A framework for future governance

There are many theories about what makes an effective sport's governing body. There are five essential ingredients – transparency, accountability, impartiality, cooperation and proactivity. To those ends a variety of specialist committees would ideally be appointed below the executive board covering a variety of areas from commercial and financial, to media, legal, marketing, scheduling, participation, technology, sustainability and expansion. There is an increasing drive towards diversity in the make up of these committees. As Nick Bitel, chair of Sport England points out, "Organisations with diverse boards have diversity of thought. That means they make better decisions, are more successful, and crucially are better able to understand and reach the audiences we want to engage in sport and physical activity." No one should be allowed to serve on any committee for long periods.

Avoiding conflicts of interest is critical. Such conflicts have caused a major controversy in football's Champions League, where Manchester City have been penalised by UEFA for breaching Financial Fair Play rules, as detailed earlier, but Paris Saint-Germain (PSG) haven't despite miraculously forking out £335m in one year for two top players (Mbappé and Neymar). They escaped on a technicality and the case was abruptly terminated. But questions were immediately raised about the fact that PSG's Qatari chairman, Nasser al-Khelaifi, is on UEFA's executive board and is also chairman of beIN Media, one of UEFA's key media partners (which is now under investigation).

Manoj: There are also often interdependencies within a sport. CVC, a UK based private equity firm, is building a dominant position within rugby. CVC first acquired an ownership stake within the domestic Premier League, and then won an auction for a stake in the international Six Nations tournament – not that surprising when you consider that the Premier League teams essentially lease or rent their players to the international boards to play in tournaments like the Six Nations. So in effect the Premier League teams have important control of star player appearances in international tournaments – an interdependency that few saw when the initial investment was made. They are now in a dominant position to control much of the sport.

While I am a strong supporter of private investment in sports, the second order and third order potential for conflicts of interest, or control, need careful reflection. Leagues must have some form of accountability to the fans and participants. If a league's motives are purely profit driven (especially if the investors have a target time period for their returns), then short-term decisions e.g. paywall television, might impact the long term accessibility of the game, and ultimately participation. Cricket in the UK, post 2005, is a case study on the effect on the games participation numbers of taking major sport off terrestrial television. Rugby in the UK could soon be the next. And sports like golf are becoming ever more susceptible to private takeover, having failed to attract the next generation of players and fans.

Another mistake sometimes made is the presence of media owners in a league. This can help launch a property, but you automatically limit the likely income from the broadcast rights (as there is only one winner), and this in turn limits your potential to attract private capital to invest in the franchises (assuming a share of media rights is part of the investment opportunity). This will be a challenge for both the kabaddi and soccer leagues within India.

Governance post Covid

Manoj: The actions and performance of governments have perhaps never been under as much public scrutiny as during this pandemic. Every action is scrutinised, every action justified, and yet no one actually acknowledges that everything is really a series of experiments, as it is impossible to have a plan, with so many unknowns. The public perhaps now realise that systematic under investment in our political structures has cost us dearly during the pandemic. The lack of long-term thinking has cost us dearly. The world will have a major reset in governance, and sport is no exception.

Sports administrators have been presented with an unprecedented range of challenges, in an impossibly short time in which to make decisions. Some have simply stuck to the 'follow government advice' mantra (almost as nauseating as the 'follow the science' mantra), some have shown themselves to have no real decision-making power, and some have simply stayed silent.

Cricket has seen the full spectrum of responses. The IPL was postponed, and the World T20 is in serious doubt (at the time of writing). The English season has been devastated, although the management, communication and proactivity by the ECB throughout Covid has been impressive. But Covid will force much introspection, and none is more important than how we govern the game, and how we develop the role of the governors. It is akin to the debate that has raged for decades, about public versus private ownership.

We need a fresh look at the annual cricket schedule, too much of which has no purpose; we need a global collaboration to deal with the gambling threat and opportunity; greater coordination of the response to Covid (which will impact us for many years); and we need a major discussion on growing grassroots participation. Boards should not limit the growth potential of teams, grounds or franchises through their own availability of capital. Cricket has an opportunity to set new standards, and create new models, as it evolves towards greater private involvement and investment in the game.

Chapter 8
Ownership Models

Balancing profit and the fan

Living the dream

Professional sport is super-expensive to stage – with the acquisition, maintenance and salaries of top players and support staff, and often large stadia to run. In the NFL, the most profitable league in the world, only one of the 32 teams is not privately owned. No UK professional football club would survive without major private investment. All but four of the 90 teams in the main English leagues are bankrolled by wealthy individuals or consortiums, and those four are funded by supporters' trusts. The genius of the IPL was auctioning ownership of the eight franchises. It raised additional investment funds to launch the league and tapped into each of those eight owners' promotional budgets and spheres of influence.

At the latest count, 62 of the world's billionaires own a sports team. Some own several. Do they do it for fun? Perhaps initially, and many have been known to leave their business brains behind at first, as passion and competitiveness take over. But possessing a sports team isn't like owning a yacht. Most of them are in it for the money. A sports team is there to produce results, and that means income as well as individual and collective satisfaction. It is a status symbol, but it is an asset to generate income too. Eventually they become as hard-nosed with their teams as they are with their businesses.

The basic criteria on which very rich people base their decision to own a major sports team is largely financial, although there is undeniable 'passion and ego' value. Increasingly, the data suggests that sports franchises in the most attractive leagues are very robust investments – the real estate of the 21st

century. Top sports franchises make money. Not necessarily immediately. But generally, after three to four years, and the return is pretty consistent and usually recession-proof. If you look at the ten-year history of ownership of American sports teams, MLB teams' value appreciated by an average of 11.3% per year, NFL teams by 12.7% and it was 17.7% in the NBA. Manchester United's share price in August 2012 was £12.20. In August 2018 it was £26.20. That's an annual increase of 13.6%. You are not going to get consistent returns like that in many markets. They hadn't even been playing well.

Manoj: Blenheim Chalcot have started 40 businesses, but there is no question that the business that attracts the most conversation and interest is the involvement in the Rajasthan Royals. In the early days, it was written off by most as a 'toy', owned because of my passion for the game. Naturally, the investment was influenced by that passion, but ultimately it was an investment decision based on economics. Since day one, we have tried to apply the same principles that we have tried to apply to all of our businesses at Blenheim Chalcot.

There is no question that sports ownership benefits your other businesses. It changes the way people see you. It is a great ice-breaker for conversation. It creates entertainment options that other forms of hospitality cannot match. And it leads to new contacts, and new opportunities. However, fundamentally, our investment had to work on a standalone basis. Every time emotion has governed a decision, which it inevitably does sometimes, it has tended to be a bad decision.

Historically, people used to describe the value within a sports franchise as 'trophy value'. That is to say, that the value was derived from the fact that it was a scarce asset, and there was always someone willing to pay more than the last buyer to have that 'trophy value'. The return on investment came from someone being willing to pay more for the 'ego value'. This was largely the case with football clubs, which pre-2000 made very little commercial sense. However, with the value of rising media rights, and the explosion in demand for content, investors are beginning to understand the real inherent value of sports franchises. The scarcity value is now derived from the fact that the only programmes people watch live (as opposed to on demand) are sports and the Game of Thrones! (NFL fans will point out that 70 of last season's games drew

audiences bigger than the Game of Thrones season finale!) Sports franchises
are now valued more like movie studios, and in the world of entertainment
where the value of content is king, you can see why their value has appreciated.

Creating an ethos

Private ownership is now everywhere in elite sport. We are not talking just
of the 70-odd teams owned by those 62 sports-mad billionaires. The list of
families, consortiums, companies and shareholder groups who own – or have
recently owned – a professional sports organisation runs into the thousands.
All are attracted by a global sports market estimated to be worth over $600bn
by 2021. The oldest owner is Virginia Halas McCaskey (96) of the Chicago
Bears NFL team whose father, the legendary George Halas, first owned the
franchise in the 1920s. The richest is Mukesh Ambani, of the IPL's Mumbai
Indians, whose net worth is somewhere north of $50bn. The most diverse is
Stanley Kroenke who owns five sports franchises – Los Angeles Rams (NFL),
Colorado Avalanche (NHL), Denver Nuggets (NBA), Colorado Rapids
(MLS) and Arsenal (EFL). He must have an amazing collection of replica
shirts. The most successful, in sporting terms, is probably John Henry with
four MLB world series titles with Boston Red Sox since 2004, a Champions
League triumph with Liverpool and, following the resumption of sport after
lockdown, sealing Liverpool's first-ever Premier League title in June 2020.

What do these owners actually do – apart from pump in vast amounts of
cash and (ideally) extract some? And, as both the risks and rewards escalate,
and the digital expansion reaches new previously inaccessible markets, what
are the best ownership models? And how will they evolve as the potential
profits from sports rise exponentially?

The style of sport's team owners is undergoing a transformation. Initially –
principally in the US – they were men of great passion and expertise (like
the aforementioned George Halas who was a fine player and coach before
he took control of the Chicago Bears). Later these types were superseded by
tycoon tradesmen who invested some of their fortunes in sports teams partly
to further their products' reputations. After that they were wealthy oppor-
tunists seeking publicity and tax benefits (football ownership in the UK used

to be rumoured to be a great mechanism for individuals that needed to 'clean' money). Now, the majority are business people attracted by the growing profile and reach of sports and the considerable potential rewards.

There are still a few individuals for whom owning a sports team is mainly an ego trip. They are in it to win it, but with little interest in the long-term health of the club, the players or the league. Many thought that Roman Abramovich, who saved Chelsea from virtual bankruptcy in 2003, was in this category. "I don't want to throw my money away, but it's really about having fun and that means success and trophies," he said when he first took over. He has now ploughed over £1bn into the club coinciding with the most successful period in Chelsea's 113-year history (11 major trophies won). This success was attributed initially to the purchases of foreign stars. Hiring and firing 16 managers didn't seem to be a strategy promoting stability. That said, in parallel, major investments were made in the academy, and the infrastructure of the club. He seems to have grown into the role. The club now seem to be yielding the benefits of that longer-term investment.

The best private investors act like growth hormones on sports teams. You can think of it in terms of a tree. The owners feed the roots, the trunk grows taller and stronger; they shape the direction and strength of the branches, and the canopy of influence is gradually established. It eventually supports a number of smaller ecosystems each of which further nourishes the main structure. By now the roots have penetrated far and wide.

With the IPL starting from scratch, the original owners had a unique opportunity to create individual cultures at their franchises – a distinctive tree, in other words. The Mumbai Indians bought many of the most glamorous players and had a star studded 'ambassador' line up. The recent Netflix documentary *Cricket Fever* provides an interesting insight into the franchise. The Royals' Jos Buttler, originally with MI, comments: "Mumbai Indians felt like the Manchester City of the IPL," Buttler says. "A massive franchise in a huge city. A big operation. There's a lot of expectation and pressure."

Ben Stokes, who played for the Pune Supergiants before the Royals, adds: "At other franchises it will only be about winning. At the Royals, the atmosphere is as much about winning, but also enjoying it, learning and having fun." The precociously talented Sanju Samson, still only 24 and a Royal since the age of 17 (he played for the Delhi Daredevils during the Royal's two-year suspension) puts it beautifully when he says "The Royals is like a university of sport, and sometimes life. We are encouraged to express ourselves. Not only do you learn to be a better cricketer, but you learn to be a better individual."

The Chennai Super Kings have been more clinical and super-consistent. Concealed behind his benign expression, the captain MS Dhoni is fiercely competitive, and the coach, Stephen Fleming, is hugely respected. They ooze power. Historically, they spent big on Indian superstars – Suresh Raina, Ravi Jadeja and Ravi Ashwin. Under the leadership of Dhoni they are fearless and competitive – they expect to win. Dhoni even strode onto the field during the climax of a match against the Royals in 2019 to challenge an umpiring decision. (The power of the Indian cricket superstar is that they can do things in the IPL for which other players would receive bans.) They are highly successful. They have won the IPL three times and featured in eight finals.

Meanwhile there is more of a free-spirited nature within the Kolkata Knight Riders, a reflection of their long-time owner, the exuberant Bollywood icon Shah Rukh Khan. His profile has helped the franchise garner massive profile, expand fan bases, and drive up their sponsorship revenues. Their revenue is estimated at $50m – not bad for a team that only plays together for two months. They are probably, along with Mumbai Indians, one of the IPL's most profitable teams.

Overall, the owners of the eight teams have invested and reinvested over $1bn into the IPL enterprise, as well as providing a huge amount of expertise, influence and publicity. There have been many benefits to the investors themselves of course, but, while there has been much trial and error, the contributions of the owners in making the IPL a success cannot be understated. However, there is an important and interesting question about what form and structure of private ownership is ultimately most beneficial for a sports franchise.

Manoj: The ownership of IPL teams has attracted almost as much attention as the cricket. Owners have been terminated, suspended and pilloried. Some have gone bankrupt, and others have been forced to flee the country. The Rajasthan Royals have had more than their fair share of controversy.

After Season 1, we were perhaps insecure about our ownership's lack of profile. We experimented with the addition of celebrity to the ownership group – experiencing both the positive and negative impacts. Celebrity is important to promote visibility. However, combining celebrity and ownership can have its challenges.

The franchise owners were all experiencing sports ownership for the first time and there are no books on how to be an owner. The IPL has numerous owner behaviour stories: from bizarre dressing room team talks; to strange additions to the support staff; to owners complaining about their lack of TV airtime during a game relative to other owners. When, after Season 1, there was a suggestion for owners to have a dugout alongside the team's, it was clear that the tournament's priorities were wrong.

The Royals have tried to keep it simple, keeping a clear line between the dressing room and the boardroom. We have not always got it right. We learnt a lot about celebrity management with the addition of Shilpa Shetty to the owners' group. When we went to South Africa, as champions, we travelled as one big extended group, and that led to more of a holiday touring atmosphere – and it made important tough decisions harder to take. We also focused too much on media management rather than on-field performance.

No one teaches you what to do, and there are some important expectations – with the media, with politicians, with officials from the BCCI. Some of the best memories are from sharing victories with the team – in the bar, after games. Great friendships are formed. But fundamentally, you need to govern these franchises as you would govern other businesses. It is as, if not more, important to have impartial non-executives, with good cognitive diversity across the board of the team. Sport is a business, in which it is hard to not be emotional in your decision making. The results are highly visible, and the feedback loops are highly public (and often personal). That is not always the case in other businesses.

Ownership roles

What other influences do owners have? Their potential impact is vast (see diagram below). They are responsible initially for key leadership appointments, not just a chief executive and financial controller but the coach and captain too. In many ways the coach in T20 is of greater importance than the captain (the reverse of Test cricket). He oversees the franchise's culture, selecting the team and orchestrating the strategy and planning the game. He gets to come on to the field twice during an innings at the 'timeout' to initiate a change of approach if necessary. He is always close at hand in the dugout. He also has to deal with a tournament where there is a lot of travel and non-playing time, so maintaining a positive environment over a seven-week period with thousands of miles of travel requires innovative ideas. He is more like a football manager than a cricket coach, though a strong captain – a Dhoni or a Kohli – will still have the final say.

Appointing the manager/coach in any sport is increasingly vital. The influence Jurgen Klopp has had on Liverpool supporters is instructive. He offers hope, charm, intelligence, passion and wit. He oozes charisma. As one Liverpool fan-site puts it: "He's the lovable uncle that slaps your butt, offers you a beer and tells you to man-up when you've fallen out of love with football." The Liverpool fans adore him. Undoubtedly that feeling is conveyed to the players. There's a good vibe around the team.

It helps if the players are approachable too. Again, that ethos is driven by the owner. If he/she is engaging and open, the players are more inclined to be. Access to players – their willingness to interact with fans and participate in events and display some humility – drives a feeling of belonging amongst the supporters. A kid's autograph book or selfie request shunned is a family alienated. Fans react best if they feel valued and respected and their views are listened to. Promises must be kept.

7 Roles of an Owner

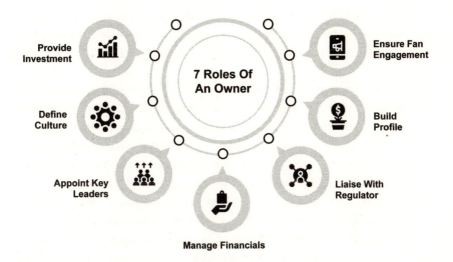

Fig. 16

Manoj: As with any business, the owners and the shareholders appoint the key leaders, who in turn set the culture for the franchise. We benefitted from the experience and complete focus and commitment of Warne, and then Dravid, in the early years. As with any business, you have to appoint the best leaders off the field, which is not straightforward. The talent pool for professional leaders of sports franchises is small, albeit growing. Too many of the candidates are simply cricket obsessed and attracted by the glamour. Or, they are senior managers looking for a 'glide path' into retirement. Or, they have simply not had the hard professional training that established industries provide. There are great examples out there but finding them is hard.

There are a growing number of institutions offering sports management qualifications (which are more than just hospitality or event management). The Royals are partnering with the Australian sports education leaders, Deakin University, to offer a sports-marketing course within India. The six month largely online foundation course is aimed at both upskilling within, and equipping those entering, the industry. It is not a total solution but an attempt at increasing the talent pool.

We now have seriously trained professionals choosing sport as a career over main-stream industry, banking, or consulting, but this is a recent phenomenon (especially in India). The salaries paid to these professionals are also catching up with other careers – although there is still some way to go to match the $34m apparently paid to the NFL commissioner, and the $20m paid to the NBA commissioner.

The same is true of coaches. The coaching talent pool in cricket is a bit one-dimensional. Most are former players with relatively conventional theories of the game. There are few innovators, or practitioners who look outside of cricket. The responses from our most recent coach selection process in 2019 were surprisingly similar – nuggets like: "I think the less you say the better"; "It's all about creating the right environment"; "Cricket is a simple game"; and "Cricketers respect coaches who have been there and done it." Part of the issue for cricket coaches is that they are extensions of the team, not managers, often spending too much time in dressing rooms with the team. In contrast soccer is starting to see the emergence of professional coaches who didn't necessarily play at the very highest level. We will see this in cricket over time, as the skills to succeed as a top player in the modern era are quite different to those required to coach. The modern coach has top class general management, commuication and teaching experience, with clear views on the 'specialist support' required.

Ensuring influence

Sport is still managed by governing bodies, and decisions made at the governing body level are still the most important determinant of success or failure. The decisions affect the welfare of players; the outcomes for fans; the investment returns for the owners. They also ensure (or not) a level playing field – especially in a tournament like the IPL, where fixture lists, stadium allocation, umpire allocation, pitch preparation, replacement player rules, auction position allocations – can all give a team a small edge.

Manoj: Communicating with the regulator – in this case the BCCI – is a crucial role for both the owner and the leaders within a franchise. We completely underestimated this when we acquired the franchise. In the early years, the IPL was a one man show. Now there is important stakeholder management across the spectrum – the BCCI, the state associations, the state governments and the central government.

The Royals have benefited from having Ranjit Barthakur as executive chairman of our Indian operating entity. We met 30 years ago, when he was a pioneer in the emerging mobile sector. He has been our leader off the field, managing our multiple challenges – and building relationships with our key stakeholders.

Balancing profit with purpose

Manoj: There is the financial responsibility to provide the right level of investment for a franchise. This is not just about profit and loss. It also means having the right balance sheet structure (the mix between debt and equity). Some sports franchises have got themselves into problems by taking on too much debt. With very predictable revenue streams, sports franchises are very attractive to corporate lenders. They also have very 'testable' market valuations. They are therefore easy to lend to, and a sensible level of debt makes sense for such businesses. But too much debt, and there is a danger. Getting that balance right is very important. The financial focus allows the teams to invest in the best players and have the best chance of winning – something every fan wants. However, a financial objective alone is not enough.

The financial objectives are important within a sport to drive clear decisions and maximise investment. However, sport has such a potential to change society, and indeed the origins of so many sporting clubs are grounded in community and charitable activity. That social purpose, as we see when the world gets hit with something as dramatic as Covid has the potential to change, improve and even save lives.

Enlightened owners can make a real difference. Influenced by the IPL, the Pakistan Super League launched in 2015. Ali Khan Tareen, the son of a self-made multimillionaire, acquired the Multan franchise in January 2018 after the previous owners defaulted. He could have treated his newly bought side as a rich man's plaything, a unique status symbol. But no. He saw it as the catalyst to regenerate a neglected, largely agricultural area. He is striving to maximise advantages for young people in the 50 million strong South Punjab, promote gender equality and improve education levels in schools. "The whole idea of this project is to bring cricket back to the region," he says. "This is where the likes of Waqar Younis, Inzamam-ul-Haq, Mushtaq

Ahmed came from but since the late 1990s there has been no young South Punjab-born player who has made it to international level. The main problem was that there was nowhere for people to play."

A fully structured local league has been created. "There was some initial resistance to league cricket but once we got one up and running it spread like wildfire," he said. "People were getting my number through friends and family and saying 'Please start a league in this town or that town, we'll give you the ground' and so on and so on." Tareen has built an academy in the Lodhran countryside too and imported a number of overseas coaches. He often returns from his business travels with new cricket equipment for the academy's young players. He has given local youth hope and aspiration in an undernourished area of Pakistan.

Although the PSL has been played outside Pakistan (in the UAE) the effects of this sort of investment are already being felt locally. The tournament is improving and Pakistan cricket has been reinvigorated. Pakistan were until recently currently the world's top ranked T20 international team and the competition has returned to the country. It is not so farfetched to suggest that the PSL might ultimately have an influence on stabilising a politically volatile region. It could have global significance. Having a really clear social purpose should be a requirement for every sports franchise. Indeed, it is exactly how many of the great soccer clubs began their existence. (Glasgow Celtic started as a church group raising money for the poor, and many other famous football clubs evolved out of church teams.)

Manoj: Now that the franchises are profitable, it is very important that the franchise owners recognise their social responsibility. In India, all companies are required to give 2% of their profits to charitable causes, but this is easily avoided or fudged. The value that resides in a sports franchise is derived from the fans, and the owners that forget that do so at their peril. We also operate in a country where 500 million people live on less than a dollar a day, so spending millions on cricketers needs to be set against that context.

Several teams have started to recognise that. RCB and MI have both dedicated one of their home matches to conservation and education. We, at RR, have focused on girls' education, child protection (from trafficking) and female empowerment. Our switch to a pink team strip was driven by first playing in pink to highlight the plight of girls and women in Rajasthan. It now seems appropriate that we have fully adopted that colour. The IPL has a unique opportunity to highlight the plight of those less fortunate. It is a huge media platform that can change awareness and change behaviours. We have a responsibility, as the IPL, to shine a spotlight on unmet needs within the region.

As we evolve the Rajasthan Royals structure, and as the IPL matures, teams should consider taking a portion of their value and giving that to the local communities. It strengthens the fan–franchise connection, but more importantly, drives a purpose (beyond profit) that can underpin the future values of an organisation. We have started with the creation of the RR Foundation, but there is still much to do.

Embracing risk

For many years the Royals continued to trade on their underdog status and use of young unknown players on the field. They failed to make the playoffs for several years. They were stuck in a rut. They were caught in that classic sporting dilemma of not knowing when to change. Should you stick with the formula that worked before, or twist, and try something new, speculate a little? Sportsmen are creatures of habit. It is never easy to shift them out of their daily methodology, to re-programme their default button. At certain times the owner – or manager – has to take the initiative. A recalibration is sometimes required. The owners (like a chairman in business) need to be close enough to the facts but distant enough to evaluate when change is needed.

Manoj: In some ways, we had an opportunity for a recalibration in 2016, when we were suspended for two years. At the time of the suspension, many of us had had enough, and we thought seriously about selling. But that would have given substance to many assumptions about our franchise. Instead, we made a series of important strategic choices. A choice to double-down on our investment and bring more of the Blenheim Chalcot resource and approach to the franchise. A choice to invest more in the brand. A choice to evolve the ownership group. And a choice to start institutionalising both the governance and the ownership structure. On the field, we have evolved our auction strategy, now fully investing our available auction purse. We are also trying to innovate our leadership structures. We will continue to invest in differentiating the Royals as an environment for young players, demonstrated by the investment in our own private ground and academy in Nagpur (in central India).

Most of the greatest success stories in sport come about because someone made clear choices and took a risk. One of the subscribers to this idea is Boston Red Sox and Liverpool FC owner John Henry. Having bought the Red Sox for $380m in 2002, he invested smartly in a team that had not won the World Series for 86 years. Two years later they were champions.

Their arch-rivals the New York Yankees greeted the Red Sox with snide banners proclaiming 'Congratulations Boston, World Series Champions 1918, 2004, 2090'. It was a little premature. Henry, a former commodities trader and hedge fund billionaire, supervised his team to another Major League title in 2007, and then another in 2013. His secret? To invest lots of money and keep reinventing the philosophy. In the years since Henry took over, the Red Sox have consistently had one of the league's largest payrolls.

Henry likes to gamble. He's committed to winning quite literally at all costs. His willingness to raze his teams to the ground and start again also contributes to extreme volatility —for instance a late-season collapse in 2011 and a last-place division finish in 2012. From the ashes of those two years, only fools would have bet on Boston to win it all in 2013. But then they proceeded to do exactly that. When they won the World Series again in 2018, they became the most successful baseball team of the century.

Henry has applied the same rationale to Liverpool. He bought the club for £300m in 2010. It took a while for his business acumen to produce results, but in 2018 he outspent even Manchester City's Emirates owners, pouring in £170m on new players despite having just reached the UEFA Champions League final. The outcome has been to win the Champions League in 2019 having invested a record £223m on player acquisitions, and now blowing every other Premier League side out of the water in 2019–20. Liverpool recently announced record profits of £42m. From a valuation of £532m in 2010, the club is now worth £2.1bn. Henry has made 61 other billionaire sports franchise owners very jealous.

Manoj: As a Liverpool fan, I've found watching the progression of the club under the Fenway Group both fun and educational. It is clear that they have a distinctive 'playbook' – control was Henry's first requirement, then clarity on recruiting the very best leadership (on and off the field), engaging with the local community and history of the club, and above all focusing on building a structure that can win, not just once but over a sustained period. It is also clear that they invest for the long term, not expecting immediate results with every decision. (As recently as two years ago, there were Liverpool fans calling for Klopp to be dismissed, pointing out that this initial three-year record was no different to that of his predecessor.) They are investing in the infrastructure – not just the stadium, but also the training facilities. And most importantly, they are developing a long-term player development and player acquisition strategy. We still have so much to learn, and as we evolve the ownership group, we must tap into the very best expertise from around the world.

The owner's dilemma

Manoj: There is a productive tension between the objectives of fans and owners, but fundamentally they are mutually dependent. Without decent owners, fans don't get match-winning teams, and they gradually lose affiliation and engagement. Without engaged fans, the franchises don't build the financial strength to compete at the highest levels. When that happens the owner gradually loses the value that they have invested. Fundamentally, their central objective is the same – to win, and that's what preserves the balance of power.

Balancing Profit and the Fan

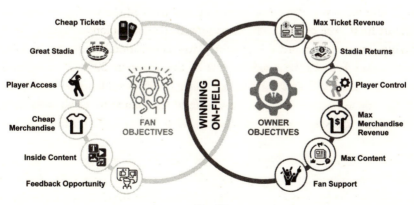

Fig. 17

There are various ways of winning over the fans exemplified by the alternative approaches employed by American owners of sports franchises. Dallas Cowboys' Jerry Jones wants to put on a great show and wow everyone with the sensational hospitality at the AT&T stadium he built. Winning is not the *only* thing. The late Phil Wrigley, of chewing gum fame, showed a more caring side of ownership by refusing to schedule evening matches for the Chicago Cubs because of the disruption to the local community they would cause. This level of altruism among proprietors is rare, however.

Some utilise their high-profile sports' purchases to enhance other divisions of their business empire. Their sports franchise is a sort of loss leader. George Steinbrenner used his ownership of the New York Yankees to create the Yankees Entertainment and Sports (YES) TV network in New York, America's most lucrative media market. Rupert Murdoch bought the LA Dodgers to prevent Disney establishing a regional sports network in California. This is all fine. But Mike Ashley, founder of the Sports Direct retail chain and owner of Newcastle United, went too far. Initially he was the shining knight who saved the club from financial ruin and endeared himself to the fans by watching the match among them dressed in a replica shirt (sold by his company Sports Direct) and drinking beer. But he was highly impatient of the team's performances, and hired and fired 12 managers during his first decade at the helm. It didn't enhance their performances. The nadir was when he attempted to rename St James' Park, the club's ancestral home, as Sports Direct.com stadium. The howls of protests from the Toon Army (the Newcastle fan club) and the media ridicule ensured the idea didn't last long, but it does illustrate the need for supporters' groups to remain vigilant and perhaps have some form of representation, or at least protection.

Manoj: Whether it's through ownership, board representation or simply supporters' clubs, it is vital that fans have some form of representation within the club. In Germany, businesses have evolved with powerful workers' councils – sports clubs must engage with such entities. The challenge is how to do this effectively.

Diversifying ownership

Sports teams cannot afford whimsical interventions from owners any more. There is too much at stake and too many involved factions. As big corporations and private equity firms hover around sports franchises, other more structured ownership models are evolving. The German Bundesliga has one of the most flexible concepts with its '50+1' rule that facilitates a spread of investment, but no more than 49% of each club can be owned by private individuals or companies. Majority voting rights (i.e. 51%) must be held by the club's members' association. This has resulted in a club like Bayern Munich being 75% owned by the fans. Just under 300,000 supporters now have a share in the club. It costs just €60 a year to be a member. So that's €18m in cashflow before anyone's bought a ticket for a game. Barcelona FC have a similar model.

The Green Bay Packers are wholly community owned by 360,584 stockholders. Despite being the smallest market in all of North American professional sports, with a population of just 104,000, Green Bay has remained solvent – and competitive – with this arrangement for almost a century. (This ownership structure has a 'grandfather's permission' and is not otherwise allowed in the NFL. All the other 31 teams comply with the NFL rules stipulating a maximum of 32 owners per team, with one holding a minimum 30% stake).

In the UK, sports governing bodies are innately suspicious of outside investment. They still try to cling on to power, but as costs spiral, their hold will be increasingly precarious. Leagues are beginning to look beyond their insular world for potential investors. Within rugby, the private equity firm CVC Capital Partners has bought a 27% stake in Premiership Rugby for £225m. It will be interesting to see how the balance between profit and the fan unfolds at the league levels. Participation within a sport is enhanced by the broadest possible broadcast of a sport – generally terrestrial television – but short-term profits are often maximised by rights sales to the paywall TV companies.

Rugby chiefs hailed their new investment as "a landmark deal" that "heralded a new era" and intimated that CVC's money would go towards improving facilities at club level and growing the league globally. As CVC look to extend their influence into the Pro14 tournament, and even the Six Nations championship, fears are growing that they will become too powerful. Will they, for instance, influence the taking of the Six Nations behind a paywall? CVC previously invested in Formula 1, buying the whole shooting match for £1.4bn in 2006. When they sold their majority share to Liberty Media 11 years later, F1 was valued at £8bn.

Meanwhile, English cricket, inherently nervous of outside investment have initially decided to keep the ownership of their new tournament, The Hundred, in house. It guarantees control but potentially stunts growth.

Manoj: There is sometimes an irrational fear of the profit motive in sports. This is not specific to cricket. The argument is normally couched in terms of protecting the good of the game, which actually means protecting the vested interests of those in positions of power within the game. All sports exist for the fans and the players. Fans want the best spectacle. Players want the best rewards for their successful exploits. That said, the profit motive alone is dangerous, and must be regulated, but it cannot be ignored.

Ensuring the best possible experience requires investment. As does attracting the best players. Investment needs a return. And without investment, competition and the profit motive, you rarely see innovation.

The people who benefit from these external investments the most are, of course, the players. There has never been a better time to be a professional sportsman. *Forbes* lists 85 sportsmen – sadly no sportswomen – who earned over $25m in 2019 alone. Cristiano Ronaldo narrowly won the bragging rights over Lionel Messi with his $105m income, $1m more than Messi. (Virat Kohli was the highest earning cricketer at number 66 in the list with $26m.) On retirement it has become almost compulsory for these athletes to declare that they 'want to give something back'. A number are now putting their money where their mouth is by becoming owners.

A host of American sports legends – the likes of Michael Jordan, Shaquille O'Neal, Magic Johnson, Wayne Gretzky and the Williams sisters have bought shares in a variety of US sports franchises. The former England footballer David Beckham, whose net worth is estimated at $400m, was part of a small consortium that purchased an expansion team for Miami in America's Major League Soccer (MLS) tournament. The franchise was recently christened Inter Miami CF, and debuted in MLS earlier this year.

"I've had a wealth of experience from playing with different clubs in different cities and cultures around the world," Beckham said at the launch of the franchise, "so that's where I can add my expertise into this ownership group. That will be my role – to bring great, talented players, but also to build this academy." He knows, fundamentally from his experience at Manchester United and 'the class of '92', that the generation of superb, homegrown talent is the best way to keep a sporting franchise solvent.

Manoj: There is no 'silver bullet' answer to the optimum ownership model, but it needs more discussion, and more evolution. At RR, we are (in close consultation with the BCCI) evolving our ownership structure. Having attempted the 'celebrity experiment', we are now embarking on a transition. We need to build for a future whereby the franchise can be owned by a broader public shareholder base. We need to bring greater diversity of thought to our ownership group. There is much we can learn from the US, and from other industries. We need to create a structure that allows for fluidity. We need to think about how we can create structures that allow people to invest, but also divest. At some point we would like to, subject to BCCI approval, create an investment structure that allows individual investors to participate.

Along with the ownership structure, we are evolving the governance structure, adding Sir Andrew Strauss to our board. Strauss brings deep expertise within the game, is universally respected, and can play a key role in coach appointment, and development of our leadership team. At some point, we need to add more Indian cricket expertise to that group. Our Indian advisory board with advisors like S. Ramadorai, who created Tata Consultancy Services, and Piyush Pandey, the creative force behind Ogilvy & Mather in India, is also a crucial part of our governance. Ravneet Pawa brings her expertise to our activity within education.

Compete, but also collaborate

There is a reason that the NFL is the most profitable sports league in the world. Although there is intense competition between the 32 teams on playing, sponsorship and marketing levels, they work harmoniously together in many areas off the field. The 31 individual owners, and representatives of the Green Bay Packers, meet regularly to discuss all aspects of the league's status and development. They are divided into various committees with diverse responsibilities and they react quickly. In early 2020 they swiftly agreed to an extra team added to the playoffs per conference and an extra percentage point of revenue to the players. There is proper collective bargaining. The league's revenue – equally shared out – is worth $255m per team. The franchises in Major League Baseball are equally collaborative and have developed a highly effective revenue-sharing model (see Chapter 9) – the source of their tremendous profit.

World's Most Lucrative Domestic Leagues

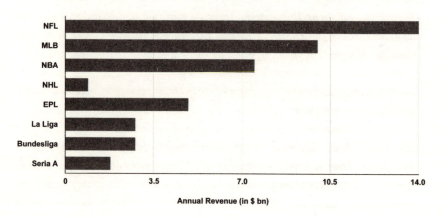

Fig. 18

While American sport boasts sums the IPL can only dream about, India's potential to affect global sport is enormous. However, until the IPL can approach the NFL's level of collaboration between teams and the governing body, it's rate of progress will be slow. There have only been a few official IPL owners' meetings in the 11 years of the competition. And, to date, they have not achieved a lot.

Manoj: Cooperation and communication between franchises is, of course, vital, and the early owners' workshops – one in Mumbai and one in Bangkok – were more like parties. Since then the collaboration amongst owners has been limited.

Tensions and competitive edges between franchises are natural, but the game could benefit from a more balanced relationship between the BCCI and the franchises, and greater cooperation between the franchises themselves. It is better to work together to have economies of scale in areas such as merchandising and sponsorship. But it hasn't really happened. Until the owners' council becomes a reality – until everyone sees the benefit of collaboration – you're going to have suboptimal development of the tournament. The Lodha reforms recommended two owner representatives on the IPL governing council, but what is most important is more dialogue.

There are multiple areas of potential collaboration. Expanding the game overseas, harnessing central licensing and merchandising solutions, developing and exploiting the digital opportunities, collaborating on technology platforms, and being an effective group to debate issues such as match footage, gaming and other innovations.

There is a fascinating opportunity emerging as the leadership of several franchises, and indeed the BCCI, passes to a younger generation. This is a microcosm of the opportunity that will present itself to India as a whole, over the next 10–15 years. The younger generation within India are often global in their perspectives and open minded to innovation and collaboration. Akash Ambani, Parth Jindal and Kaviya Maran represent an exciting new generation of IPL owners. Venky Mysore, Raghu Iyer and the Diaggeo team at RCB represent a modern generation of professional leaders.

So, the role of a sports franchise owner is complex and multifaceted. There is no manual on how to be an owner. It was part of the motivation for creating this book. But an owner's approach and strategy not only makes a huge difference to the success of a sporting franchise, it defines the brand. It is vital to get the right person or collective.

The tournament is only 12 years old – barely an adolescent – yet already it is experiencing a second phase of ownership now, with a more rigorous, focussed approach as the franchises start to turn a decent profit and attract outside investment. This is the great advantage of private ownership. Each has his, or their, own approaches and spheres of influence that help the franchises grow. The competition is almost as intense off the field as it is on. That is a healthy situation for a league, each pushing each other to higher achievement.

Manoj: Twelve years of being the Rajasthan Royals' lead owner has been a rollercoaster ride. We didn't anticipate court cases, terminations, suspensions, spot-fixing and government fines. Equally, we didn't assume that the tournament, and our brand, would become so big. And there is no better feeling for mere mortals, who are not skilled enough to play at the highest level, than to experience victory as an owner – however small your stake.

But you have to keep things in perspective. It is sport. Yes, there is money at stake, but it is not life and death, and anyone who invests in sport should do so with capital that is a part of their overall portfolio, and you need an ability to lose, or emotion overtakes rationality in the decision making. It has been an extraordinary privilege to be involved in the creation of one of the world's biggest sports tournaments. The learning has been immense, and much like any other venture in life, we have made many mistakes, and learnt a great deal.

To privatise or not, post Covid?

Manoj: One of the inevitable consequences of the Covid pandemic will be a recession. Governments around the world have responded with significant financial support but it will simply soften an inevitable hard landing.

This will reshape the world, transform the corporate landscape, and for many sports, accelerate the inevitable increased involvement of the private sector within sport. The previously undiscovered sport investment opportunity is now universally recognized. The emergence of sports focused investment funds epitomise this trend. Family offices have been investors for years. Many private equity groups have dedicated sports practice groups. More will follow. And the institutional investors will eventually arrive. All will be focused on how they can get a share of valuable media rights, in a world where live sports have never been more valuable, and where Big Tech has enormous chequebooks. Some sports bodies look challenged, some (especially in the US) are already run by private owners, and others refuse to accept the inevitable. It is not a question of either/or, but a question of how and when.

Covid is putting huge financial pressure on sports bodies, and sports teams. Advisors will follow the dollar – and there will be more transactions, divestments and recapitalisations in the next three years, than took place in the preceding thirty. In some parts of the world cricket has been hit very hard. The ECB, with its professional leadership team, will be an interesting barometer of this change. English cricket needs to embrace private investment at multiple levels – to help the debt-laden Test match grounds, to create a proper franchise T20 league, and to monetise undervalued rights. Australia is no different, and the Indian experiment, with the IPL will probably be expanded. The era of private ownership within cricket will probably be accelerated.

Chapter 9
Embracing the Digital Revolution

Digital innovation is creating a new era of commercial growth in sports

Sailing downstream

"Bam!" is the sound a cricket ball makes on West Indian Chris Gayle's bat when he sends one into orbit. There was a lot of that the day the self-styled Universe Boss blasted 175 from 66 balls for the Royal Challengers Bangalore in IPL Season 6. He bludgeoned the fastest hundred (from 30 balls) ever made in professional cricket. He stood with bat aloft, like baseball's greatest left-handed slugger Babe Ruth, and flogged the bowling literally to death. He resembled a comic book villain, swatting away intruders with his club – biff, bosh, baaaammmm!!!

The word has very different connotations in baseball, although it has made a similar impact and is gradually following suit in cricket. BAM is the name of one of New York's fastest-growing tech start-ups since the Millennium. Baseball Advanced Media specialises in providing sophisticated, segmented streaming services of matches to the fans. Not only is live coverage offered to any subscriber's device through the app, but there are split-screens enabling the viewer to watch several games at once, easily accessible highlights packages, layer upon layer of statistics, individual in-game player trackers, realistic digital recreations of match action and expert analysis. If you just want to watch all the home runs, or all the great defensive plays, you can do that too. The BAM app is described as the espresso of baseball – 'pure concentrated action'. Vitally there is also a ticketing tab making it not only simple to book a seat and actively engage with the team but also for the franchises to track and interpret supporters' decisions and preferences.

The development of BAM is very relevant to sports franchise owners. After the dot-com bubble burst in 2000, the MLB franchises were worried about increasing costs of websites and streaming their many games, so they clubbed together, each investing $1 million a year for four years, to put all their operations under one roof and share profits equally. BAM was formed and all 30 baseball parks were linked by a fibre-optic network to HQ, a former biscuit factory on Manhattan's west side, opposite the New York base of Google, as it happens. By 2014 BAM employed 700 people and generated $800m annual income. A spin-off, BAMTech, majority owned by Disney and looking to expand their expertise into other markets, was recently valued at $3.76bn.

So, for an investment of a mere $125 in BAM you can get every one of your favourite MLB team's 162 matches (and 2270 played by the other teams if you so wish) streamed to your mobile device, and all you wanted to know about baseball besides. In return the franchises get to know everything about their fans individually and collectively. And that's where the real money is...

Digital is the new goldmine for sports. A report by IT giant Tata Communications Services (TCS) identified 2019 as "the tipping point for the global sports industry as digital innovation kick-starts a new era of unprecedented commercial growth for all stakeholders." Loosely translated this means achieving constant and diverse digital engagement is where the future profits lie.

The fact is the modern media consumer expects to be in control of their viewing schedule and for content to be available in multiple forms, at any time and on any device. Sports broadcasters have to segment their approaches to viewers like never before. Sports which have been used to fans tuning in to traditional forms of broadcast at pre-set times are now recalibrating the way they distribute content to increase both fan-bases and engagement. Those who don't will quickly fall behind. Marcus Parnwell, director of product at DAZN, a streaming service for live sports says, "All viewers, but especially younger viewers, expect to watch content any time, on any screen, and be able to pause, rewind or watch highlights. Our platform is popular among younger viewers who do not want to pay subscription fees or be tied to a device. They want the freedom to watch and pay as they go."

The mushrooming growth of OTT (Over-the-Top of traditional TV transmission) network platforms like Netflix, Amazon Prime, Facebook and DAZN that transmit their content over the internet rather than via traditional broadcast methods, are at the cutting edge of this development. They present both opportunities, and risks, to sports. They allow the governing body to go straight to the consumer without the middleman (the broadcaster) and potentially spread their net far and wide. The English Premier League are making no secret of their future plan to stream matches to lucrative overseas markets (Premflix?). It promises vast potential income. But it will need considerable investment and marketing and there will be no guaranteed lump sums paid in advance as they are accustomed to receiving from current broadcasters.

Cricket is slowly catching this technological wave. It is a complex game to cover, with intricate and expensive production requirements. There is streaming of domestic cricket in England, but it is mostly a rather unsatisfactory two fixed-camera job (Surrey were planning a trial of a four-camera production in 2020) and the monetisation is minimal. It will be interesting to see the impact of New Zealand cricket recently selling all their domestic rights to streaming service Spark Sports.

Smart communication

A challenge for the IPL's initial streaming ambitions was the slow take up of mobile technology in India. In the first few years of the competition less than a quarter of the population owned a mobile phone, and that was just a basic handset for texting and calling. iPhones were way too expensive, and the cheap imitators hadn't arrived.

A crucial intervention by the mobile phone operator run by Mukesh Ambani, the owner of the Mumbai Indians, effected a dramatic transformation. In 2016 Reliance Jio slashed the prices of data-roaming on a 4G network to virtually nothing (see chart). Mobile-data packages in India suddenly went from being very expensive to among the cheapest in the world. All that time-consuming 'buffering' of video is no more. This has been the catalyst for an exponential rise in smartphone ownership in India, from 30m handsets in 2012 to a projected 829m in 2022.

Crashing Data Prices and Smartphone Penetration

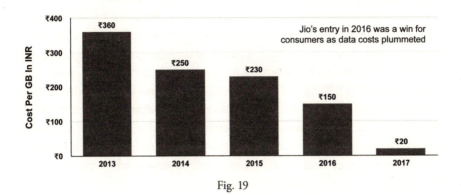

Fig. 19

Smartphone Penetration and Data Costs in India

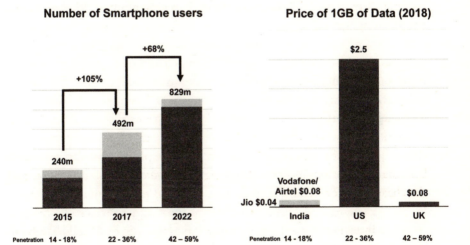

Fig. 20

This coincided with the bigwigs of the digital world trying to muscle in on the auction for the IPL digital media rights in 2017. Facebook, Amazon and Twitter were all in the mix and, yes baseball's BAMTech too (they were ultimately rendered ineligible). Star TV – now owned by Disney – stole the lot (TV and digital) with their whopping $2.5bn bid. They soon made their new acquisition count too.

"A key driver of our investment in 2017 was to use the IPL to drive the subscriber growth of our Hotstar streaming app," says Sanjog Gupta, Star TV's executive VP. "Through our Hotstar digital channel we enabled viewers to stream the match free on their smartphones with a five-minute delay. We built-up the interest with a pre-match show, with dedicated reporters at grounds and special features and packages before the match. We integrated a layer of gaming into the feed, so you could try to predict what would happen before the game began, or answer a trivia question, earn points and ultimately win a car. The engagement levels really took off. There were 35m digital viewers of the IPL in 2016. In 2018 there were 150m. You'd see rickshaw drivers stopped by the side of the road watching the match on their phones."

This symbolises the rapid transformation of India. Five years before, many rickshaw drivers probably had no telecommunications of any kind, not even a landline at home. The plummeting cost of data (and therefore of the handsets) means now they all have smartphones. It's been a fabulous advance. Not only can the drivers stream the latest IPL match and interact with their team but also they can accurately locate the route to their passengers' destination rather than having to stop every five minutes to ask someone the way as was their tendency before.

The value of these networks has most recently been illustrated by Facebook investing $5.7bn for a 9.99% stake in Reliance Jio Platforms (an investment that has been followed by a who's who of global private equity investment firms). If there had ever been any doubt of the long-term value of IPL franchises, that deal confirmed that the only way is up. The deal made Facebook the largest minority shareholder in the Indian telecoms network, and it marked the largest investment for a minority stake by a technology company in the world, and the largest foreign direct investment in the technology sector in India. With Facebook's 400 million WhatsApp users, 300 million Facebook users, and the Reliance 500m smartphones, this is some turnaround for Facebook, who had previously incurred the wrath of Indian regulators, with its failed Free Basics programme.

Content factories

So how do individual sports franchises monetise this explosion of digital demand? The key is creating interesting content that can be shared and discussed and thus increase engagement – perhaps 'attachment' would be a better word – to a player, team or brand. Video on an individual's mobile phone is, by definition, more personal, more intimate. The idea is to try to get the viewer closer to the inside of the world that fascinates them, to linger in a player's personal, semi-private space. Sponsors are keen to have access to this world – it personalises, almost humanises them. Social media has opened up a whole new sphere for them – a planet of opportunity.

Manoj: Content is of course where we started with Investors in Cricket – creating Cricket Star. Cricket Star was our entry point into Indian cricket. After our first season victory, we shot a documentary of that year – Road to Victory – and when the second year was transferred to South Africa, I had a DVD of it in my bag. We gave it away free to the TV company. They had nothing to broadcast, so it was played constantly, which was brilliant for the Royals. It helped build a profile in a country that was given five weeks to launch IPL Season 2. That said it was a cheaply produced, horrible documentary!

This was before the development of all the OTT platforms and the take-up of smartphones in India. Mobile devices have changed everything. Accessing content for mobiles opens a whole new world for sponsors and franchises. It increases the commercial value of the megastar players. If you've got charismatic superstars who captivate TV viewers, it makes a huge difference, Players who are big box office draws will command higher sums. In the same way Real Madrid announced their shirt sale income on the back of the Ronaldo signing, franchises will start to value a player's digital content value. You're buying into their brand – and there's a cross-pollination between them and the franchise that should work productively for both. Historically, building a media profile was something that players worried about later in their careers. Now they will be thinking about it from the start.

The two Spanish footballing rivals Real Madrid and Barcelona are world leaders in this area. For a start they had the two most marketable players on the planet with the largest social media interactions in sport, see below (the figures within which were undoubtedly a contributory factor in Ronaldo's transfer price of £105m to Juventus in 2018).

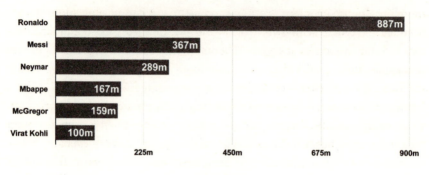

Top Sportsmen's Social Media Interactions
January – Jul 2019 (millions)

Fig. 21

Both clubs have the most social media followers of any sports organisation – each over 200m if you combine their Instagram, Twitter and Facebook accounts (almost twice as many as the next in the list, Manchester United). Exploiting this digital mass, Barcelona partnered with a creative agency – Fastory – to create a video quiz surrounding Lionel Messi's performances in El Clásico games, relay some unusual stats and encourage people to register as a Barca fan. The key is interaction. The fans don't want to be passive digital supporters. They want a feeling of belonging.

Facebook Live was utilised effectively in the build-up to the 2017 El Clásico, getting closer to the players, driving 27m views from over five hours of content broadcast by the two teams. Between Barcelona and Real Madrid, the most valuable social media post was Barca's 'Full Time Final' video on Facebook Live which was watched by over 4.3 million viewers and generated over $186,000 for sponsoring brands. There are fewer restrictions for sponsors on social media than there are on traditional TV platforms which have to follow strict guidelines. Also, a sponsor's reach is far more measurable in terms of 'hits' and 'likes'. "With social media adding over $5m in total value to Barcelona's sponsors, this shows just how critical a medium it has become," said Max Barnett, Nielsen Sports' head of digital. "The $186,000 generated by both teams in the El Clásico highlights the importance of social media for an away team. It's a tool to generate value for partners when there is no possibility for exposure through traditional in-stadium advertising."

Real Madrid used Ronaldo and his (then) 130m Instagram followers to build more personalised content. His site is populated by lots of professionally shot moments – stylised windows on his world – and short, sponsored video content behind the scenes at fashion shoots or training sessions. It is light and snackable. Individual videos get millions of views and likes. Virat Kohli, the Ronaldo of cricket – cool, driven, super talented, mega-rich, 50 million Instagram followers – has similar material. There are promos for Puma footwear, energy drinks, fragrances and fashion labels. They are quite honest and personal, almost off the cuff. They also reach millions of eyeballs. These social media heavyweights are a godsend to brands (and therefore franchises). They are a direct line to mass market. Kohli knows it. That's why he charges $700,000 a day to promote something. Ronaldo is probably double that.

At baseball's New York Yankees there's a different approach to digital engagement. It is based round the history of the franchise – dating from 1913 – with great games replayed (Yankees Classics) and great players recalled (Yankeeography). *Ultimate Road Trip* is a film following a group of Yankees fans through the entire season. The range of content emphasises the depth and integrity and longevity of the team. It relays the subliminal message that it is a life choice to be a Yankees fan, a choice that gives you a sense of pride and privilege and a deep connection to the past. Even oneupmanship. It gives you a sense of superiority being a Yankee.

It helps that they are highly successful (they have won a record 27 World Series overall though none recently) and place great emphasis on purchasing the best players. In a recent study, four factors were correlated with loyalty to a team: pure entertainment value, authenticity, fan bonding and history. The Yankees ranked highest when it came to entertainment value, and history. The combination obviously works. The franchise was valued at $4.6bn in 2019, the second-most valuable sports team in the world.

Essentially big sports franchises are becoming media operations, placing a lot of emphasis on generating video content and then distributing it on their various social channels which are built on the players' own growing followings. The reach is enormous. Not only is that growing a team's global viewership in terms of volume, making it more attractive to brand partners, but they can drive a more personal level of engagement among fans, creating a far more compelling value-proposition for sponsorship and advertising. As TCS concludes, "by harnessing the power of the latest digital technologies, all players in the global sports ecosystem are able to unleash new opportunities for growth."

Without the history or playing record or, initially, the megastar players, the Rajasthan Royals had to find other angles that would engage their potential audience. Their USP is their inclusive, family-type atmosphere and ability to uncover and develop hidden talent. There is a fund of stories to be generated from that. Tazeen Syed was their head of digital in 2017, recruited from Facebook. "From growing an audience point of view the issue all franchises face is that the IPL lasts less than three months," she says. "We wanted to go beyond that. There is so much going on pre-tournament. Our trials start in December. Some great stories come out of that. Hopes and disappointments, loads of emotion. Getting to know the families of new players. Going behind the scenes as we build up to the season at training camps and away days. The content must be authentic though."

They build awareness of and engagement with the players – creating characters – and then blend the sponsors' messages into the videos. "Mobile phone content has a more personal feel than programmes on TV," Syed adds. "As a result, traditional ads don't work on mobiles. You have to find other ways of getting the messages across." Sponsors are increasingly buying into the concept that less is more.

Red Bull, for instance, made a three-part documentary with the Royals' Ben Stokes, following his progress around India during the 2019 IPL. They are not over-indulging the product message. There are just occasional glimpses of the logo or Stokes taking a swig from a can. He's also filmed on his visit to the relief centre for the Rajasthan victims of child trafficking. This is a much more effective approach.

Behind the scenes documentaries are something the American sponsors and networks do very well. Journalists and broadcasters have been allowed into the US sports teams' locker rooms since the 1980s, as the recent Netflix series *The Last Dance*, following Michael Jordan's iconic career, exploited. There is something more sacrosanct about cricket dressing rooms (at the moment). It is a sort of no-go area for outsiders. A private refuge. But barriers are gradually being broken down, as the Netflix series on the Mumbai Indians shows. Sponsors can subliminally benefit from this as the viewer enjoys the privilege of being allowed into a hidden world.

Manoj: In 2020 the Royals have shifted to a new digital brand look that plays on the heritage of Rajasthan and the Royals brand. We are combining this with an increase in innovative video content. Our new video production team will join the squad at all training camps, embedded with the team throughout the IPL. We want to tell the players' individual stories and showcase the highs, lows, elation and despair that comes from the sports field. Teams who have the strongest social teams make fans feel more intimately part of the journey. They give a peek behind the curtain. They capture candid, simple moments. We plan to be invest heavily in this area, with docuseries and 'behind the scene' stories.

Through better content and greater engagement, we can learn more about our audience and deliver the right message at the right time through entertaining content. This will enable us to leverage data in a way to monetise across ticketing, retail, academies and provide our commercial partners with the insight they require.

Fan participation

In the last decade the television coverage of sport has scaled new heights. The high definition cameras, the super slo-mo replays, the interactive graphics, the mic-ing up of players and coaches and the in-depth analysis has brought the armchair viewer closer to the action than ever before. You can almost feel the hits when two giant rugby forwards collide in the tackle, though the artful use of sound to further enhance the experience is still inferior to movies or nature films. And, increasingly, this experience is portable on phones or tablets. Viewers have reported following sporting events in places as remote as a tropical jungle, halfway up a mountain or in mid-ocean. (When an England cricket fan watching the third 2019 Ashes Test at Headingley on board the Bosporus ferry screamed euphorically at Ben Stokes' winning boundary, the ship's crew initially thought he was staging a terrorist attack.)

The downside of all this superb quality and access is it can dissuade supporters from actually attending events. Not only would that represent a major loss of revenue but also broadcasters – whether traditional or digital – would be dissatisfied. A capacity crowd gives an event status and atmosphere even on TV. A half-empty stadium is a turn-off (something the pandemic is at least temporarily reminding us of). Much emphasis must still be placed on making the spectators' visit worthwhile and memorable.

> *Manoj: We still have a long way to go in the IPL. The integration of stadia into an all-round globally competitive entertainment experience is at best patchy. When the franchises start to be more deeply integrated into the creation of the fan experience, we will see another step change. Digital is not a real threat to live sports, as there is so much that digital can transform to enhance the live experience. Ticketing, parking, getting drinks and food, finding your seat, getting information during a game, connecting with other fans and recording. Those unique moments can all be significantly enhanced by digital.*

The American sports do this highly effectively through the quality of their stadia – the giant screens, the pre-match entertainment, the hospitality suites, the food and drink brought straight to your seat, the interactive installations, the whole buzz of the event. Everyone is engaged in one way or another. Formula E, the new electric car-racing circuit is using digital technology to take fan engagement to another level through its unique, and much-debated, FanBoost feature.

Fans at the track are given the opportunity to vote for the driver they wish to receive a FanBoost before the race. The three drivers with the most votes receive a power boost of 30kw, which lasts for five seconds at a time and provides extra speed which can be used to perform a crucial overtake. It is a bit like the power-up blocks you can click-on the video-racing game Mario Kart. It is marrying Formula One live sport with gaming in a brilliantly inventive way.

Cricket can profit from this technology. Already coverage of the IPL encourages viewers to participate in votes for most valuable player or best death bowler or predicting if a certain batsman would play a match-winning innings, and there have been in-stadia opportunities to decide whether a player has been dismissed in say a tight run out. There will be increasing links with gaming and betting (circumventing the fact that gambling is illegal in India) through predictive apps. We've seen how one of the major sponsors of the IPL is now Dream11, the gaming app that encourages you to select which players from a match will perform the best with the reward of points and a 'ranking' if you predict accurately.

Virtual Reality (VR) technology is also developing fast. IBM Watson is a VR concept that allows the 'viewer' to actually be on the field with a goalkeeper or quarterback for instance and replay a real match situation wearing a headset and look at it from various different angles. VR advances will allow the casual fan to experience an over that has just been bowled in the match in full 3D glory. Via an app on a smartphone they will also be able to capture and watch the live play from any on-field location, and right up close, minimising the disadvantage of seats that are far away from the action and at an unfortunate angle. Facial recognition technology (at present mainly used for police forces) will also be increasingly available to learn more about individual players – pointing your phone at say a nearby fielder will generate a torrent of information, data and video highlights. With the boss of Microsoft Satya Nadella, a passionate cricket fan (he played for his school team in Hyderabad) all these developments will materialise sooner rather than later.

Digital platforms give sports the ability to create more emotional connections, which makes them 'stickier' from a commercial perspective – fans are more likely to buy TV and streaming subscriptions, more willing to attend events and more likely to buy merchandise. The commercial power of the human element makes the presence of and access to the sport's leading stars fundamental to its growth. The more supporters can identify with the big personalities, the more likely they are to become active fans. Lalit Modi knew this from the start. But what he didn't know was how the digital revolution could and would deliver on his vision. Digital platforms offer so much scope for direct engagement, and, even more valuably, provide a wealth of information on each consumer on their behaviour and preferences. That's one of the reasons Amazon makes $3bn a year. The digital opportunity has helped convert start-up sports franchises into potential media monoliths with the big tech companies slathering all over them. And the buying power of these is astronomical.

Market Capitalisation of Tech / Media Companies

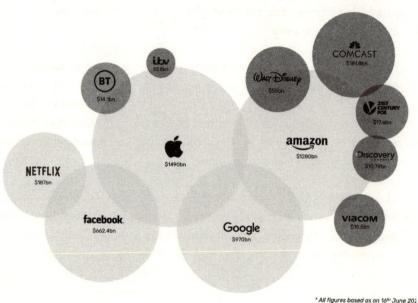

* All figures based as on 16ᵗʰ June 20¿

Fig. 22

Covid induced digital acceleration

Manoj: Whether it is the impact of grandparents using Zoom, healthworkers consulting via Skype, companies running on Microsoft Teams, the pace of digital acceleration through Covid-induced lockdown has been startling. Since 1997, we have been talking about digital transformation, but the events of the past few months, have accelerated that by years. Working from home, closing deals through video conferencing, shopping completely online and living with-out terrestrial television – these will all be commonplace by the end of 2020.

The digital acceleration will be very evident within sport. Matches behind closed doors are forcing stadium investments to be completely rethought. Stars forced to be at home during lockdown mean digital content being vir-tually delivered. Restrictions on gatherings have forced events like the NFL Draft (which took place virtually this year) to be completely renegotiated. Monetisation of multiyear, multimillion sponsorship deals are being com-pletely restructured. And the value of future rights between traditional TV and digital will be completely rethought.

Cricket lends itself to digital delivery but its exploitation of digital rights has been limited. Think back to the impact of the relatively basic Hawkeye technology. Let your mind imagine what could be possible and you will see the potential of digital. Cricket must embrace gaming. Cricket must embrace more technology within the playing of the game. Cricket must create handheld experiences for fans watching the game.

Cricket is the only game that can deliver the huge South Asian market poten-tial to the big technology giants – Facebook, Amazon, Microsoft, Apple and Google – two of which are now run by Indians!

Chapter 10

Innovate or Stagnate

New ideas and inventions will continue to make the game dynamic

Art becomes science

Cricket is the most innovative sport in the world. Think of all the developments in the game over the last 30 years: coloured clothes, white balls, floodlights, neutral umpires, third umpires, match referees, Hawkeye, the decision review system, Hotspot, stump cameras, day-night Tests, T20, pink balls, drop-in pitches, four-day Tests, flashing bails, T10 and now The Hundred. That's before we even start considering all the fancy new shots and funky deliveries. Cricket's longevity is a factor of its adaptability. Compare that with football, still debating whether 4-4-2 or 4-3-3 is the best formation and uncertain about the use of technology (Video Assisted Reviews – VAR) almost two decades after it was introduced into cricket.

Manoj: The debate about VAR in football is an example of how sport can be slow to change. The issue is not whether it should be used, or whether it is 'killing' a free-flowing game. The issue is that everyone, referees included, need to have a clear and quick method for using it. Anything that improves the accuracy of decision making in high-stakes sport, even by small margins, has to be adopted.

Innovation is both cricket's strength and its weakness. Because it is essentially a more complex game than football it has to keep reinventing to maintain public interest. If it doesn't, its popularity wanes. The intriguing aspect of its evolution is that it is the sporting metamorphosis of art becoming science. Test cricket is art – exploring character, allowing vivid individual expression.

T20 is the scientific offshoot. Everything is about angles and calculations, permutations and probabilities. It may look, superficially, as just a slogathon. Actually, as we've seen, there is a lot of careful analysis and preparation in every shot and every delivery. As the leading T20 league in the world, the IPL has driven that development.

T20 is now not a game of five days or 100 overs or four hours duration. It is a game of 240 balls. Each one of those balls is an event. Each one of those balls could be decisive, the one that could win or lose the game (bear in mind that the margin of victory in many T20 matches is less than ten runs). Whatever you achieve with that one ball – a four, a wicket, a brilliant boundary save – effectively counts double because of the shorter time frame. Dot balls are priceless for the fielding side, a dangerous extravagance for a batsman. Risk is not only important, it is compulsory.

Manoj: Even in the space of 12 years, the sophistication of the approach and the quality of the preparation has transformed. Everyone is focused on ever-smaller margins. The depth of the support staff has grown with analysts, fitness coaches, nutritionists, specialist coaches – the list goes on. It feels quite different to the captain-coach combination of Shane Warne, with 16 players – five of whom had never played first class cricket – in our first year. A nutritionist was not high on the agenda! The investment in our support staff has grown from $100,000 to $1.5m a season in a decade.

The batting orders in T20 are meticulously worked out. Some batsmen are naturally better at utilising the powerplay overs (1–6) – hitting strong, orthodox shots to the unprotected boundaries. Think Chris Gayle here, for instance, or India's Rohit Sharma – using big levers or supreme timing to get the ball through, or over, the infield. Or they batter it with uncompromising force and will, like David Warner or Jason Roy. Other, more dynamic batsmen are better suited to the middle overs where they can use their supple wrists to manipulate the ball where the fielders aren't: men like Kane Williamson and Virat Kohli. And then there are the guys with the outrageous repertoires – Glenn Maxwell, Jos Buttler, MS Dhoni of course – who, importantly, do not overtly feel pressure or fuss about playing themselves in. They can cut direct to the chase.

Failing to get these batsmen in their appropriate places can cost you 20 runs an innings, usually the difference between winning and losing. And the same applies to choosing the right bowlers for specific overs and stages of the game. Some just don't have the discipline or confidence to bowl at the beginning. Others don't have the variety or composure to bowl at the death (end of the innings).

Manoj: The value of different roles within the teams has also changed over time. Initially, there was huge prominence placed on aggressive opening batsmen, then allrounders attracted the biggest prices, then domestic talent, and now the value of high-quality 'death' bowling attracts a premium. Traditionally, India has always produced more high-quality batsmen than seriously fast bowlers but that is starting to change. The supply of Indian talent in specific roles will drive the value of the overseas star imports. A player having at least two skills is now almost a given, and in years to come there will be very few pure batsmen or bowlers. It will be a question of where you bat, and what you bowl. Players will be expected to have a new level of mental agility enabling them to bat in multiple positions.

Because of the brevity of a T20 match, the standard index of evaluating batsmen and bowlers – averages – do not work. There isn't the time to make consistently big scores or take lots of wickets. So the data boffins come up with other metrics, using special algorithms that compare performances in different phases of the game, and against different types of opponents.

Teams are increasingly seeking this kind of detailed information when planning T20 matches, especially as batsmen develop ever-greater repertoires. The amazing range of shots is matched by the specific and dedicated way they are rehearsed. After endless repetition of the various smashes, sweeps, ramps and paddles, batsmen practice each shot against a random supply of deliveries to make sure that once they have preselected their shot in a match situation, they can play it to any ball that materialises. Batting in T20 revolves around field manipulation. It emphasises the essentially premeditated nature of this form of the game. Calculations, angles, prediction are at the heart of it. The most successful teams are the ones who best combine their dexterous skills with applied mathematics.

Manoj: For over a hundred years, the names and location of fielding positions within cricket have been a given. You are taught at a young age that you must have a 'ring' of fielders, with distinctive names for each position – like 'cover', 'silly mid on', and 'long leg'. There are a number of typical field settings, and naturally some variation, for type of batsman, situation etc. Everything is assumed and preconceived. It is only recently that mapping where the ball actually goes in T20 has been undertaken. Many of these traditional field positions are redundant in the modern game, and there are new ones that have not yet been given a name. Coaching needs to keep pace with these developments. Gradually we will see more mathematically derived field settings.

So now there are an army of data boffins working on the IPL. You can see them milling around Indian hotels having meetings with small groups of players or coaches. Their interactions produce new ideas and strategies. So much more thought goes into an IPL game than in other formats. There's practically a scenario for every ball. Players can then go away and rehearse these plans. Matches don't begin until 8pm. Increasingly with wearable tech, the analysts will have even more information to indicate a player's suitability for certain tasks.

The IPL's vital ingredients are time and money. Time to explore, time to prepare, time to train and experiment and, most importantly, time to talk. And money to support the investment in the people, technologies and knowledge – that make that time useful. That has been at the heart of the IPL's rapid evolution. There is a constant exchange of ideas, both before games and afterwards when the teams and coaches mingle at the regular post-match parties. It is a global cricketing conference. The standard of play has risen exponentially.

Big Data

Much has been written about the use of data to select players and analyse performance. The ability to generate data and analyse it is affecting every part of sport, as it in every business, and indeed everyday life. Business people talk about the digital revolution, but it is really the explosion of data, combined with increases in computing power, allowing faster analysis – 'Big Data' – that has changed our world. *Moneyball* brought alive the application of data to player selection. The next generation of Billy Beanes are analysing every aspect of sports performance. Coaches are now using data to make real time decisions e.g. substitutions in rugby and soccer, much the same way Formula 1 uses real-time data across every aspect of its decision making. Data is used in preparation for cricket matches – most typically relating to the opposition or the pitch. But we are still scratching the surface on the application of data within sport. Kal Somani, a US tech entrepreneur, bemoans the lack of simulation technology. "With all of the data, AI, robotics, and VR technology now available, the missing link in sports technology is still effective simulation."

Manoj: We are using data and robotics within our net practice sessions. One of the challenges for modern bowlers is the extent to which batsmen move in the crease. We have used AI to model the movements of certain players, which we feed into a robot, that then moves across a wicket as the bowler is executing their delivery. The task of hitting the ground just before the robot (as if you were executing the 'yorker' (ball at a batsman's feet) is then simulated). Creating that real simulation in a typical net-practice session is very difficult. That said, there should be a note of caution. Plenty of players look very good in the 'nets' (practice) but then struggle in the middle of the pitch! Cricket needs strength of mind, as well as skill.

Top soccer clubs are investing in data to determine the optimum diet for athletes. *Times* journalist Matthew Syed is currently researching the area, and says "For years, the world has believed that there are such things as good diets and bad diets. However, the reality is that these 'optimum diets' are all based on statistical analysis that looks at the impact on averages. Individuals react differently to different diets, and the differences between two ends of a spectrum that yield an average can be quite stark."

Manoj: Diets and nutrition are an interesting area, as the impact on performance is significant. One of the challenges for IPL franchises is that we only have the players for eight weeks, so the ability to influence diet is limited (although better with the domestic players). Anecdotally, you see very different approaches, but there are such advances in dietary – DNA matching technologies, that this will almost certainly be an area of investment for teams.

Off the field there is data about fans, experiences at the game, on the game itself, on consumption during a game – the list goes on. One of the other aspects that makes sports franchises so valuable is their ability to generate what marketeers call 'first party data'. As concerns about data privacy grow, there is an irreversible trend towards consumers (fans) owning their data. One of the most ironic aspects of the rise of Big Tech – Google, Facebook, Amazon, etc. – has been that their value has almost entirely been created by consumers' unconscious willingness to give away their data for nothing. As this changes, brands, apps and companies that can access that data (with the consumer's permission) will grow in value.

Manoj: At Blenheim Chalcot, we are very focused on businesses that have proprietary data. Technology, and the systems that people often see, are largely replicable. Access to proprietary data is not replicable. Sports franchises can build unique 'data pictures' as fans are so emotionally connected with a brand. (Liverpool certainly know a lot about my family's buying preferences, for example!) The most valuable sports franchises will capture that data and analyse it in a way that helps fans and further engages them – what the industry calls CRM (customer relationship management).

There are also other applications of data innovation. This year, we used our machine-learning business – Fospha – to study the bidding behaviour of every franchise in the past 12 years. We processed hours of video footage and used AI to make behavioural predictions that could benefit our auction planning.

So, data really is the new steroid for sports teams. While data can never replace human knowledge or instinct, as competition gets tighter between the best teams, data is sure to become a more fundamental aspect to getting that competitive edge.

Virtually perfect

On the horizon is something that will enhance it even more. It doesn't require a pitch or a ball either. Just a headset and a bat connected wirelessly to a computer. Experimenting with it in a studio in Shoreditch, East London, was so realistic it transported me back to my old life standing at the wicket at

169

Lord's to face a tall, ferocious fast bowler. It was a reminder of why so many batsmen rely on sports psychologists.

Wearing the wraparound headset you take your stance holding a full-size bat with a sensor on the handle and a transmitter in your back pocket. Software then transports you to the middle at Lord's, Chennai or wherever you desire, for a virtual reality experience that will revolutionise batting practice, and open the way to a whole new gaming opportunity.

The 'bowler', an avatar of an unidentified West Indian, stood at the end of his run at the Nursery End. The Lord's media centre and stands loomed up beyond him. The keeper and slips were ready behind as I turned to look at the field. The scoreboard said 12 to win. I could hear the buzz of expectation in the crowd through the headset's speakers. The virtual reality bowler approached the crease. He sent down a slippery 'delivery' which later registered at 130kph on the big screen. I moved late and thrust my bat where I thought it was. It whizzed past my edge and through to the keeper. The bowler looked aggrieved and went back to his mark.

He ran in and bowled again. A slower ball which I punched into the covers. A 'fielder' converged on it, picked it up and threw it back to the keeper. The virtual reality ball smacked into his gloves. There was some muttering in the crowd. Cue the next delivery. A shorter ball. I flailed at it, feeling a sensation on the bat as it then skewed into the offside. Two fielders pursued it to the Tavern boundary, one stopping it just short, the other hurling it in. The runs required on the big screen decreased to 10. The next ball was a bouncer. I ducked so vigorously the headset nearly fell off. He followed up with a fuller, quicker one. I poked at it but heard the 'death rattle' (when the ball hits the stumps) almost before I got the bat down. The bowler clenched his fist and the mid-off fielder punched the air with delight. It reminded me why I had a batting average of 11.

It felt incredibly realistic, with the bowling in real time, a full 360-degree view of the ground as I turned around, the noise of ball on bat in my headphones when I actually managed to hit one and, best of all, avatar 'fielders' who moved and swooped on the ball as professionals would, and fizzed it back to the 'keeper'. The pace of the bowling was lively. It did feel real.

Working in TV coverage, I have tried for years to impart the drama, the speed, the apprehension of facing a really fast bowler to the viewer. This could do it.

Using CGI of the kind more familiar in animated movies, this system has been developed by Cathy Craig, a renowned professor of experimental psychology, and her programming team at Incisiv, a company specialising in next generation 'action intelligence' at Queen's University Belfast. Still in development, the potential for this technology is boundless.

In collaboration with Hawkeye data of actual deliveries bowled, this VR will enable a batsman to 'face' any international bowler and their whole spectrum of deliveries, or a real over they've bowled in a match. More than that it will also place the player under the severest pressure, exposing them to real match situations accompanied by a hyped-up crowd. Their responses and heartrate will be measured and calibrated – a true record of their ability to handle a pressurised environment. You can imagine a future where a batsman, next man in to confront the alarming speed and angle of Mitchell Starc or the deceptive spin of Rashid Khan, can actively prepare for it by 'facing' their virtual reality deliveries in the dugout.

It is a potentially transformative tool for batsmen. It will allow them to become accustomed to a bowler's visual cues, or experiment with risky or dangerous shots – the 'ramp' to a quick bowler for instance – without the risk of getting injured. An England opener could explore how well he copes with the awkward lift and trajectory of Jasprit Bumrah in the key opening overs of a Test match, and assess how he manages his heart rate and concentration. A batsman obsessed with hitting 1000 balls before the match could do so in the training room without exhausting the bowlers or the coach's throwing arm. They could even accurately replicate the experience of facing a mystery spinner with men around the bat and the wicketkeeper muttering distracting observations.

Ultimately it will also accelerate the development of the next generation of batsmen too. A 14-year-old kid could test his skill and reflexes against Bumrah in his bedroom, then click a button and watch the replay. And anyone who could afford the headset and software could experience what it was really like to face a 90mph bowler.

Manoj: There's absolutely no reason why the skills derived from practising in a simulator that is as close to reality as possible cannot be transferred into real life. Just look at pilots – they train on flight simulators and that counts towards their licence. Surgeons practise their operations in VR. Much of a Formula 1 driver's training is done in virtual reality. There's no reason, once we improve the system a bit, that you couldn't do it for cricket, or any other sport for that matter.

IBM has developed a similarly immersive experience with its Watson AI system. In the not too distant future, all cricket academies will have this technology, and maybe even school kids too. And because batsmen will be battle-hardened and bristling with intent from their VR practice in the dugout, T20 scores will climb ever higher to the ecstatic roars of the capacity crowds and the exclamations of the TV audiences who will be experiencing – perhaps even 'facing' – VR replays on their giant screens. And by then it will be the bowlers who'll be needing the sports psychologists.

Game on

But the greatest opportunity that this new tech offers for cricket is in the gaming world. Part of sport's future prosperity sits on an Xbox console in your kid's upstairs bedroom. Gaming is the fastest growing form of entertainment in the world, revenues increasing at roughly 10% per year. An estimated 2.5 billion people play video games. The FIFA eWorld Cup has been running since 2004. The finals drew a capacity crowd at Wembley and the winning team earns £250,000. Each English Premier League club has a team in the ePremier League. The final is covered live on Sky Sports. Gareth Bale recently invested in an esports team – Ellevens – to compete in tournaments including the FIFA eClub World Cup (in which they lost the final on penalties – well it couldn't be a British-based team without that happening, could it?).

The numbers are staggering. The big esports are not electronic versions of real sports (e.g. football). They are fantasy or first-person shooter games. An American teenager, Kyle Giersdorf won £2.3m after taking the top prize in a Fortnite tournament – more than the prizemoney on offer at Wimbledon or the Masters. By 2018 the various versions of the FIFA video game had sold 260 million copies. To make progress up the global ladder you have to buy points to purchase packs of players. The manufacturer of FIFA, EA Sports, has made more than $1bn from microtransactions such as these points.

If that makes the parent-in-you shudder to think how much money (and time) your teenager might waste on computer games, it might reassure you (slightly) to know there are now esports university courses with a legitimate degree on offer. The one at the University of Chichester in Sussex features everything from competitive gameplay and game analysis to sports science and psychology to the business side of the industry. The leading FIFA players also actually have coaches and mentors.

And playing a game like FIFA does have benefits. Teenagers, like our sons Billy and Ravi, say they get really excited actually controlling brilliant players they see on TV. "Being able to play at such a high standard online inspires me to go and train and try and match those standards on the pitch," says Billy. Rio Ferdinand even credits FIFA and other similar games with contributing to Manchester United's unprecedented era of success. "How people would play in a FIFA game, those traits would come through in football," he said. "It also helped with team bonding and was a big, integral part of our success."

'Esports may even be the future of all sport' explains William Collis, author of *The Book of Esports* and owner of top esports pro team OXG. 'Today there remain unsolved problems holding back the competitive gaming industry, such as incentive misalignment between publishers (who control the games themselves) and league operators (who control esports media).'

Manoj: 'One of the challenges for esports promoters is how they make the shift from a mindset focus on maximizing micro transactions to a mindset focus on maximizing the value of their nascent media properties. These conflicts should resolve themselves, as more sophisticated operating models evolve. There are genuine benefits to esports – such as limited risk of physical injury, and accessibility to a population for whom physical sports are less appealing – which will ensure that esports plays a big role in the future'.

Cricket is not even scratching the surface in this field, with the latest video game release, Cricket 19, feeling pretty basic compared to a massively resourced phenomenon like FIFA. But using the latest VR technology, a whole new gaming experience could be created taking the player right into the middle of one of the great arenas to pitch their joystick/bat skills against the world's fastest or craftiest bowlers, or bowl a virtual ball at a batting legend. In time, IPL franchises will own e-teams and there will be stars of the eIPL and even greater, all-year round interaction with the fans of the various T20 teams.

Manoj: I have been surprised at the relatively slow development of cricket video games. More generally, the major gaming companies have been slow to pick up on the vast mobile growth in South Asia. When you look at the quality of products like the FIFA20 and NBA2K games, it is not hard to see how much potential remains within cricket. The mobile-first games will be the ones that dominate South Asia, and when you look at the exponential growth of games in South East Asia, it is not hard to imagine a cricket-equivalent in India soon.

More than a club

With all this gaming and AI knocking about, the operation of a sport's franchise is changing. We have already seen how the digital opportunity is transforming the approach of the Royals. Franchises have become content creators – and data collectors – as much as they are cricket teams now. With their star players and coaches and ambassadors and personalities (and future esports players) they can generate daily stories for the benefit of fans and sponsors. They will – or are – establishing academies and talent nurseries and with increasing use by wearable tech they become research centres for testing new technologies or investing in development projects.

Manoj: The growing interest in sports franchises of global technology funds, and technology entrepreneurs, is because sports franchises are indirect investments into the growth of digital. As digital and mobile take over more of our lives, the value of those sports brands in connecting consumers with products will continue to grow.

Barcelona FC is a good blueprint. Barca's mantra is Mes Que un Club: more than a club. It has 83m Instagram followers and 9m subscribers to its

YouTube channel. A simple video introducing new player Frenkie de Jong with a fun quiz got almost 3m views. There are iPhone clips of Lionel Messi arriving and warming up pre-match which get 100,000 views in a few hours. There are numerous events and exhibitions and opportunities for tours or to play on the pitch. Its website is a cornucopia of offerings and links and mission statements about values. The Barca Innovation Hub promotes and nurtures an ecosystem for the sports world.

Manoj: Building on our partnership with Dubai Expo 2020, we plan to launch an RR Innovation hub within our Nagpur academy later this year – to create a 'safe space' to learn, experiment and apply these innovations. This is where having multiple colts and women's teams and academies will be very helpful – allowing us to create real life learning labs.

La Masia – 'the farmhouse' – Barcelona's junior academy runs research programmes as well as nurturing talent. There are tie ups with Barcelona University. The Innovation Hub describes itself as "a renowned sport innovation and knowledge centre, committed to promote and collaborate in new scientific research projects and services, and enhance future professionals in the industry through our digital platform, master programs and conferences." It encapsulates Barca's philosophy – it *is* more than a club, it's a way of life.

Its shirt sponsor is Rakuten, the Japanese version of Amazon, which paid over $200m for a four-year association. You can see the synergy there between a club wanting to expand its influence far and wide and an e-commerce platform with instant access to millions of potential customers. But perhaps the most interesting bit of all is that Barca is owned by the fans – 144,000 of them pay a minimum of €140 to belong. (That's a basic €20m in income.) And recently they introduced tokens which supporters can buy to enable them to participate in decisions on certain club matters (like what music to play when a goal is scored). All in the interests of increased fan engagement. This must be the model that IPL franchises eventually emulate.

Manoj: Digital innovation will bring the fan closer to the game, and closer to the players. Social media is not always helpful, but players have woken up to the development of their own brands. Franchises have to stay at the cutting edge of development, and ultimately franchise brand value will trump sports star brand value because of its longevity.

But technology is also impacting sport in areas of performance, and this is where franchises will also need to invest. Whether it's preparation, recovery, diet or mental relaxation – new apps and tools are emerging all of the time. At a recent FA technical advisory, board members were discussing the advent of DNA mapping technology to personalise player diets. Dave Brailsford – the legendary cycling coach – discussed technologies which he is importing from Formula 1, and the science behind coaching is developing all of the time.

Coronovirus demands experimentation

Manoj: For years at Blenheim Chalcot, we have argued that the reason big institutions struggle with innovation is their inability to experiment – because of an overdependence on the 'planning culture' (and a reality that experiments often fail, which investors rarely reward). My business partner wrote a recent blog on how government's failure to deal with the uncertainty that Covid has created, is 'partly because of its overreliance on 'being advised by the science'. What we forget is that much of this science is developed through series of experiments. Governments (and many big companies) are designed to take decisions, based on proof, often placing more investment in the management and removal of risk, than in the idea itself. This is not an approach that works in environments of huge uncertainty. You have to experiment, and to be prepared for those experiments to fail'.

In the world of digital venture building, we are constantly dealing with uncertainty – testing the ability to change customer behaviour with new apps; dealing with new competitors every month, (given the low barriers to entry); managing sudden and new shifts in regulation; and managing uncertain and cash-constrained financials. So experimentation is what we do.

In sport, the media can be punishing on new experiments – look at football and VAR. Sports journalists often criticise change and punish innovations that have teething problems (which all innovations do. I remember the attitude of many cricket journalists when the IPL started…) All this does is breed a culture of risk aversion. Sports bodies have inadequate technology and innovation expertise within their composition. As the acclaimed writer and speaker, Matthew Syed would say, there is a complete lack of cognitive diversity – which breeds group think. Sports boards are often populated by people with a history in the game, political power or who have worked for a big company – that mix does not always breed entrepreneurial, innovative ideas. Covid is taking sport into a period of massive uncertainty, and will force a rapid acceleration in how we think about innovation, risk and experimentation. It will force a rethink about the skills franchises and administrators need. And it is a unique period of time, in which fans will willingly embrace experiments, because we are all so desperate to see sport again. The organisations that embrace innovation, and all that requires, will be the ones that thrive post Covid.

Chapter 11
The T20 Takeaway

Extending the IPL's global reach

Acronym overload

In the midst of our interview, Lalit Modi reviews videos on his phone of early IPL promos and random dramatic moments, stunning catches, booming hits and dancing cheerleaders. Despite being banned for life from the IPL he looks and sounds proud. He should be. He has unleashed a power that cricket didn't know it possessed.

In 2007 there were only three official short-form cricket tournaments around the world. The Australian version, the predecessor of the Big Bash, was the KFC T20. There was something eminently appropriate about Kentucky Fried Chicken as an active sponsor. T20 cricket seemed then so lightweight and insubstantial. A tasty snack, but unmemorable and leaving you hungry again a couple of hours later. The IPL wasn't just a different recipe for T20, it had far more lavish ingredients. A cordon bleu version, if you like. Still with the breadcrumbs on the outside but much richer within. The IPL's phenomenal success has spawned many imitators, both within cricket (around the world), and within India (across a variety of sports). From the Big Bash in Australia to The Hundred in England, cricket is transformed.

India's broader sporting landscape is also radically altered, with professional leagues from soccer to volleyball to badminton, with home grown sports like kabaddi transformed by the professional league. Cricket still dominates that sporting landscape accounting for 85% of the Indian sports economy (with the IPL accounting for two thirds of the Indian sports revenues). That said, sports like soccer are growing in importance at a rapid rate – especially in particular geographies.

Manoj: Within India, sport has become an acceptable pastime, rather than its historic positioning as a diversion from study! The division between work and play has always been clear in Indian families, with sport seen very much as play. It was a rational notion, as a sports career was seen as a high-risk choice, one in which being successful was not a guarantee of making a living. Indians have generally tended towards more certain career choices, such as medicine and engineering. Now there are a multitude of sports leagues within India – all heavily influenced by the IPL.

Examples of Other Sports Leagues in India

Premier Badminton League
Sport: Badminton
Launched: 2013

Hockey India League
Sport: Hockey
Launched: 2013

Indian Super League
Sport: Football
Launched: 2013

Pro Kabaddi League
Sport: Kabaddi
Launched: 2014

Pro Wrestling League
Sport: Wrestling
Launched: 2015

Pro Basketball League
Sport: Basketball
Launched: 2015

Pro Volleyball League
Sport: Volleyball
Launched: 2019

Premier Futsal
Sport: Futsal
Launched: 2016

Fig. 23

Within cricket in 2020 there are more than 30 professional short-format competitions (the best-known arranged below), all deadly serious and all with confusingly similar abbreviations: from the APL through the BBL and the BPL to the CPL and the PSL. The IPL teams are referred to as the RRs, RCB and KKR. The teams in England's new tournament, The Hundred, will doubtless be referred to as BP (Birmingham Phoenix) and TR (Trent Rockets). There are even T20 leagues in Canada, Hong Kong and Nepal

– known appropriately as the Everest Premier League (the world's other EPL) – and a highly successful T10 tournament in the UAE. There are three televised women's T20 competitions too. The USA are launching a professional short-form league by 2021, backed by two media companies – Times of India group and Willow TV. All they now need is a 'visionary entrepreneur', and support from some of those Indian CEOs – Satya Nadella (Microsoft), Sundar Pichai (Google), Indra Nooyi (Pepsi) and Ajay Banga (Mastercard) among them – some of whom have invested.

International T20 Leagues

Fig. 24

For an adaptable cricketer, without a heavy international schedule and preferably single, the global T20 calendar is like a kaleidoscope, spangled with blocks of colour depicting the various playing opportunities. The best cricketers from Afghanistan, a country only recently awarded Test status and with therefore moderate international commitments, have probably benefitted most. Over a period of 16 months between August 2017 and December 2018, their brilliant young leg spinner Rashid Khan, appeared in 115 T20 matches

180

for nine different franchises. It is no coincidence that he is currently the top ranked T20 bowler in the world. His emergence blazed a trail for other Afghanistani cricketers to be hired by overseas franchises, and the country has surged up to seventh place in the T20 international rankings – ahead of the likes of Sri Lanka and West Indies – as a result.

Manoj: The story of Afghan cricket, first highlighted in the brilliant 'Out of the Ashes' book by Tim Albone, demonstrates the pools of undiscovered talent that exist across the subcontinent. Everyone talks about the 1.3 billion people in India, but most ignore the 450m in Pakistan, Bangladesh, Afghanistan and Nepal. With the advent of so many T20 leagues, players are getting more opportunities. Everyone focuses on the $1m contract in the IPL, but the trickle-down effect is also important. A $25,000 opportunity in the Bangladesh Premier League that puts a young player in front of an IPL franchise talent scout can be as life-changing.

The T20 explosion has been a bonanza for many players. It has provided ageing stars with a fabulous new lease of life. The West Indian Chris Gayle, the self-titled Universe Boss, still clubbing bowlers into orbit in his 40th year, regained his appetite for international cricket after successful spells with various T20 franchises. T20 was his stimulant. Ex-Indian Test stars Harbhajan Singh and Yuvraj Singh are still sought after, approaching their cricketing dotage. Plying his trade for 16 different franchises over the last two decades, and adapting from dashing opener to nerveless finisher, Australia's Brad Hodge got a recall into the Australian one-day side after his IPL stint with the Royals. He only finally stepped off the T20 merry-go-round in 2018 aged 43. And then stepped back on it straightaway as a TV commentator.

T20's expansion into other new territories has uncovered exciting players and stirred the embers of the game in unexpected locations. Sandeep Lamichhane, was a budding 15-year-old Nepalese leg-spinner who attracted the interest of some visiting Hong Kong players. Lamichhane was promptly recruited for Kowloon Cantons in the Hong Kong T20 Blitz. Young wrist-spinners are priceless in short-form cricket, especially those no one has seen before. Just over a year later he was playing in the IPL and the Big Bash.

Associates' ascent

Lamichhane's rise is a microcosm of what is happening in the cricket world. There was a clamour in some quarters for cricket's ruling body, the ICC, to get a grip and douse the spread of the T20 bushfire as it raged supposedly out of control across the globe. Instead, in a rare moment of enlightenment, they fanned the flames by reversing the three-nation (India/England/Australia) 'heist' of international cricket's broadcasting income in 2014. (Those three countries had negotiated to receive the lion's share of the revenue.) In January 2019 the ICC announced that all 105 of their members would be granted T20 international status.

Soon afterwards countries as far removed as Belize, Samoa and Serbia had played a T20 international against another member country. The most recent entrants to this expanding circle were Portugal and Gibraltar who played in the three-nation Iberia Cup (won by Spain) at La Manga, prolonging the European cricket season right to the end of October. And in December 2019 Bhutan took part in a tri-series with Nepal and the Maldives. There are now 71 countries who have played a T20 international. Four of these fledgling cricketing nations – Oman, Papua New Guinea, Netherlands and Namibia – qualified for the preliminary stages of the ICC World T20 tournament, originally scheduled for October 2020 in Australia. Thailand was one of the ten teams in the recent women's ICC T20 World Cup.

The ICC belatedly saw that T20 was the platform to properly globalise the game. The longer the format the more infrastructure is required to sustain performance. A Test playing country needs at least six first class teams, top class grounds with A-grade practice facilities, five-star hotels, and, not least, wealthy TV production companies with broad capabilities. A decent T20 team can be generated by a much less sophisticated system. With lots of enthusiasm but few resources, Afghanistan, for instance, have shot up the T20 international table from Division 3 of the World Cricket League alongside the likes of Argentina and the Cayman Islands to seventh place in the ICC T20 rankings, above Bangladesh, Sri Lanka and the 2016 World Champions West Indies. In T20 one player can win a game literally off his own bat in a matter of balls. It renders the history and reputation of an opposing nation almost redundant. It makes for compelling unpredictability. It makes for a niche game becoming truly global.

Certainly, the T20 phenomenon has impacted on some countries, notably the West Indies who have experienced a talent drain as players choose T20 franchise cricket over playing for their national team. They estimate that for every junior cricketer who reaches international level, around $1m has been invested. And then some of those players disappear and much of the benefit of all that development ends up in T20 owners' pockets. While the likes of Gayle and Dwayne Bravo were making money in the PSL, their West Indies colleagues were battling away in the 2019 World Cup qualifying tournament in Zimbabwe. Luckily, they got through. But you could see it another way.

Manoj: People bemoan the demise of West Indies Test cricket, but without T20, and with the pressure of US sports leagues attracting so many of their ball-playing athletes, we would have seen even more rapid contraction of West Indian cricket. The IPL, and the CPL that followed, have 'provided' a vital lifeline. The harsh economic reality is that many countries can't sustain multiple formats of the game. Many of the smaller boards are only viable due to the income from a series of matches against India. This leads to an unnecessarily packed schedule, and an inevitable situation (given the law of big numbers) that India will soon only have a few teams that can consistently challenge it, and that India might have multiple teams playing in different formats.

It is impossible to prevent countries from running their own T20 tournaments. Why would you anyway? They are a money-spinner (at least some are) and they are vital for player development. What the ICC will need to do is create 'windows' in the international calendar for T20 leagues to operate. These would be April–May (Asia), mid-July–mid-Sept (UK and Americas) and Dec–Jan (Australia, NZ, SA). This would leave six months of the year to play Tests and short-form internationals. It would also mean certain T20 leagues – especially the Asian ones – would run simultaneously. Market forces would decide which ones prevailed. There also needs to be a standardised amount – related to the player's purchase value – paid from the franchise to his state/county of origin.

Manoj: What we are seeing in smaller countries is the resurgence of cricket, because of a more competitive and more accessible format. Even traditional Test playing countries like South Africa and Sri Lanka will struggle to sustain multiple formats of the game. The issue now is not the proliferation of T20 leagues, but rather the coordination of them. The more leagues, the more opportunity for aspiring cricketers, but this is where scheduling is so important. Over the next few years, the game has to confront the fact that it has too many formats. To ensure that the international game thrives, and to manage player welfare, there can be only three major T20 leagues – and logically, they would be in Australia, India and England. Ultimately they all need Indian players if they are to provide the required economics to support the best players in the world.

There is too much emphasis on competition between the leagues. The dominance of the IPL is inevitable, so rather than compete, or reinvent formats, the other leagues need to recognise that their value is ultimately derived from the future value and financial position of the IPL.

The way to give the second-tier leagues real purpose is through a recalibrated Champions League. The previous version gave the IPL teams too big a playing advantage. A Champions League featuring all the domestic T20 tournament winners, with a focus on a level playing field, in September/October might initiate another broadcast rights opportunity, which could be shared around the world.

The one other opportunity that all of the major countries should lean into is the US. It is a huge market. It is a hotbed of sports innovation. It will raise global entertainment standards – redefining accepted cricket norms. And it has a powerful South Asian diaspora with deep pockets to fund a sustained launch into a highly competitive sports market.

The pressure placed on the governing body from all these T20 leagues has forced another positive change. The ICC, who had been sitting on their hands ever since the idea of a World Test Championship was first mooted in 1997, finally jumped up and got it organised. It started in July 2019 with each of the top nine Test teams playing six of the others home and away. The top two will play off in the final – at Lord's – supposedly in 2021. Another championship is then scheduled 2021–2023.

It is not a perfect arrangement but it at least gives most Test series context and ensures that even dead rubber matches (i.e. those played after a series has been decided) are important. It will perhaps maintain interest, possibly even increase interest, in Test cricket. The IPL effectively jumpstarted the initiative.

Visual enhancement

You don't have to look too hard for the beneficial impact of the spread of T20, in spite of the chaos of the cricket calendar and the pressure on the Test format. Has the game improved as a result of all these new competitions? Indisputably it has. The best T20 leagues are a melting pot of cricket's sharpest players, coaches, trainers, analysts and thinkers. Ideas are exchanged, new skills acquired and enhanced, an ultracompetitive environment challenges talent to explore the outer reaches of their ability. There's lots of time to spend honing skills – cricketing workshops if you like – and then an intense environment – the match – in which to expand them. If you use good ingredients, you invariably get a better product.

There are still grumpy luddites in England and elsewhere who believe that T20 is evil, an ogre that has trampled all over their beloved sport. In fact, not only has it rescued cricket, bringing in new fans and unprecedented levels of revenue, but it has also enriched the international game. Batsmen have become like avant-garde artists, imaginative, daring, almost anarchic. Picassos in pads. Batting has become a combination of cricket, baseball, hockey, tennis and golf. I have seen young players enhance their hand speed hitting balls with a hurling stick. The power of modern batsmen is astonishing, forcing coaches to wear helmets when they are giving throwdowns. Bowlers work overtime to unearth new deliveries and find fresh disguises and try (and usually fail) to conceal their emotions if they don't work. Boundary fielding – a mix of gymnastics and circus – is a stunning spectacle. Cricket has become entertaining and fun again.

Manoj: Innovation happens when you combine the best in the field with an environment for them to learn. An example of this was Steve Smith's arrival, and impact on our approach to fielding training. (He was a prime target for Rahul and Zubin in the 2014 auction, but they were not convinced our budgets would stretch to get him.) He was both obsessive and innovative about his practice. Back in 2014 I saw a group of our players (domestic and international) watching in awe as he practiced one-handed catches on the boundary rope (and this was well after the main training session had finished). Horizontal one-handed catches, like the one that Ben Stokes took in the opening game of the 2019 World Cup, are now more regular rather than an exception.

The talent and spirit of players like England's Jos Buttler and Ben Stokes has been enhanced by T20 and their supreme skills and stunning range are an excellent adornment to a Test match. Never mind Stokes' superhuman effort in the World Cup final, his ability to play an innings of such adaptability and audacity as the one he produced to win the 2019 Ashes Test at Headingley must have been helped by exposure to the intensity of the IPL. He encapsulates one of cricket's greatest strengths – its versatility.

Survival rates

Despite the general disruptiveness of the T20 explosion, it has enhanced the Test format. In the last decade Test match scoring rates have risen by, in some sides, almost one run per over meaning, potentially, an extra 80 runs a day. Those frankly rather dull days when a team not so much scored as secreted 200-4 in 90 overs are mostly a thing of the past. And because of the atmosphere of general positivity, the likelihood of a boring draw has been significantly reduced. To reassure the purists who love a backs-to-the-wall scrap to parity, draws still happen, but in the last ten years their incidence has halved.

There have been some one-sided Tests, it is true, brought about largely by a visiting team's lack of preparation. That, in turn, is due to the players' crammed schedules as they leapfrog the world clocking up franchise air-miles. Once the windows for T20 leagues have been established, the pressures on the players will be lessened. And the overall product will be improved.

But let's be frank, Test cricket is unlikely to survive in the long term, at least not in certain places. In countries like Sri Lanka and West Indies, with small populations and therefore limited scope, it's economically unsustainable. The crowds for Tests have dwindled to virtually nothing. The income from Tests is negligible. In developing nations like Pakistan and Bangladesh with people who are time-poor, it is ultimately going to be a struggle too.

For a country to be successful at Test cricket requires infrastructure – in other words a healthy first-class system – and resources. The ECB spend £40m annually on the England team. It is logical to assume that by say 2030, only England, Australia, India, South Africa and possibly New Zealand – countries with populous middle-classes (a euphemism for people who can afford to take time off work to spend at sports events) – will be prepared to spend large sums on maintaining a Test team. Test cricket will become a little like rugby, with England, Australia, South Africa, New Zealand and India competing in five-Test series for a biennial trophy: The Five Nations? Those who appreciate the finer things in life will still get their long-form cricket fix. But it will be a more rarefied experience.

Manoj: It is hard to see a long-term future for Test cricket, in its current form. It is my favourite form of the game, but I am not the future. It has a unique ability to create compelling narratives, with ebbs and flow, like no other competition. Players see it as the ultimate form of cricket, but in most countries, Tests aren't paying the bills, they're accumulating them. A game that consumes that amount of the schedule, that has such limited following amongst the youth... it is unlikely to be sustainable outside of the major countries.

Olympic salvation?

Some might accuse the IPL of initiating international cricket's slow death. In fact the opposite could be true. The intent should be to harness a reduced Test championship with 50-over and T20 World Cups as now and make one short format an Olympic sport. Now that there are a multitude of nations playing the same game, the International Olympic Committee (IOC) can hardly refuse – as long as they can all agree on one format. Rugby sevens has managed it, so has golf, even breakdancing is being considered for the 2024 Olympics. Surely short-form cricket will merit inclusion by 2028 in Los Angeles?

Sir Clive Woodward, architect of England's 2003 Rugby World Cup triumph, cites the expansion of rugby after the incorporation of the sevens format in the 2016 Games as an important guide to cricket's future. World Rugby reported 16m new fans to the sport after that event.

"If I was running cricket, top of my wish-list would be to get cricket to become an Olympic sport," Woodward said. "I sit on an IOC commission and I am often asked 'how do we get India?' The way is to get T20 into the Olympics. That would be absolutely brilliant. You get the Olympic rings attached to cricket and surely India would totally buy into it. China too. You'd be amazed how you could grow the game. It's a bit like sevens. Rugby did a brilliant job in pitching sevens to the Olympics. The politics involved is huge. But it's worth it. The sevens event in Rio was fantastic, not just the matches themselves but the way the athletes engaged in the village. The IOC loved it. It could transform cricket too and there's no logical reason why you couldn't have T20 in the Olympic Games." There is one important difference between rugby and cricket. Rugby Sevens had limited commercial value in terms of rights, so giving it to the IOC was an easy decision. T20 is cricket's highest-value product, so having it in the Olympics could dilute value to the current stakeholders. It is not a straightforward offering.

Manoj: The IOC are slowly realising the economic significance of India, and South Asia more broadly. The IOC's income is derived from the value of its media rights, and the way that you capture such a critical part of the world is simple – cricket. With the added participation of Pakistan, Bangladesh and the rest of the subcontinent you've got an extra two billion pairs of eyeballs there. Getting cricket into the Olympics should be a top 5 priority for the IOC.

The way T20 matches have now expanded, often taking four hours, it may be the T10 format, introduced in 2017 in the UAE, and winning support from many players, commentators and spectators, that might work better as an Olympic sport. Matches are completed in 90 minutes and some of the scores in the 2018 competition were staggering – Northern Warriors made 183-2 in their ten overs against Punjabi Legends in Sharjah. T10 is certainly a version of the game that will encourage the many associate cricketing nations as it doesn't require vast playing resources or infrastructure or supreme fitness.

Featuring eight teams, some with names derived from ethnic communities and a couple that were more generic, it was a universal success from the players' perspective. The whole thing is done and dusted in 12 days, there was no 7am air travel after a late night to get to the next venue and the standard of play was high.

Eoin Morgan, who captained Kerala Knights, loved the concept. "'The T10 format is brilliant," he says. "It's probably the closest cricket will get to baseball. It exposes a different aspect of cricket. It also attracts a different fan as well in the sense that you'd probably find a lot of people there who wouldn't go to a normal cricket match. It's so easy to understand because it's arguably as simplified a cricket match as there possibly could be. I'm a huge fan." That said, the quote needs context as ultimately a World Cup winning captain wants to play for as long as possible in front of true cricket fans – but it shows that the modern player understands the importance of making the game accessible.

The league was founded by the billionaire industrialist and keen cricketer Shaji Ul Mulk, descended from the landowning Nawabs of Kurnool in India, but who settled in Dubai and was actually in the 15-man UAE squad for the 1996 World Cup. Business interests forced him to withdraw. Each team was bought for between $4m and $10m – so small-fry compared to the IPL – on a ten-year lease. Ul Mulk likes the 90-minute time frame for a match because it equates with football. "Football has 3.5 billion viewers on average each year," he says. "It delivers all the human emotions – anger, happiness, sadness and excitement – in 90 minutes. But in the end, it is just putting a ball in the net. Cricket is so much more complicated. It's sophisticated. It's just too long." Hence the T10 idea, although the comparison with football may be somewhat premature.

But is it profitable? "We wouldn't be doing this if we couldn't make money out of it," says Mulk. "And each franchise owner knows they can make money from it in turn. India is of course a major market." They are already in discussion. But his focus is actually on the USA. "That's the real market to believe in. Ninety-minute cricket and the US are a perfect fit. We're already talking to the US Cricket Board. And if we get into the US, then the whole world will play ball."

USA Cricket is keen to be part of the craze. "Newly released global research shows there are more than 20 million cricket fans in the United States," said the board's new chairman Paraag Marathe, formerly the director of football at the San Francisco 49ers, so increasing cricket's connections with the NFL. "A well-run professional league is the platform needed to engage existing fans and grow new ones to support the bullish vision this Board has for cricket in the US." There will be a trial competition in 2020, with the full league launching in 2021. The investor group is impressive.

Manoj: There is no question that now is a unique moment in time for cricket to embrace the opportunity in the US. It is not just about the scale of the market, but also the economic significance of the diaspora within that market. To work, it will need engagement and support from the BCCI – as fans want to see current Indian stars. To fund the investment, there is no shortage of cricket-mad capital in the US. The number of Indian CEOs in the Fortune 500 is at an all-time high. Also, the geographic concentration of the diaspora within the US makes that opportunity even more compelling.

Mass participation post Covid

Manoj: As competition for the decreasing consumer leisure pound will intensify during a Covid-induced recession, all participants will be forced to seek new fans. Broadening the appeal of many sports from a gender perspective has been painfully slow, but finally, the impact feels real.

Cricket's inaccessibility has always been part of its exclusive appeal. However, in a world where retailers who rejected online must now embrace online, where doctors adapt from physical to virtual consultation, where businesses operate without physical space, all assumptions must be challenged – and everything must be made more accessible. Cricket can be no exception.

The IPL is a form of cricket which cities and countries around the world – in new markets like the US – want to host. It is a form of cricket that has revitalised women's and girls' cricket. These gender and geographic extensions will ultimately determine whether cricket truly becomes mainstream or remains niche. The IPL has made sport accessible to millions of Indians, and the proliferation of new sports leagues is an important part of the tournament's legacy.

How the IPL extends the geographic reach of cricket is equally important. Attempts so far have had mixed success, but if successful in places like the US, then the overall global financial viability of the game could be raised. The IPL has to be one of India's best ever exports!

Chapter 12

A New Innings

How Coronavirus might accelerate
a new future for cricket.

PC World

Since the arrival of the coronavirus pandemic, one of the most oft used phrases has been the 'new normal' – for the way that we now live, we work, we socialise and we govern. The virus has arrived at an extraordinary pace, caused incredible pain to families with unprecedented human loss across the world, and the full impact will be impossible to evaluate for many years. Post coronavirus (PC) world presents challenges across the board – sport is no exception.

In February 2020, for most of the cricket world, life felt pretty normal. Players were gearing up for IPL Season 13, and overseas cricket tours were still in flow. Then suddenly – global lockdown. Everywhere, normal life – office work, education, construction, travel, socialising and all sport – totally suspended as the virus swept the globe. The Wimbledon tennis championships were cancelled, the Euro 2020 football tournament and perhaps most significantly the Olympics postponed. The month of April 2020 saw the modern world's first-ever sporting blackout as almost half the planet – over three billion people – remained largely indoors. Covid-19 has had an even more devastating effect on international and domestic sport than World War Two. (At least then football – the Wartime League – continued in the UK, though county cricket was abandoned – and Major League Baseball carried on in the US throughout the early 1940s.)

While sportsmen and women have conjured up innovative ways to remain fit and focussed despite being confined to their homes, the administrators are grappling with unprecedented logistical and financial challenges. While trivial in the context of the loss of human life, the cost to sport will be in the billions, the damage to some irreparable. Teams, franchises, clubs, even whole tournaments might be no more. Playing staffs may be ravaged. Broadcast contracts could be cancelled. Sponsorship deals renegotiated and repriced. Live events redesigned. Player contracts redrawn. Leagues restructured. Fan expectations changed forever.

"It's the end of something," wrote the veteran film critic Todd McCarthy when the entire US movie industry shut down in March. "What the next something is seems less knowable than ever." In the next few pages we will analyse what the 'new innings' might look like for cricket, with implications for sport more generally.

As we suggested at the start of this book, the most successful sports and businesses are the ones that can adapt best to their ever-changing environment. Coronavirus has been a once in a lifetime transformation. For 50 years or more cricket has constantly innovated to remain relevant while also retaining its authenticity. The IPL was its most recent reinvention. It transformed the structure, organisation, finances, skills, aspirations and public perception of a game that was battling to retain its status in the world.

As the thirteenth season of the IPL was about to start, we were writing this book pondering what would be the next chapter in cricket's rich and chequered history? Where would the game be in another decade? And what or who would be the drivers of that evolution? England, where cricket originated? Australia, one of cricket's early innovators? Or India, the dominant financial force, and the modern disrupters? Or perhaps the burgeoning women's game, or even the emerging US game?

In fact, it will be none of these. The driver of cricket's and sport's next steps will be a microorganism a thousand times smaller than a human hair – the virus parasite that causes the disease Covid-19. Cataclysms like this global epidemic – causing unprecedented disruption, social isolation and worldwide economic chaos – marginalise all but essential services and force the business community into making hard choices, ones that, in the good times, have been constantly deferred. Harsh realities suddenly must be faced.

Cricket, one of the world's oldest sports, first codified 150 years before football or rugby, which has survived world wars and pandemics and many other global crises, must not shirk this challenge. Its dominant position in one of the world's highest potential growth regions gives it the opportunity to lead the way. Its racial and ethnic diversity, its global reach and its sense of social responsibility simply adds to that potential, but much as in all aspects of life, potential is only realized with the right choices.

Sporting Importance

There are few who can deny missing sport during the lockdown – whether playing or watching. The yearning for freedom to exercise and play has never been greater. The yearning for friends and team mates to play with has never been greater. And the yearning for, and recognition of the value of, sporting content too. The viewership figures for *The Test* and *The Last Dance* docuseries tell broadcasters everything that they have ever needed to know about the value of sport's 'content'. The feeling of triumph with the restart of the English Premier League – and not just Liverpool fans! – has been illustrative. Nothing creates drama like live sport. However, post Covid the nature and the presentation of these games will change with game rules and fan presence affected in a pre-vaccine PC world.

> *Manoj: Live sports will obviously change in a post-Covid world with closed-door or partially attended events. Innovations in production will mean that they still air, and they will still attract huge numbers of eyeballs, albeit on their sofas. The media rights may rise more slowly in the short-term, but as a category of content wanted by the majors (broadcasters and Big Tech – Facebook, Amazon, Apple, Microsoft and Google) the appetite will be unchanged, especially in growth economies like Asia. Cricket has the perfect 'hedge', balancing the downward pressure on price of rights from struggling corporates, with the post-Covid unabated rise of Big Tech and the continued growth of India's middle class.*

The ability of sport to create unique narratives remains unparalleled – who could have written that 2019 World cup final denouement? Or the 2019 IPL final script? Or Ben Stokes's heroics at Headingley? Media rights will continue to grow, with some short-term bumps (caused more by the desperation of some sporting bodies, rather than the long-term attractiveness of those rights). Broadcasters will be forced to innovate even more quickly, creating solutions to the loss of 'stadium atmosphere', generating ever-more personalised experiences (the recent NBA deal with Microsoft will be fascinating to follow), with channels and production segmenting fans ever more narrowly.

Manoj: The forced lockdown has driven all-time viewing records on major streaming platforms. That trend is now irreversible. Streaming platforms are truly mainstream now. The NFL's recent decision to grant exclusivity to Amazon is proof that consumers accept streaming as the norm. The identity of the new 'Big Buyers' in the content world have fundamentally changed, but not the value of live sports rights. Viewing content will also become increasingly personal.

While live sports will continue, the value of their rights in many leagues can still be greatly enhanced. The design of the IPL had many attractive characteristics, but placed the value of the media rights as a central objective. And at the centre of that strategy was a focus on ensuring a level playing field between teams to ensure as many unpredictable outcomes as possible. Large private investment helped provide the funds to secure the best players in the world, but much of the investment only came because of that focus on the 'level playing field' between teams. The auction and the salary cap ensured the balance and therefore exciting unpredictability. With calendar exclusivity, this maximises fan potential, driving up media rights income, which continues to guarantee the income to secure the world's best players. It is a virtuous circle. All major leagues should now regard this as the blueprint.

Simplify to Grow

Many important figures have had their say about what will be the 'new normal' and the way forward for the post-Covid world. The man who made the IPL explode into life – Brendon McCullum – puts it succinctly. "This whole situation makes you more aware of the things you don't properly appreciate in life, and also what you do and you don't really need. You can live a simpler life and still enjoy yourself."

How do you translate that into planning cricket's future? McCullum's 'simplicity' might be the key, which initially means – for cricket – one main format. There are few major sports that pursue the different durations and formulas that cricket allows. Part of this is historical, part natural evolution, part romantic attachment (players and administration) and part the result of deferring those tough choices. Certain versions of the game cannot continue to survive on sentiment alone. They have to be financially sustainable too. This is the blunt truth now confronting cricket chiefs – the same truth confronting business bosses across every industry.

Manoj: If you suggested pre-Covid that last summer's World Cup would be one of the last ever 50-over World Cups, people might think that you were mad. But now it has to be a possibility. It was memorable because of that final, and because the home team won. But how many people followed it throughout the six weeks? How can the player schedule accommodate a World Test Championship, a 50-over World Cup, a 20-over World Cup and a Champions Trophy. What's next, a Hundred (ball) World Cup? Or a T10 World Cup?'

There were too many formats of the game even before the virus took hold. No other global sport supports as many versions. Covid will bring financial viability into sharp focus for all industries and businesses – making it much harder to continue with parts that do not generate cashflow. It will potentially accelerate the transformation of the longer format versions of the professional game. While subsidies to promote participation in amateur grass roots cricket will always be vital, subsidies to fund professional forms of the game (that fans will not pay to watch) will become harder to justify. Tough choices must be made with respect to Test cricket. To save it, at a minimum, it perhaps needs to be reduced to four days, and played between fewer nations, with clearer long-term planning, to allow organisers to create, market and capitalise on these 'special events' (as opposed to increasing the frequency of the marque events e.g. an Ashes every two years). The number of Test matches that finish within four days has grown from 25% in 1990 to 55% in 2019. With respect to World Test Championships – few fans have any idea who is participating, let alone winning.

Confusing fans with tweaks to formats serves to make an already complicated game more complicated. Innovation is important, but the cost of creating new formats (or what retailers would refer to as 'categories') is expensive – and too expensive for cash strapped cricket boards. It also has the potential to confuse players and fans.

With all cricket's myriad formats, it is not just the fans who are suffering from confusion, the players are increasingly struggling to adapt. Before the global lockdown for instance, some England players were going to be playing at Test match tempo in a half-empty Sri Lankan stadium one afternoon and then attempting to smash it around in front of 50,000 screaming spectators in the IPL four days later. It requires extraordinary mental and physical agility to do that. As the skill levels increase, and practice becomes more specific, and the margins between teams smaller, players' preparation time will become more important. Would Jurgen Klopp or Pep Guardiola tolerate players arriving two or three days before the start of the Premier League having been playing a different format of football elsewhere in internationals?

Protect your assets

The games's assets are the players and the fans. Abuse either, and the game eventually suffers. The top players are massively overstretched. They are vital assets. Almost appearing to enjoy the enforced break, Virat Kohli admitted recently that he had to take occasional timeouts from cricket because "there are too many games that have no relevance." Cricket's first post-Covid step is to severely streamline international and domestic scheduling, or the strides made by T20 will be nullified. Something has to give. Many players will have had an important reset and many of the top players will have had a chance to rethink their personal priorities over the next few years.

Manoj: Crises tend to bring disparate factions together to work for the common good. Covid should be the catalyst for cricket's two powerhouses, ICC and the BCCI, to work in harmony for the future of the game. In the past the BCCI guarded their cricketers closely for fear of devaluing the domestic game. Meanwhile the ICC has populated the schedule with multiple international tournaments. Player burnout and spectator ennui are inevitable if cricket's governing body insists on scheduling at least one annual World T20 and Champions Trophy, not to mention fitting in World Cups and World Test Championships, between now and 2031 as they suggest they might.

It is time for proper collaboration. The ICC should encourage the first and second-tier domestic T20 leagues further, constructing windows in the international calendar and creating joint incentives for a reconstituted Champions League. This, featuring the top two teams of each of the premier national leagues, could be a jointly-owned competition played for a month every September/October – the quietest time in the global cricketing calendar. With its greater emphasis on domestic players it would take some of the pressure off the overworked international players.

However, there is also the issue of wealth distribution amongst players. A professional sportsman's life is a short and stressful one. The earnings of a 20-year old French *wunderkind* like Kylian Mbappé who scores goals for fun are therefore disproportionately high. The players should still be amply rewarded and their sheer marketability will continue to set their price. But Covid has shown that perhaps the market for pay should also be recalibrated. The earnings of some sportsmen has become stratospheric. *Forbes* lists over 80 sportsmen – playing for a team – earning over $25m in 2019 (though of course only some of that revenue is derived from the sport itself). We asked what is the appropriate level of player revenue from a league? Is it right that a Premier League footballer earns a hundred times a player in League Two, or that Virat Kohli is paid $2m by Royal Challengers Bangalore and a team-mate $40,000?

Manoj: Another aspect of Covid has been the realisation that income inequality needs recalibration. Many issues have come under greater focus – the income of a US CEO versus an average staff member; the income of an average investment banker versus those of key health workers; the almost unstoppable wage inflation in big sporting leagues. The proportion of the economics in many sports taken by players (e.g. in the top tier of football) will perhaps change. The only way to manage such a recalibration is through salary caps and minimum levels for different categories of players – an area in which the IPL has led multiple innovations.

All major team-sports leagues need enforceable and transparent salary caps. These caps would allow a fairer share out of the total income, ensure a more balanced competition, but would also help prevent clubs desperate to climb the ladder getting into precarious financial positions. Most importantly, these caps drive up the ultimate value of the league's media rights, increasing the revenue for the whole sport. The issue remains as to 'how that pie gets divided', but at least it is bigger. The Kohli's and Ronaldo's can claim a greater skill level and fanbase and therefore financial pull than the rest, but they also could not be what or where they are without teammates, previous clubs and other support staff assisting them on the way to the top.

Total player earnings must be proportionately less of a league's turnover than they are currently in some sports. The major leagues vary between 40 and 60% of rights revenue. It is time to link player earnings from a league to the media income for those leagues – building greater alignment. Initially, this may cause some discontent in some sports, but if the financial savings were placed in a pot marked 'future of the game' the arguments would soon subside. Post Covid, the lavishly rewarded stars must be seen to be making a proper contribution to the opportunities for the next generation.

And while we must protect the players, we must protect the grass roots of the game. This is where the fans are created, nurtured and this is where the value of the game is created. The coronavirus-inspired Thursday night ritual in the UK to stand on your doorstep and applaud the National Health Service staff reminded us all of the forgotten heroes who protect us. People who put responsibility and care of others above salaries and safety and other personal concerns. Their vital efforts were previously rarely acknowledged. They are often paid a pittance.

There are many similar types in cricket. They may not save lives, but they do enrich them. We are talking here of the volunteer coaches, the umpires, the scorers, the match-managers, the fixture secretaries, the 75-year-old guy who still lovingly cuts and rolls the pitch down at the club three times a week. People dedicated to the game they love. They are the lifeblood of cricket. Its fertiliser. They rarely get any recognition. Some of the vast sums the game now generates should be redistributed to them. It's time for more investment from the bottom up rather than the top down. These players all began somewhere. Without nourishing the roots, the plant will not flourish. Or put differently, you won't get the mass participation that builds the fan base to ensure valuable media rights.

The England cricketers did not wait long to do exactly that. They donated £500,000 to the ECB in the midst of the pandemic and expressed a wish for it to be passed on to the lower reaches of the game. "Without grassroots cricket we're nothing really," said Jos Buttler, who also donated his World Cup winning shirt to an auction for a hospital charity. "Those are the people we're trying to inspire. I know the players are very strong on wanting that money to help grassroot structures and pathways because we need to bring people into the game and make sure that is very strong."

Embrace India

Manoj: One aspect of cricket that makes it different to some of the other major global sports is the dominance of one country within the game's economics. All cricketing nations need to embrace India, and India knows it. The country's income from cricket is well over double that of any other, and over 85% of the game's income comes from games involving India or Indian teams. International tours to, or by, India turn most of the other cricket economies from red to black. Three T20s against India (in India) nets $20m in broadcast revenue. The presence of Indian players in any league amplifies the media rights value of that tournament. While many fans are happy with Ben Stokes, rights buyers want MS Dhoni or Virat Kohli. Young Indian players will also help boost interest, as the IPL is accelerating their star power. The impact of the IPL has resulted in the Indian subcontinent constituting 90% of the one billion global cricket fans under 65.

In 2019, the global cricket economy was estimated (in a report by the former IPL CEO) to be around US$ 1.9bn, with nearly $1.2bn (approximately two-thirds) generated through games in India ($800m), or games played against India in other countries ($300m). The IPL is the biggest event, generating more than $600m revenues (about a third of global cricket revenues). IPL 2019 tournament revenues were estimated to be 30% higher than that of the 2019 ICC World Cup.

Estimated Annual Revenue from Cricket (Pre-Covid)

Country	Cricket Revenue	% Broadcast	% Match Day
India (inc. IPL)	860m	70%	5%
England	280m	40%	40%
Australia	280m	70%	20%
Others	530m	80%	4%
Global Total	1.9bn	70%	10%
IPL	600m	70%	5%

Fig. 25

The mix of broadcast, sponsorship and matchday income varies significantly, in different markets, with matchday income accounting for only 5% of cricketing revenue in India. Clearly, the impact of Covid will be felt most directly with matchday income in England and Australia, and with near-term sponsorship income pressure. However, the postponement of the IPL shows that India is not immune from the pain.

Manoj: Attracting India player participation should be a priority for major domestic cricket leagues. From a playing perspective, exposure for young Indian players to overseas conditions creates a compelling proposition to encourage Indian participation. Generating attractive economic opportunities for Indian stars in their later years is another attraction. However, this requires a mindset shift of collaboration rather than competition between the governing bodies. The 'exam question' is to how to structure this in a way that benefits India, Indian players and Indian cricket.

For non-Indian players the earning potential in the IPL will still completely overshadow any other opportunities. In 2019 Sam Curran, the exciting 20-year-old allrounder from Surrey, was bought by Kings XI for $800,000. That is considerably more than his late father – the feisty competitor Kevin Curran, who played in two World Cups for Zimbabwe – earned in his lifetime. Sam played nine games for Kings XI, and bowled 33 overs. Effectively he earned $4,000 a ball.

The pandemic will have a short-term impact on player earnings. However, for the top players, the prospects still look good. India's middle class has more than doubled in number in the last ten years. By 2030, a massive proportion of the world's middle-class population will be Indian. Before Covid, India's economy was set to grow tenfold. Those projections will now be reduced, but the country will still have more purchasing power than any other nation in the world. And what do you think they are going to spend their money on? Well, for the foreseeable future, anything that Kohli recommends.

Growth of India's Middle Class (in millions)

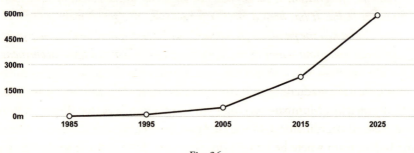

Fig. 26

Kohli is very much a child of the IPL, someone who played in the very first match (he made one solitary run, like all his Royal Challengers Bangalore teammates being totally dumbstruck by the Brendon McCullum show) and has grown into an immense figure, in parallel with the tournament itself. And he is a magnificent role model, not just in the manner that he wins matches for his team but just in the way that he *is*.

He is a symbol for his generation with his gym-honed body and his low-carb high-protein diet, his intense work ethic and his incredible desire to win. Through his exploits and his 65 million followers on Instagram he is stimulating the reshaping of Indian culture from a population riddled with health issues, self-doubt and corruption to a fitter, fairer, more focused nation. Kohli's lifestyle and attitude sets the ultimate benchmark, and the results are obvious. Kohli is the number one batsman in the world and his country are the number one team. He has been the torch bearer for New India. He, and his teammates, have given his nation a tangible feeling of self-confidence. You can see it in the TV adverts for cosmetics and fashion and other lifestyle enhancements.

Manoj: The IPL has not just changed cricket, it has changed Indian society. It has liberated young, modern India. It has created an environment where young Indians can express themselves – out of the home, talking exuberantly, singing, dancing (even having the occasional drink). It has contributed massively to a health and fitness culture, especially in urban areas, that was non-existent years ago. It has turned sport into an aspirational professional career. Its scandals have helped modernise governance in areas beyond cricket and expose wrongdoings. It has been fantastic for tourism, and greater international integration. It has been a catalyst for the development of other sports within India. It has been a positive for business, for government and for the fan. And when the pandemic has passed, the importance of health and hygiene in India will grow – and so too, the importance of sport in the subcontinent.

India have been gradually building on Kohli's legacy through the IPL and specifically men like Mumbai-dwelling John Gloster, the Rajasthan Royals' physio and medical coordinator. Gloster, an Australian, began as the head physio to the Indian team where he found it tough going. Since starting work with the Royals, he has been on a mission not only to harden his players' physiques but also to influence the nation to get fit. He recognises the responsibility these superannuated cricketers have for enhancing the lives of their billion fans. And that new focus has been influential in the nation's economic uplift.

The detail Gloster applies to the Royals players' wellbeing is more typical of the regimes followed by elite Olympic athletes. He is a sort of fitness evangelist. "Cricket is the vehicle driving this message, and it is incredible to see the transformation in the fielding and the fitness of Indian cricketers in the past decade," he says. "In the 2016 Olympics in Rio, India won two medals and ranked 65th in the medal table. With properly organised systems India could become a real Olympic power. That helps drive the economy. A recent Australian government paper has a 100-page section recommending investments in Indian sport."

The structures and personnel that franchises like the Royals have put in place is helping to professionalise India. It *should* lead to even greater growth. And even stronger self-belief. That is important. If the pandemic had arrived a decade ago, India would have been in a fragile state. But now the country is established as an economic, technological and sporting power, and with the right reforms, it is resilient enough to survive the current economic recession and grow even stronger in tandem with a gradually expanding IPL.

Manoj: Most accept that India is the 'New Home' of cricket, but how productively India interacts with the rest of the cricketing world will be a central issue that determines the growth of the overall game. Collaboration and productive partnerships, with simplified schedules will ultimately benefit all – but require compromise. The rest of the cricket world's partnership with India is a huge issue for the game.

Rewire Digitally

Covid has undeniably accelerated the shift towards a digital economy. The dominance of Amazon, Microsoft, Facebook and Google has been accelerated (These companies were already massive pre Covid, but now account for over 25% of the U S stock market and continue to be largely unregulated). The Covid effect will make these companies even stronger.

With matches in empty, or sparsely attended stadiums, traditional revenue lines will be severely disrupted. Digital has been and will be the saviour. There are numerous solutions for cricket, building substantially on the successful streaming services in the IPL, Major League baseball and football. Virtual crowds will be the new norm. The impact of Covid will ensure that, in 2020, digital coverage of sport will explode.

There will be new conditions for events. For matches behind closed doors, stadia will have to be bio-secure (so those with hotels onsite will have an advantage) and have certificates to declare they are Covid-free. Once crowds are allowed back in, screening systems will be in place to certify patrons as healthy or non-infectious, so arriving at a match will be similar to the x-ray procedure at an airport. (US venues are looking at thermal cameras which can detect if supporters have a fever.) Ticketing systems will need to be adapted to ensure social distancing in the stands. The queuing system at food and merchandise outlets will have to be carefully monitored (or items delivered to individual seats).

> *Manoj: We will need to very quickly transform how we organise and stage live events, because we are going to play a lot of games behind closed doors. Then when the fans are let back in we will have to change how we check and screen people coming into a stadium. Sport is already playing a vital role in solving the challenges of live event management in a post-Covid world. Technology will be a saviour for live sports.*

But digital will also change the experience at home. Take as one example an intriguing new partnership between the NBA and Microsoft. For the forth-coming 2020–21 season, NBA broadcast coverage can be customised to the preferences of the individual consumer. So if a viewer watching a game wants more analysis of a specific incident, or a deeper insight into a particular player, or highlights of that player's best games, or specific data feeds, or to watch the match with 'ref-cam', or to join a group chat about the game, all this will be instantly available. Artificial intelligence will offer a whole range of options and choices specifically tailored to them. Essentially it is personalising sports cover-age. Instead of traditional 'one to all' coverage, it is 'all to one.' Headsets will also be increasingly used to fully immerse the viewer in the sporting experience.

> *Manoj: Suddenly we are all living our lives in the digital world, commu-nicating with our families and friends on Zoom, and ordering everything online. Rural communities are worrying about broadband connections. The digital transition has rapidly accelerated and the growth of digital sports con-tent will be exponential. It will be a really important new (or at least grow-ing) source of revenue and engagement, especially with so many games played behind closed doors.*

'Engagement' is the watchword for the sports business and Live Chat is a rap-idly growing phenomenon. Research by Google has shown that 80% of sports viewers are using a second device at the same time as watching the game, look-ing at stories or videos or communicating with friends. The key for franchises and leagues is to direct that social networking traffic through their own chan-nels to improve spectator experience and interaction, and to drive revenues. New partnerships could supply all these options via one screen – the match on one half which you are sharing with your friends on a Zoom-type call on the other side, or various data feeds and social-media posts regularly popping up on screen. Older age-groups may want to retreat to a darkened room at these prospects, but Generation Z are already used to this multiple interaction on their Xbox consoles playing Fortnite or Minecraft or watching movies in virtual groups on Netflix Party. The reality is that, in this new, socially distanced world, digital is bringing people back 'together'.

More importantly for the sports themselves, this technology will build fantasy elements into the coverage – in harness with those gaming companies mentioned earlier – to offer the spectator countless opportunities to engage with the action. Data will be fed to the viewer from a multitude of sources – motion-tracking cameras located in the stadium, microchips in players' helmets or footwear, real-time data from athletes' bodies, a stream of relevant stats processed and interpreted by bots – creating a huge range of markets to participate in. And that's where the revenues are generated. Almost half of this participation will be done on a smartphone. One click and you've just put a tenner on Mbappé to score in the next ten minutes.

Manoj: Cricket, which incorporates so many different facets and skills and data sets, which, as an individual sport within a team game, generates so many miniature stories and duels within the overall narrative, is perfectly set up to maximise and exploit this technology. It would develop a whole new layer of integration with the fans, and vitally keep the much sought-after younger generation engaged. Digital is now the 'silk road' for sports in general, and cricket in particular.

Sports teams are digital content factories. The players have established even bigger fanbases with their various posts and activities during lockdown. More and more franchises and professional clubs are participating in esports. It will make the best cricket leagues highly marketable properties. Big Tech companies will be even more anxious to form alliances with the franchises, enabling them to mine all that invaluable information about customer behaviour and preference. Big Brother is going to go on a sports' shopping spree.

Announcing the Microsoft partnership with the NBA, Adam Silver the CEO, a forward-thinking governor who showed great initiative in the early days of the pandemic by shutting down the NBA before any other major sport, said: "The way to keep people of any age watching longer is to create more engagement with them, to deliver to them more of the content that they want. Whether that be on a separate screen or whether that be part of the telecast itself, it can be deeper content about particular players they're interested in, data around those players and in some cases, gaming content, and that can either be fantasy content or sports betting content. I think we just have to adapt for younger consumer habits because those younger fans are watching more screen time than any generation in the history of media."

Manoj: Facebook's recent $5.7bn investment in [Mukesh Ambani's] Jio mobile, is intriguing. It's a tie-up between a social media giant that wants more access to the Indian population and the subcontinent's dominant mobile phone operator that wants applications and content. National teams, clubs and franchises will all be creating stories for the major platforms. This year TikTok has transformed the social media world, and more platforms will evolve. However, content will remain king. And that is why sports franchises are so valuable. It also highlights the importance of India to Big Tech, which is in turn, very important for the global game of cricket.

Build the Extensions

Reconstitution will be the immediate priority for sports when lockdowns are eased. Getting the show back on stage will be the main focus, initially. But growth – including putting that show on the road – will still be on the agenda in the medium term. The 'extension' policies of US sports have been clear for a while. London was a major target. This was the back page of London's *Evening Standard* in April 2019:

Major League Baseball presents
Boston Red Sox v New York Yankees
London Stadium 29/30 June 2019

This was right slap bang in the middle of the Cricket World Cup – Australia were playing New Zealand at Lord's that weekend, followed by England against India. American sports muscling in on the UK seeking to develop an overseas fanbase is nothing new – the NFL first experimented with staging matches in London in 2007, and a record crowd of 85,000 attended the match between the Philadelphia Eagles and the Jackson Jaguars at Wembley Stadium in 2018. Last year two NFL games were played at Tottenham Hotspur's new stadium in which the grass football pitch can be quickly retracted revealing the Astroturf of an NFL surface beneath. Each game attracted a crowd of over 60,000.

NBA teams had also been playing in London. They have an office in Shanghai. And their most ambitious venture – the Basketball African League featuring 12 teams drawn from all over Africa – was due to launch in Senegal in March 2020. Inevitably it was postponed, but the intent is clear. And the event listed above, Major League Baseball's first venture into Europe in London in 2019, drew a total of 120,000 fans for a double-header between the sport's two most famous teams. It emphasises how important it is in this ultracompetitive world to continually look to expand your market. The two biggest football brands – Manchester United and Barcelona – have also been doing this for years. Almost half United's estimated 659 million fanbase are from Asia (315m).

Global expansion has always been on the agenda for the IPL. That was the idea of the 2008 Champions League – bringing together the best T20 teams from around the globe to play a tournament in India in November. It was postponed because of the terrorist attacks that month. No IPL franchise has since successfully developed their brand abroad, although Kolkata Knight Riders and Kings XI Punjab have established partnerships with Caribbean Premier League teams.

But, once the pandemic is overcome, IPL franchises will start to properly spread their wings. They will look to play exhibition matches, and eventually IPL games, overseas. They have a captive market – the vast South Asian diaspora (see graph below). There are an estimated 31m people born in India, or of Indian descent, living abroad. The US has the highest number – over 4m. That's greater than the entire population of New Zealand. You can bet that at least 75% of them are cricket lovers. And if they're not, some of the most influential CEOs in the US – Sundar Pichai (Google CEO), Satya Nadella (Microsoft CEO), Indra Nooyi (Pepsi CEO), and the Indian CEOs of Mastercard, Nokia, Diageo, Motorola, IBM, Citigroup – will soon convince them of the importance of cricket. Microsoft is even constructing a cricket ground on its superb new campus in Redmond, Washington. Some Caribbean Premier League matches have already been staged in Florida with decent support. Indians and their expats make up the vast majority of the global cricketing fanbase.

The US is perhaps where cricket's most exciting new prospect exists. Microsoft's Nadella thinks so, as he has invested personally into the league. There is a ready-made audience, superb infrastructure, sponsors galore and a nation ready to do business with the UK and the subcontinent and get involved in a global sport. On a special visit to India in February 2020, President Donald Trump proudly consecrated the new 110,000-seater cricket stadium at Ahmedabad, even if he did mispronounce the name of India's greatest player ("Su-Chin Tendoolkaar"). Cricket, with its increasing reliance on science and data, is the perfect vehicle for the US sports fan and their tech-giant backers. All they need is a version to play.

Indians Living Abroad by Country – 2017 (in millions)

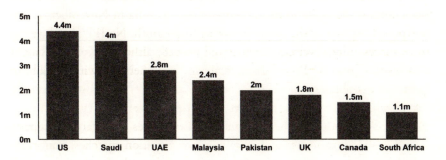

Fig. 27

The women's game should be properly invested in. Indeed, it is a brilliant asset with huge growth potential, and a place to test and discover new innovations.

Manoj: The Women's World Cup final at Lord's in 2017 was a watershed moment for the game. Cricket has always been a family game – in parks and on beaches – and there is no reason that it should not be the case in all aspects of the game. Amateur clubs would grow if parents could drop off all their kids, not just the boys. Memberships would swell if you embraced both halves of the population, and ultimately the game would attract new broadcasters and broader sponsors.

The ICC Women's World T20 final between Australia and India in March 2020 drew a crowd of 86,000 at the Melbourne Cricket Ground, close to a world record for a women's sporting event. For the first time women's T20 cricket is included in the line-up for the Commonwealth Games in 2022 in Birmingham. When order is restored there will also be a four-team women's mini-IPL to be staged alongside the men's competition. The newly created men's teams in The Hundred will also have parallel women's sides.

These are very important developments for the future of cricket. Not only will it attract more female fans but also 75% of all schoolteachers in developed countries are women. The more females that understand and appreciate cricket, the more they might encourage their pupils to play the game rather than any number of other sports or pastimes. That opens up a huge new market for the game. There are now female commentators on the men's game, female analysts and administrators.

As well as building these extensions, cricket must continue to invest in bringing children into the game. Cricket has not always been the most accessible sport, not least because of the infrastructure it requires, but also because the way we coach and teach has changed very little in the past thirty years. In the spring of 2019, the Royals became the first IPL franchise to open an academy abroad, building on the relationship with the outstanding coach Sid Lahiri (who has developed players like Ollie Pope). Building on his partnership with Reed's school in Surrey, the Royals have set up a facility training kids during and post school hours. Shane Warne, now a Royals' ambassador, attended the launch and was impressed with some of the young talent on show. There is a tie-up with the Royals' own high-performance centre based in Nagpur. There will be an exchange of coaching methods, coaches and talent between the two, with more academies planned across the world.

> *Manoj: Our academy development strategy is an important route to connecting with the next generation of cricket fans. The kids are excited to go to a place where they are taught T20 skills, and we have a steady stream of youngsters, many from the diaspora, now attending our camps in Nagpur. The partnership in the UK is another innovation, and we hope to find other like-minded academy partners all over the world. We want to develop a new curriculum of cricket coaching, a new approach to teaching, and ultimately contribute to a new philosophy of how the game is played.*

Broadening the Ownership

Who owns the game? This has been a question often asked in sport. The answer should be – the fans and the players (amateur and professional). And yet it is an open question as to how represented they feel by those making the decisions.

> *Manoj: The issue of who owns the game is really a question that should shape how the game is regulated. Sometimes it gets confused with the question of who can and can't own the franchises, or who can or cannot invest in leagues.*

As we've seen, throughout the cricket world all nations have looked enviously at the success of the IPL and tried, in some way, to replicate it themselves. Australia's Big Bash was originally planned to be a franchise tournament with privately-owned teams, but Cricket Australia got nervous and ultimately retained control. The teams are owned by the state associations. The novelty value, reliable Australian weather and excellent stadia made it an initial success, but, now in its ninth year, it has over-expanded and under-invested. The 2019–20 competition lasted far too long and the low-level salary cap ($1.7m per team) was inadequate to attract many of the world's best players. The tournament lacked star quality. There were many half empty grounds and media revenues suffered a significant drop. The same was true of South Africa's Mzansi Super League which was poorly marketed and lost a colossal amount of money.

England, still ruing missing the T20 goldrush first time around, attempted to innovate with a new format – The Hundred, involving various time-saving devices like shorter innings and blocks of 10 deliveries from one end. It is a novel idea but perhaps the wrong solution to an important problem (the problem being the increasing time taken to complete T20 games). Eight new city teams were created to, theoretically, supersede for six weeks in high summer, the old county system which has been the bedrock of the domestic game for 130 years. It was a brave and widely unpopular move, even after those counties were promised an extra £1.3m each annually from the bonanza £1.1bn media rights deal.

Coronavirus ensured it was stillborn, in 2020 anyway. This may be a blessing in disguise. This is a huge opportunity to reset and rethink. Two short format leagues in the same country in the same summer makes no sense. It is political compromise. Private investment for the teams in The Hundred is now critical – alleviating pressure on the ECB for whom the tournament is already costing £60m, and helping future-proof the competition, and raise the teams' budgets thereby securing the world's best players. At present the highest salary band is £100,000. Virat Kohli doesn't even get out of bed for that.

Covid will pressurise and possibly change the situation. There are few alternative options. Even a venerable institution like the MCC has begun to realise that the only secure way of financing new developments is through private fundraising – selling lifetime memberships. The private investment bit is non-negotiable. Professional cricket is unsustainable without it. The pressure on many already debt-laden English counties – several who haven't made a profit for a while – is now extreme. For some, they will need private investment into their grounds and facilities at the very least. For others this is judgement day and a realisation that they can probably only survive, fully professionally, as a T20 outfit. For England and Australia, the time has come for private investment into their franchise T20 leagues. A revamped T20 Champions League might also breathe life into the smaller T20 leagues – giving them purpose and financial opportunity.

Manoj: I think private ownership is the best model for team and franchise ownership, but not necessarily for league ownership. The American model has deficiencies, and where leagues are fully run by 'owner consortia' the profit motive can become all encompassing. Private investment drives innovation. But private investment without regulation is dangerous – as we have seen in the last 30 years in business.

The extra costs of staging sport will put an extra burden on the fan, and the volunteer further down the line, making it even more important that franchises and teams recognise and reward their commitment. If there was any doubt before that these 'tribes' should be incentivized through the growth in the value of the teams – Covid should dispel it. Cricket can get on the front foot here to show how the wealth creation in sport can be appropriately shared. The issue is less public versus private ownership, and more about broadening the ownership, and applying the right model to the right part of the game.'

Sports clubs also have the ability to have huge social impact, and franchises should have a broader purpose than pure profit (and if needed, regulated as such). The fact that Covid-19 preyed particularly on the unhealthier sections of society catapults the community sports-club to a new level of importance. The eager take-up of a plethora of fitness videos is just one example of the obvious dearth of knowledge about health and fitness. The failure of governments to prioritise sports education has had catastrophic consequences. Intrepid individuals and charities are attempting to fill the breach, but when you hear stories of cricket coaches visiting state schools in London to discover that the 45 minutes of weekly sports activity in one establishment is 'walking', and you see the levels of obesity amongst Generation Z, you realise how much work there is to be done.

Manoj: Sport is a great platform for education and changing behaviours. Whether issues related to health, education, inclusion, conservation or poverty, sport is uniquely placed to drive change. All participants have a responsibility. The impact of English Premier league players 'taking the knee' to show support for the 'Black Lives Matter' movement; the impact of players donating to grass roots organisations; the impact of franchises giving visibility to charities – these are all great examples of what could be common place for sport. As a player or a franchise, having a clear social purpose should perhaps become as important as the profit motive. The recent ECB support for the Ruth Strauss Foundation with the 'Red for Ruth' day is a great example.

Regulate the 'game'

Covid has highlighted the challenges with governments around the world. Global crises illuminate governing body deficiencies more than ever and place a great emphasis on decisive and honest leadership. The pandemic has further highlighted the imperative that sports have able, independent and publicly transparent governing bodies to direct strategy and allocate critical investments. The areas of their responsibility continue to expand from solvency and maintaining standards of behaviour and authenticity – never easy with the increasing encroachment in sports of the gaming industry – to player welfare, scheduling, social purpose, safety and public image post Covid. In a world where private ownership is growing rapidly, and finances are pressured more than ever, regulation becomes even more important.

Manoj: Governance is probably the single, toughest and yet least evolved issue within sport. Any change requires support from the vested interests that run it. Unless governing bodies can embrace changes to their structure, sharing of their control, evolution of their roles, then sport's rate of innovation will slow – as investment will be deterred. Most importantly, the governing bodies have to invest in the professionals that run the sport. Regulators around the world will have to find ways of attracting (and retaining) the best talent or they will always be outsmarted by the companies and investors in that industry. It is not easy, and we have often failed in politics. However, until we invest in our regulators, we will get poor, compromised, lowest common denominator decision-making.

The IPL had an important intervention from the courts, but that cannot be the long-term answer. Not enough people within the game (fans and players especially) realise the importance of this issue. Ironically, it is probably only these two constituency groups that can effect change.

Never mind judging how and where to restart these sports in a newly fragile world, another major post-Covid challenge will be managing the increasing involvement of the gaming and gambling industry in all sport. These income streams will become even more important. In addition to technology groups, the other inevitable sports partners will be the big gaming companies. They are awash with cash. The global sports-betting market is valued at $250bn (and that's just the legal version). That value will escalate even more with the legalising of sports-betting in the US and we are already seeing big tie-ups between major leagues like the NBA and gambling giants.

> *Manoj: Covid will force difficult choices – how we embrace gambling and how we channel that income into the sport is crucial. 'Fixing' is the other virus that threatens the game, and governing bodies can only solve the issue in collaboration with the industry and government.*

In-play gaming/betting (call it what you will) – powered by technology companies and software agencies – will boom, alongside the rapid expansion of digital sports coverage. Sport will be forced to embrace this new income. With the growing use of data in cricket, such associations will multiply. The enthusiasm for gaming (and gambling) in India is, of course, massive. Around $750m is rumoured to be wagered on each IPL game. Legalising this activity would produce a tax windfall for the Indian government. But more importantly, it will allow the regulators, the gaming companies and government to work together to stop nefarious activity – such as spot-fixing. Strong, independent regulation will be fundamental to control these partnerships and maintain the sport's credibility and authenticity, but so too will new government regulation in India.

The next chapter

The IPL has not only made cricket sustainable, but hugely enjoyable. And this is just the start of what is possible. Although sport and cricket have been rocked by the impact of coronavirus, cricket will thrive over the next decade. This will be ensured by the economic growth of South Asia's middle class along with the global growth of the South Asian diaspora. As a game, it lends itself to the increasing use of technology, from enhancing performance to enhancing the viewer experience. However, for a game synonymous with tradition, the greatest challenge will be to increase the pace of change, without totally abandoning the traditions that have defined the game over the past 200 years.

Manoj: In writing this book, the imperatives outlined for the game of cricket, and indeed for sport more broadly, feel both urgent and important. The intent has been: to share learnings from the roller-coaster ride of owning the Rajasthan Royals; to share perspectives on the opportunities and challenges facing the game of cricket; and to perhaps stimulate broader awareness and discussion about the imperatives we highlight.

Having focused the book on cricket's last major reinvention by the Indian Premier League (IPL), we did not expect the game to be hit by one of its most existential crises weeks before publication. We would argue that the pandemic has simply accelerated many of the highlighted changes and increased the rate of change that is required by leagues, franchises and governing bodies across the world. The short-term challenges will be numerous: cancellation of matches and tournaments; playing in empty stadia; ensuring player and staff safety; managing falling revenues; and continuing to engage fans. However, the long-term prospects for the game of cricket have never been more positive. Cricket is the world's second most popular sport. The opportunity for growth alongside the emergence of a new and economically stronger South Asia is immense. The growth within the existing core fan base of the game is something that any global sport would envy. The additional growth offered by the increasingly global south Asian diaspora and the opportunity for growth with the less traditional younger and female audiences is enormous, given the popularity of the shorter formats of the game amongst those segments. However, there are critical choices, which will determine the extent to which the game of cricket seizes those opportunities.

There is an important debate to be had about the number of the game's formats, along with the number of, design of, and inter-relationship between tournaments. The game must focus its investment to maximise growth. Simplification will help protect the game's most important assets, which are the fans and the players. Schedules would benefit from more certain calendar slots, creating greater fan anticipation and excitement. Schedules would benefit from fewer meaningless games. The debate about the future test cricket needs balanced discussion. At a minimum, Test Matches (and their associated schedules) need reconfiguration.

'Less can often mean more' in sport, with the media rights value of many of the best sporting events heightened by their scarcity. The value of media rights is the most objective metric to test the effectiveness of tournament and schedule design. These media rights are accelerating in value with the advent of digital, which both creates opportunities to create new content, reach new viewers and to enhance the fan experience. Cricket, as with all sports, needs new strategies to deal with the with the major technology giants, whose market dominance will further accelerate post Covid. Digital technologies and 'Big data' will improve player performance, improve the fan experience, and allow even closer access to the players and the action.

Cricket will benefit from the changing economic balance within the world. The game must embrace India collaboratively and productively, by respecting the criticality of that market, and the diaspora, to the game's growth. India, too, needs to manage its power as the new 'Home of cricket', and lead the expansion of the world into new territories, and new segments, such as the women's game. India must also lead on the threats posed by illegal gambling and fixing within the game. This remains a major threat. India's ability to lead the global game will be a major determinant of future success and growth.

Cricket has been slow to embrace private investment, but it must do so strategically. Private investment, unchecked and unregulated, is not the answer. Broadening ownership, and connecting it with the players and the fans, to create new models is a priority for all sports. Cricket has the potential to lead in this area.

Cricket, as with all major sport, has the power (and therefore the responsibility) to effect major social change. Hence, social purpose must be built into the structures of the game at every level. It is a truly multi-cultural and multi-racial sport that can unite. It must lead the way in changing racial intolerances, which still blight society. It is the dominant sport in South Asia, where over half a billion people still live in extreme poverty on less than a dollar a day. At the time of publishing, Coronavirus is ripping through South Asia with a devastating impact, which will be felt for several years. Cricket depends on this region and must play a role in helping the recovery. Financially, cricket has the power to transform lives. In business, it is fashionable to talk about 'responsible capitalism'. Cricket could lead the way.

*Cricket, as with many sports, needs a richer debate about the role, accountability and structures of its governing bodies. The choices made by the 'governors of the game' affect us all. However, to grow and innovate we also need private investment, which creates the potential for conflicts of interest. This is not a challenge unique to cricket. Fans and players have a responsibility, and an incentive, to pose these questions. Many will realise that these debates are as important to our continued enjoyment as the sporting debates about 'who should bowl next or who should bat in what position?'. This book might hopefully stimulate the ongoing debate about the future of the game. We have presented ideas. Some will be right, and some will be wrong. There will be other ideas, and better ideas, out there. So, realizing that this book is outdated the moment that it is published, we have created a place for the ideas and the debate to continue at **anewinnings.com**. We hope that you will subscribe and contribute to the debate, which will hopefully continue!*

*Cricket has a great opportunity to grow, but it will need new levels of collaboration, and greater diversity in its thinking. We have all realized how important a role sport plays in life. If the sport's key stakeholders work together to continue building on the reinvention of cricket by the IPL, and use the fast, unexpected changes to make tough choices, then there is much to be positive about. We will then fast forward a 'reset' of the game, and we will stride towards an exciting **'New Innings'**.*

Author Biographies

Although Simon Hughes had a successful 15-year professional cricket career with Middlesex and Durham, winning nine titles with Middlesex, he is best known in the game as The Analyst for his unique work on TV and radio explaining the game. It has earned him several national awards and his innovations and style have been copied on TV coverage of sport all over the world.

As well as his broadcast work he is well-known as a newspaper columnist and author having written nine previous books on cricket, including the best-selling A Lot of Hard Yakka (1997), and he is also editor of The Cricketer Magazine. He has attended numerous IPL games both as spectator and pundit, follows the tournament avidly and has been a regular visitor to the sub-continent for 40 years.

***

Manoj Badale was born in Maharashtra but educated in England and studied economics at Cambridge University. Since 1998 he has co-founded over 40 businesses – mostly technology-related – through the venture-building group, Blenheim Chalcot, that he set up with Charles Mindenhall. A cricket lover, he set up a consortium to purchase the Rajasthan Royals IPL franchise in 2007 and the team won the inaugural tournament in 2008.

As the only English-based lead owner of an IPL franchise, Manoj has a unique perspective on the business of cricket, and sport generally, and advises a number of major sporting bodies. He is also heavily involved in charitable activities, particularly as founding chairman of the British Asian Trust and was awarded an OBE in 2018. Married with three children, he has immersed them all in his twin passions of cricket and Liverpool FC.

Index

Sreesanth 105
Sri Lanka ix, 8, 69, 111, 181, 182, 184, 186
Narayanaswami 92
Narayanaswami Srinivasan 92
Srinivasan viii, 92, 118, 119
stadiums 13, 46, 65, 90, 96, 101, 204
Star 8, 9, 11, 15, 36, 46, 59, 60, 61, 68, 154, 155
George Steinbrenner 142
David Stern 12
Dale Steyn 99
Stoke City 111
Ben Stokes 1, 3, 52, 74, 78, 80, 86, 102, 131, 158, 160, 186, 194, 200
Andrew Strauss 145
streaming 43, 150, 151, 152, 154, 161, 195, 204
Sunderland 50
Sunrisers Hyderabad 39
Super Bowl 43, 49, 91
Supreme Court 112, 116, 118, 119, 123
Surrey 10, 63, 152, 201, 210
sustainability 125
Swansea 50
Matthew Syed 168
Andrew Symonds 28, 39, 51

T

T20 2, 5, 7, 8, 9, 10, 11, 13, 14, 15, 16, 28, 30, 34, 35, 39, 40, 51, 58, 62, 63, 69, 70, 72, 73, 74, 75, 79, 80, 81, 83, 92, 101, 108, 109, 122, 127, 134, 138, 149, 164, 165, 166, 167, 172, 174, 178, 179, 180, 181, 182, 183, 184, 185, 186, 187, 188, 197, 198, 208, 210, 211, 212, 213
Imran Tahir 71
Praveen Tambe 69
Sohail Tanvir 29, 36, 40
teams viii, 3, 5, 8, 10, 11, 14, 17, 18, 20, 21, 22, 23, 24, 25, 27, 28, 29, 32, 38, 40, 41, 44, 46, 47, 48, 49, 51, 52,

53, 54, 55, 61, 62, 65, 68, 69, 70, 72, 74, 77, 78, 79, 81, 82, 83, 87, 90, 91, 95, 99, 100, 101, 108, 109, 112, 116, 117, 121, 125, 128, 129, 130, 131, 132, 137, 138, 139, 140, 141, 143, 146, 149, 151, 156, 157, 159, 166, 167, 168, 169, 174, 175, 179, 182, 184, 189, 195, 197, 198, 200, 206, 207, 208, 210, 211, 212, 213
Big Tech 67, 149, 169, 194, 206, 207
Technology 169, 205
Sachin Tendulkar 6, 9, 13, 24, 33, 65, 71
Test cricket 35, 38, 134, 164, 183, 185, 186, 187, 196
World Test Championship 184
Toronto Blue Jays 94
Tottenham Hotspur 95, 208
tribes 103, 104, 213
Twitter 153, 156

U

UAE 110, 138, 180, 188, 189
Shaji Ul Mulk 189
Ultratech Cements 62
unpredictable outcomes 17, 18, 47, 48, 53, 67, 102, 195
Paddy Upton vii, viii, 82, 106
USA 180, 189, 190
US Cricket 189
Robin Uthappa 28, 51, 82

V

VAR 164, 176
Michael Vaughan 70
Virtual Reality 161
VR 161, 168, 171, 172, 173

W

Shane Warne vii, viii, 3, 25, 27, 32, 69, 93, 98, 101, 116, 165, 210
David Warner 68, 102, 165